1999
Joanne Scott
CALGARY, AB

D1387977

Dolls' House Needlecrafts

Dolls' House Needlecrafts

OVER 250 PROJECTS IN 1/12 SCALE

VENUS A. DODGE

David & Charles

A DAVID & CHARLES BOOK
Copyright © Venus A. Dodge, 1995

First published 1995
Reprinted 1996, 1997, 1998

Venus A. Dodge has asserted her right to be identified as
author of this work in accordance with the Copyright,
Designs and Patents Act, 1988.

The designs in this book are copyright and must not be
made for resale.

All rights reserved. No part of this publication may be
reproduced, stored in a retrieval system, or transmitted, in
any form or by any means, electronic or mechanical, by
photocopying, recording or otherwise, without prior
permission in writing from the publisher.

A catalogue record for this book is available from the British
Library.

ISBN 01753 0169 1

Colour photography by Jonathon Bosley

Typeset by ABM Typographics Ltd, Hull
and printed in Singapore by C. S. Graphics Ltd
for David & Charles
Brunel House Newton Abbot Devon

Contents

KEY TO SYMBOLS

Each project is introduced by a symbol indicating the main technique you will need to complete the item described. Where a combination of techniques is required this is shown by a combined symbol.

 Needlepoint

 Embroidery

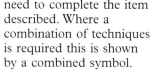 Knitting

 Crochet

 Quilting

 Patchwork

 Appliqué

 Assembly with glue

 Sewing

 Sewing and assembly with glue

 Woodworking and sewing

 Ribboncraft

 Macramé

 Woodworking and assembly with glue

Introduction

When I began to plan *Dolls' House Needlecrafts*, I hoped to include everything I could think of that dolls-house owners might want to make, because I believe it is the homemade items which give the dolls' house its character and charm, and make it so emphatically personal. Everyone has different talents, so it seemed a good idea to offer as wide a choice of projects as possible so that every reader could use her (or his) own skills. Very soon, I realized that achieving this aim would need a team of contributors – to make those things I cannot make, or cannot make well enough – and that is how the book developed.

The contributors I chose are all acknowledged experts in their field, with international reputations for originality and quality. We have worked together for more than a year to produce *Dolls' House Needlecrafts* and it has been a delightful experience for me, as I have a profound respect for the skills and professionalism of each member of the team. I owe them my warmest gratitude for making my job as author so very enjoyable. Between us, we have designed patterns for more than 250 items to make for your dolls' house – from simple, quick projects to miniature heirlooms – in every kind of needlecraft.

In Chapters 1 and 2, you will find knitting and crochet projects from Isobel Hockey and June Stowe, which range from quick and simple cushions and rugs designed for beginners, through blankets and bedspreads, to fine clothing for children and adults. You will also find some very desirable accessories, including dressing-table sets, a tea-cosy and a hot-water bottle cover, which will add a personal touch to your dolls' house.

Chapter 3 concentrates on needlepoint and embroidery projects, mostly from Sue Bakker and Dora Lockyer, beginning with cushions in each technique and working through samplers and small furnishings to beautiful bedspreads, rugs and carpets. There is something here for every house from the Tudor period to the present day.

In Chapter 4 you will find projects in patchwork, quilting and appliqué from several members of the team. There are cushions, furnishings and bedcovers in a variety of techniques suitable for both beginners and more advanced needlewomen.

Chapter 5, which covers soft furnishings, also includes projects from several team members. You will find methods for making curtains, bedding and household linens, including a mattress, sheets, towels and lampshades.

Chapter 6 deals with dressmaking, and has simple patterns and methods which can be used to make clothes for adults and children to wear, or to display in the dolls' house. I have also included a range of costume accessories, such as slippers and stockings, hats, gloves and umbrellas.

Chapter 7 gives patterns for simple furniture projects like stools and screens, and authentic upholstered furniture from Joan Ince, including a leather-covered wing chair, a Victorian sofa and chair, and a chaise-longue.

In Chapter 8 you will find a range of crafts, including beadwork, ribboncraft, macramé and basketwork. The projects range from a hookah pipe and a feather duster to a picnic hamper and fishing equipment - and there is even a hammock!

Each needlecraft is discussed in the introduction to the relevant chapter, in which members of the team offer advice on the materials and tools to use for the best results and pass on tips which will help you to achieve professional results. All the projects are shown clearly in the colour photographs and are explained thoroughly in the patterns and instructions. At the back of the book you will find a list of UK and US suppliers, and dolls-house books and magazines which you may find useful. If you wish to trace the furniture, wallpaper, etc shown in the photograph, or any of our doll 'models', you will find details in the Acknowledgements.

A word of warning about copyright. All the patterns in this book are intended for private use. It is illegal to reproduce any pattern for commercial purposes without the specific written permission (licence) of the author.

We all hope that you will enjoy *Dolls' House Needlecrafts* and find it useful, and that you will make lots of lovely things for your own dolls' house.

VENUS A. DODGE
DORSET, 1995

— CHAPTER ONE —
Knitting and Crochet

If you enjoy knitting and crochet, have a sound basic knowledge of the craft, patience and good eyesight (or a good magnifying glass), working in miniature needs only the right tools and materials. We use double-pointed steel knitting needles, 6–8 inches long, which are known as 'lace' needles, though you may prefer to use the smaller needles with wooden handles which are sold by miniatures suppliers. The patterns require size 1mm (size 18 or 19) or 1.5mm (size 16) needles which can be bought from the UK stockists listed on page 189. The US equivalent sizes are 3/0 (000) and 5/0 (00000), and these are available from the US stockists listed. Crochet patterns are worked on 0.75 and 0.60mm steel hooks which are available from the same suppliers.

The patterns are made up in wool, silk, or cotton yarns, specified in each pattern. Though wool has more flexibility, in this scale it splits easily and can break. Silk produces beautiful results but is slippery to work with. Cotton also produces good results and is easier to use so we particularly recommend it for beginners. For very fine work, we like 1-ply 'cobweb' Shetland lace wool which is available in $\frac{1}{2}$ ounce hanks from Jamieson and Smith in white which can be dyed with a weak solution of cold-water dye, though it is fragile. Stronger, 1–1½-ply wool (the thickness varies from colour to colour),

ABBREVIATIONS

The following standard abbreviations have been used throughout the chapter:

KNITTING

alt	alternate
beg	beginning
dec	decrease (work 2 sts together)
foll	following
gs	garter stitch (k plain on every row)
inc	increase (work into front and back of same st)
k	knit
k2 tog	knit 2 together
k wise	knit-wise
m1	make 1 st (by picking up strand between the needles and working into it)
M	main colour
ms	moss stitch (k1 and p1 alternately, on subsequent rows the sts are reversed)
p	purl
p2 tog	purl 2 together
patt	pattern
psso	pass slip st over
p wise	purl-wise
rem	remaining
rs	right side
rep	repeat
s1	slip one
st/sts	stitch/stitches
ss	stocking stitch (1 row knit, 1 row purl)
single rib	k1, p1, on every row on even no of sts
tbl	through back of loop
ws	wrong side
yf	yarn forward
yon	yarn over needle
yrn	yarn round needle
ytb	yarn to back
ytf	yarn to front

CROCHET

US readers should note these equivalents:
double crochet = USA single crochet
treble crochet = USA double crochet
half treble crochet = USA half double crochet
double treble = USA treble crochet

ch	chain
dc	double crochet
dtr	double treble
htr	half treble
rep	repeat
rs	right side
sp	space
ss	slip stitch (or single crochet)
st/sts	stitch/stitches
tr	treble
ws	wrong side
yoh	yarn over hook

from Golden Key, or DMC Medici fine embroidery wool from Mace and Nairn, are both excellent, and are available in 25 metre skeins from the suppliers listed.

The Gutermann Perivale silk thread we recommend is available in 50 metre spools in a range of colours in both the UK and US. Cotton yarns, including Fil à Dentelles 80 from DMC and Coats/Anchor in 97 metre balls, also in a range of colours, are sold by the same suppliers. US readers will note that one metre is a little more than one yard.

Tiny buttons or beads, and fine silk ribbon are available from miniatures suppliers (see Stockists) and shirring elastic can be found in most haberdashery (notions) departments.

It is almost impossible to produce a pattern which will work the same way for everyone every time. The slightest variation in tension, needles, hook, or yarn in this scale can make a difference, so it is not practical to give a tension guide but this is not a problem when you are making a cushion, blanket, or household item. If you drop a stitch while knitting a plain pattern, it is possible to pick it up with a crochet hook. It is also possible to rectify a mistake on a more complex pattern, but we usually find it is quicker to simply abandon the piece and start again. Crocheted mistakes can be unravelled back to the error and reworked. If you are making one of the more advanced projects, we recommend that you count the stitches as you knit each wrong-side row so that mistakes and dropped stitches can be spotted and corrected immediately.

It is best to work little and often, when you are not tired, and in natural daylight if possible. Dark colours are harder on the eyes than lighter ones so we suggest working with a piece of white cloth over your lap to help you see what you are doing.

When you start and finish a piece of work, the loose ends should be neatly darned-in rather than knotted, and if you are using more than one colour leave the loose ends at one side so that you can darn them in or catch them into a seam when making up the finished work. Join seams with small oversewing stitches in matching yarn. For the best results, gently wash the completed work in tepid water with liquid soap, rinse well and ease it into shape. Leave it to dry naturally on folded paper towels on a cake-cooling rack. Don't leave white wool items in sunlight because this will cause them to turn yellow. When dry, press the work gently under a dry cloth with a warm iron.

CUSHIONS

SIMPLE CUSHION
(Shown on page 11)

This simple knitted cushion is a good first project for the beginner and, made in the appropriate colour, could find a place in any room in the dolls' house. Isobel has used DMC Fil à Dentelles cotton thread in grape colour for one version, and a random-dye to make a striped effect for the second version. The cushion cover is knitted on 1mm needles and is approximately 1¼ inches square.

To make one side of the cushion cover: Cast on 22 sts, k 4 rows, slipping first st of each row.

Patt row 1: s1, k to end.
Row 2: s1, k1, p to last 2, k2.
Row 3: s1, k1, ★ k1, p4, k1. Rep from ★ twice, k2.
Row 4: s1, k1, ★ p1, k4, p1. Rep from ★ twice, k2.
Rows 5 and 6: Rep rows 3 and 4.
Rows 7 and 8: Rep rows 1 and 2.
Row 9: s1, k1, ★ p2, k2, p2. Rep from ★ twice, k2.
Row 10: s1, k1, ★ k2, p2, k2. Rep from ★ twice, k2.
Rows 11 and 12: Rep rows 9 and 10.
Work the 12 patt rows one more time, then work rows 1 and 2 again.
Work 4 rows k. Cast off. Make a second side in

the same way. Stitch the two covers together, wrong sides facing, with small oversewing stitches and matching thread around three sides. Stuff the cushion lightly with kapok or polyester and oversew the fourth side.

SET OF CUSHIONS
(Shown on page 11)

This set of three cushions is knitted in complementary shades of colour used in different combinations so that the cushions co-ordinate rather than match. They look particularly effective grouped together on a sofa, and can be made in any colours to suit your room. June has made one set in shades of blue and lilac, and another set in rusts and brown. The cushions are knitted on 1mm needles and you will need oddments of 1–1½-ply wool (yarn) in four toning shades.

Make the front of the cushions first, then knit the plain backs to fit. The slip stitches in the pattern mean that fewer rows are necessary for the backs – but the pattern should be adjusted to suit individual needles, tension (gauge), etc.

Patt (cushion front): Rows 1 and 2, k.
Row 3: k1, ★ s1, k1. Rep from ★ to end.
Row 4: k1, ★ ytf, s1, ytb, k1. Rep from ★ to end.
Rows 5 and 6: k.

Rows 7: k2, ⋆ s1, k1. Rep from ⋆ to last st, k1.
Row 8: k2, ⋆ ytf, s1, ytb, k1. Rep from ⋆ to last st, k1.

CUSHION 1: Cast on 25 sts in M and work rows 1 and 2 of patt.
Join in second colour and work rows 3 and 4 of patt.
Work rows 5 and 6 in M, and rows 7 and 8 in second colour.
Continue working rows 1, 2, 5 and 6 in M, and rows 3, 4, 7 and 8 in second colour until 40 rows (5 complete patts) have been worked from beg.
Work rows 1–4 inclusive again, and cast off in M.

CUSHION 2: Cast on 25 sts in M and work rows 1 and 2.
Join in second colour and work rows 3 and 4.
Work rows 5 and 6 in M.
Join in third colour and work rows 7 and 8.
Continue working rows 1, 2, 5 and 6 in M, rows 3 and 4 in second colour, and rows 7 and 8 in third colour until 40 rows (5 complete patts) have been worked from beg.
Work rows 1 and 2 again in M and rows 3 and 4 in second colour. Cast off in M.

CUSHION 3: Cast on 25 sts in M and work rows 1 and 2.
Join in second colour and work rows 3 and 4.
Join in third colour and work rows 5 and 6.
Join in fourth colour and work rows 7 and 8.
Continue as for first 8 rows until 40 rows (5 complete patts) have been worked from beg.
Work rows 1–4 inclusive again. Cast off in M.

CUSHION BACK: In plain colour, cast on 24 sts and work into backs of sts on first row. Work 34 rows, beg with a p row. Cast off.
Press the pieces lightly under a damp cloth and make up each cushion by joining three sides with matching yarn. Stuff lightly or insert a cushion pad and join the fourth side.

CROCHETED CUSHION *(Shown on page 11)*

This pretty little cushion is crocheted in random-dyed DMC Fil à Dentelles 80 cotton thread, edged with black. Isobel has made one version in shades of rust and one in mixed colours to demonstrate how the choice of variegated colour can be used to make a patchwork effect appropriate to the colour scheme in your room. The cushion cover is worked with a 0.60 crochet hook, and the finished size is approximately 1 inch square.
In variegated thread, make 5 ch. Join into ring with a ss into first ch.
Round 1: (Right side) 3 ch, 2 tr into ring, (2 ch,

3 tr into ring) three times, 2 ch, join with a ss into third of first 3 ch.
Round 2: 3 ch, then turn work so ws is facing you. Into first 2 ch space, work 2 tr, 2 ch, 3 tr, 1 ch, then into each of the next three 2 ch spaces, work 3 tr, 2 ch, 3 tr, 1 ch. Join with a ss to third of first 3 ch. Fasten off and cut thread.
Round 3: Turn work so rs is facing you. Join black thread into any 2 ch space, work 1 ch, then work 1 dc, 3 ch, 1 dc into this same 2 ch space – this is a corner. ⋆ (1 dc into each of the next 3 tr, 1 dc into the 1 ch space, 1 dc into each of the next 3 tr. For the corner, work 1 dc, 3 ch, 1 dc into the next 2 ch space). Rep from ⋆ three times, but omit the last corner on the last rep. Join with a ss into the beginning dc. Fasten off thread.

Make eight squares as described. Oversew four squares together with matching thread to make each side of the cushion cover. Matching stitches and corners, with wrong sides facing, oversew the covers together around three sides. Insert a cushion pad, or stuff lightly with kapok or polyester and oversew the fourth side.

Crocheted cushions for a Windsor chair

TIE-ON SEAT CUSHION *(Shown on page 11)*

This crocheted seat cushion makes any hard wooden chair more comfortable and looks very attractive on a Windsor chair in the dolls-house kitchen. Isobel has chosen a random-dyed DMC Fil à Dentelles 80 cotton thread in shades of rust, edged with black and tied with fine black ribbon. The cushion is worked with a 0.60 crochet hook and is approximately 1½ inches square, but can be made larger or smaller by working more or fewer rounds.
To make each side: In variegated thread, make 4 ch. Join into ring with a ss into first ch.

THE CUSHION COLLECTION

1 Simple cushions, 2 set of cushions, 3 crocheted cushions, 4 tie-on seat cushion (Chapter 1), 5 Tudor rose cushion, 6 Victorian flower cushion, 7 spray of berries cushion, 8 Tudor foot cushion, 9 Georgian cushion, 10 Indian cushion, 11 Tudor lozenge panel (Chapter 3), 12 quilted cushion, 13 log-cabin cushion, 14 folded-star cushion (Chapter 4), 15 ribbon cushions (Chapter 8)

Round 1: 3 ch, 2 tr into ring, (2 ch, 3 tr into ring) three times, 2 ch. Join with a ss to third of first 3 ch.

Round 2: ss into next 2 tr, ss into next 2 ch space, 3 ch 2 tr, 2 ch, 3 tr into same 2 ch space, (1 ch, 3 tr, 3 tr into next 2 ch space) three times, 1 ch. Join with a ss to third of first 3 ch.

Round 3: ss into next 2 tr, ss into 2 ch space, (3 ch, 2 tr, 2 ch, 3 tr) into same 2 ch space, (1 ch, 3 tr into next 1 ch space, 1 ch, 3 tr, 2 ch, 3 tr into next 2 ch space) three times, 1 ch, 3 tr into next 1 ch space, 1 ch. Join with a ss to third of first 3 ch.

Round 4: ss into next 2 tr, ss into 2 ch space, 3 ch, 2 tr, 2 ch, 3 tr into same 2 ch space, ★ (1 ch, 3 tr into next 1 ch space) twice, 1 ch, 3 tr, 2 ch, 3 tr into next 2 ch space. Rep from ★ three more times, (1 ch, 3 tr into next 1 ch space) twice, 1 ch. Join with a ss to third of first 3 ch.

Round 5: ss into next 2 tr, ss into 2 ch space, 3 ch, 2 tr, 2 ch, 3 tr into same 2 ch space, ★ (1 ch, 3 tr into next 1 ch space) three times, 1 ch, 3 tr, 2 ch, 3 tr into next 2 ch space. Rep from ★ three more times, (1 ch, 3 tr into next 1 ch space) three times, 1 ch. Join with a ss to third of first 3 ch. Fasten off.

Join in black thread at any corner 2 ch space. 1 ch, work one row dc around the edge, working 1 dc into each tr and each 1 ch space, and 4 dc into each corner 2 ch space. Join with a ss to first ch and fasten off.

Make two squares as described. With wrong sides facing, oversew together around three sides. Insert a slim cushion pad or stuff very lightly and close the fourth side. Stitch lengths of ribbon to the back corners to make ties.

BLANKETS

LAP OR TRAVEL RUG

(Shown on page 15)

This is a neat little rug which can be used to keep the legs warm on cold evenings, or taken on picnics in the summer. June has knitted our rug using two skeins of terracotta-coloured 1–1½-ply wool (yarn) on 1mm needles.

Cast on 57 sts. Work 7 rows in gs.

Patt row 8: s1, k to end.

Rows 9 and 11: s1, k3, p to last 4 sts, k4.

Row 10: s1, k4, ★ p1, k1. Rep from ★ to last 5 sts, k5.

Rep the last 4 rows twenty-eight times (123 rows from beg).

Work 7 rows gs. Cast off and darn in loose ends. Press the rug lightly under a damp cloth.

SMALL RUG OR THROW *(Shown on page 154)*

In any Victorian dolls' house, where the heating is not very efficient and there are draughts, small rugs or throws are essential. Our lacy knitted throw is pretty enough to drape on a chair or sofa, ready for the lady of the house to wrap around her shoulders when the evening turns chilly. The finished throw is approximately 4 inches square, so if you wish, it can also be used as a cot (crib) blanket. To make the throw, you will need one ball of DMC Fil à Dentelles 80 cotton thread (or similar), in the colour of your choice – Isobel has used plum colour (no 3686). You will also need 1mm knitting needles

and a 1.5mm needle for casting off.

Slip the first st on every row except the first. Cast on 55 sts. K 8 rows then continue in patt as follows:-

Patt row 1: k6, k2 tog, yf, ★ (k3, yf, s1, k2 tog, psso, yf). Rep from ★ to last 5 sts, k5.

Row 2: k8, ★ (p3, k3). Rep from ★ to last 5 sts, k5.

Row 3: k4, p4, ★ (k3, p3). Rep from ★ to last 5 sts, p1, k4.

Row 4: Rep row 2.

Row 5: k4, p4, ★ (yon, s1, k2 tog, psso, yrn, p3). Rep from ★ to last 5 sts, p1, k4.

These 5 rows form the patt. Rep them a further nineteen times, then k 8 rows. Cast off loosely, using a 1.5mm needle, and darn in the loose ends. The throw is reversible, so there is no wrong side. Pin out to shape, and press very lightly under a dry cloth.

BABY BLANKET

(Shown on page 15)

This small blanket can be used as a baby's shawl or as a cover for a small cot (crib) or cradle, including the Moses basket on page 179 and the draped cradle on page 145. You will need two skeins of wool (yarn) in the colour of your choice – Isobel has used pale pink – and 1mm knitting needles. The finished blanket is approximately 4 x 3¼ inches.

Slip the first st on every row except the first. Cast on 51 sts. K 12 rows, then continue in patt as follows:-

Patt row 1: (Right side) k7, ★ (k2 tog, yf, k1, yf, s1, k1, psso, k3). Rep from ★ to last 12 sts, k2 tog, yf, k1, yf, s1, k1, psso, k7.

Row 2: k6, p3, ★ (s1 p wise, p7). Rep from ★ to last 10 sts, s1 p wise, p3, k6.
Rows 3 and 4: Rep rows 1 and 2.
Row 5: k11, ★ (k2 tog, yf, k1, yf, s1, k1, psso, k3). Rep from ★ to last 8 sts, k8.
Row 6: k6, p7, ★ (s1 p wise, p7). Rep from ★ to last 6 sts, k6.
Rows 7 and 8: Rep rows 5 and 6.
Rep these 8 patt rows a further nine times, then k 12 rows. Cast off fairly loosely and darn in the ends. Pin to shape on an ironing board and press lightly on wrong side using damp cloth.

SIMPLE BLANKETS
(Shown on page 114)

Knitted blankets are very appealing on dolls-house beds as they tuck in nicely and look plump and cosy. Our simple single- and double-bed size blankets are knitted on 2mm (size 14) needles using thicker yarn so that they can be made quickly. These are the ideal choice if you do not want to spend a lot of time making blankets which will then be covered by a bedspread. June has used one ball of white 2-ply wool (yarn) for each, as this is widely available from department stores and wool shops, but you may prefer a colour. The finished single blanket is approximately 6 inches square and the double, 6 x 8 inches.

SINGLE BLANKET

Cast on 69 sts. Work one row into the backs of the sts to make a neat edge.
Patt row 1: (Right side) s1, k to end.
Row 2: s1, k4, p3, ★ k5, p3. Rep from ★ to last 5 sts, k5.
Row 3: s1, p4, k3, ★ p5, k3. Rep from ★ to last 5 sts, p4, k1.
Row 4: As row 2.
Row 5: As row 1.
Row 6: s1, p3, ★ k5, p3. Rep from ★ to last 4 sts, p3, k1.
Row 7: s1, k3, ★ p5, k3. Rep from ★ to last 4 sts, k4.
Row 8: As row 6.
Rep the 8 patt rows twelve more times (114 rows). Cast off loosely and darn in ends. Pin out to shape, and press lightly under a damp cloth.

DOUBLE BLANKET

Patt row 1: s1, k to end of row.
Row 2: s1, p to last st, k1.
Row 3: s1, ★ p1, k1. Rep from ★ to end of row.
Row 4: As row 2.
Cast on 89 sts and work the 4 patt rows, twenty-two times (88 rows). Work row 1 again. Cast off loosely on wrong side. Press as single blanket.

COT BLANKET

(Shown on page 22)

This little blanket will tuck in neatly in any standard-size cot (crib) to keep your baby cosy. June has used 1mm needles and two skeins of 1–1½-ply wool (yarn) in sky blue – but baby girls may prefer pink.
Cast on 58 sts and work 3 rows in gs.
Patt rows 1 – 6: gs.
Rows 7 and 9: k5, ★ m1, k2 tog. Rep from ★ to last 5 sts, k5.
Rows 8 and 10: k5, ★ yrn, p2 tog. Rep from ★ to last 5 sts, k5.
Rep patt of 10 rows, thirteen times (143 rows from beg).
Work 9 rows gs. Cast off loosely and darn in loose ends.

PET BLANKET

(Shown on page 138)

This cosy blanket for your household pet will fit the pet basket on page 178. Made in a light, pretty colour, the pattern will also make a small baby blanket which will fit the Moses basket on page 179. To make the blanket you will need one skein of wool (yarn) in the colour of your choice – June has used dark rust – and 1mm needles.
Cast on 43 sts. Work 12 rows gs.
Next row: s1, k7, work next 27 sts in ms beg p1 and ending p1, k8.
Rep last row 61 times.
Work 12 rows in gs.
Cast off loosely and fasten off neatly.
Press the blanket using the steam setting on your iron, and tuck it into the pet basket, secured with a few stitches if necessary.

SMALL LACY BLANKET *(Shown on page 38)*

This light lacy blanket will fold neatly at the end of the bed as an 'extra' blanket and will also tuck in well on any single bed including the divan on page 143. You will need three skeins of wool (yarn) in the colour of your choice – June used beige – and 1mm needles.
Cast on 60 sts and work 15 rows gs.
Patt rows 16 – 19: gs.
Row 20: k8, ★ k1 winding yarn twice round needle. Rep from ★ to last 8 sts, k8.
Row 21: k8, k next 74 sts normally, dropping extra loop, k8.
Rep last 6 rows eighteen times (129 rows from beg). Work 14 rows gs. Cast off loosely and darn in loose ends. Press lightly.

COT COVER
(Shown on page 22)

This delicate crocheted cot (crib) cover would make a beautiful addition to any dolls-house nursery, and can also be used as a shawl. Isobel has chosen white Guterman Perivale pure silk thread trimmed with pale blue, but you may prefer pink for a baby girl. You will need two spools of white thread and one spool of colour, and a 0.60 crochet hook. The cover is approximately 3½ inches square and will fit any standard-size cot.

Make 33 white squares and 16 coloured-centre squares.

White (W) squares: Make 5 ch, join into ring with a ss into first ch.

Round 1: (Right side), 3 ch (counts as first tr), 2 tr into ring, (2 ch, 3 tr into ring) three times, 2 ch, join with a ss into third of first 3 ch.

Round 2: 3 ch, then turn work so ws is facing you. Into first 2 ch space, work 2 tr, 2 ch, 3 tr, 1 ch, then into each of the next three 2 ch spaces, work (3 tr, 2 ch, 3 tr, 1 ch), then join with a ss to third of first 3 ch. Fasten off and cut thread.

Round 3: Turn work so rs is facing you. Rejoin thread into any 2 ch space, work 1 ch, then work 1 dc, 3 ch, 1 dc into this same 2 ch space (this is a corner). ★ (1 dc into each of the next 3 tr, 1 dc into the 1 ch space, 1 dc into each of the next 3 tr. For the corner, work 1 dc, 3 ch, 1 dc, into the

next 2 ch space). Rep from ★ three times, but omit the corner on the last repeat. Join with a ss into beginning dc and fasten off.

Coloured-centre squares: Using colour, work as white squares to end of round 1 and fasten off coloured thread. Using W, join into one of the 2 ch spaces and complete as for the white squares.

Darn in the loose ends on each square. Matching stitches and corners, use white thread to oversew the squares together in rows of seven, then join the rows together as shown.

Edging: Join white thread into any corner space, 2 ch, 2 dc in same corner space, then work 1 dc into each dc and each corner space of each square across one side edge to the next corner. Work 3 dc into the corner space and continue in the same way around the other three sides. Join with a ss in the second of the first 2 ch.

Next round: ★ 3 ch, miss next dc, 1 dc into next dc. Rep from ★ to end. Join with a ss to third of first 3 ch.

Next round: ★ 3 ch, 1 dc into next 3 ch space. Rep from ★ to end. Join with a ss, fasten off and darn in the loose end.

Wash the cot cover gently and press it on the wrong side, while it is still damp, using the silk setting on your iron.

BEDSPREAD
(Shown on page 22)

This lovely bedspread is crocheted in the same way as the cot cover above, and Isobel has used the same colours to complement the colour scheme in our nursery. You may prefer to make the whole bedspread in one pastel or one stronger colour to suit any bedroom. You will need six spools of white Guterman Perivale silk thread, and one spool each of pink and blue or colours of your choice, and a 0.60 crochet hook. The finished bedspread is approximately 8¼ inches square and will fit any standard-size single bed, including the divan bed on page 143.

Use the method described above to make 120 white squares, 33 squares with pink centres, and 16 squares with blue centres. When completed, join the squares in rows of 13, and join the rows together as shown.

Work the edging and press the bedspread as for the cot cover described below.

Crocheted cot cover and bedspread – plan for coloured squares

CROCHETED AFGHAN *(Shown on page 18)*

Our colourful crocheted afghan is worked in individual squares, joined together on completion so you can make it as large or small as you wish.

A COTTAGE GARDEN
*Simple cushion, baby blanket, lap or travel rug
(Chapter 1), layette dress and bootees (Chapter 2),
straw hat (Chapter 6), macramé hammock, Moses
basket (Chapter 8)*

Traditionally, afghans were made to use up odds-
and-ends of yarn in the same way that patchwork
used scraps of fabric, so it will look most authentic
if the colours are fairly random – though you might
choose colours to complement a particular room.

Isobel's pattern, based on a lifesize afghan which
belonged to June's mother, is 4¾ x 4 inches in
size, and can be used as a lap rug or a cot cover.
Our afghan is worked in Guterman Perivale silk
thread and you will need one spool each of maroon,
grey, pink, crimson, pale yellow, pale lilac, mauve,
dark green, rose, pale blue, wine, pale gold, pale
green, red, gold, dark rose, beige, green, orange and
pale mauve to make the squares, and two spools of
blue to edge and join each square, or your own

choice of colours. You will also need a 0.60
crochet hook.

Make 4 squares in each colour, making a total of
80 squares, and use the same colour (blue) to
edge each square. Darn in all loose ends.

To make each square: Make 5 ch, join into a ring
with a ss into first ch.

Round 1: (Right side) 3 ch (counts as first tr),
2 tr into ring, (2 ch 3 tr into ring) three times,
2 ch, join with a ss into third of first 3 ch.

Round 2: 3 ch, then turn work so ws is facing
you. Into first 2 ch space, work 2 tr, 2 ch, 3 tr, 1
ch. Then into each of the next three 2 ch spaces,
work (3 tr, 2 ch, 3 tr, 1 ch). Join with a ss to
third of first 3 ch. Fasten off and cut thread.

Round 3: Turn work so the rs is facing you, and
make the edge of each square (in blue).

Join thread into any 2 ch space and work 1 ch,
then work 1 dc, 3 ch, 1 dc into this same 2 ch
space (this is a corner). ★ (1 dc into each of the
next 3 tr, 1 dc into the 1 ch space, 1 dc into each
of the next 3 tr. For the corner, work 1 dc, 3 ch,

1 dc into the next 2 ch space.) Rep from ★ three times, but omit the corner on the last rep. Join with a ss into the beginning dc and fasten off the thread to finish each square.

When all the squares are completed, use the edging colour (blue) and with right sides facing, oversew the squares together with small stitches, carefully matching the stitches and corners. Join the squares together into ten rows then join the rows together.

To work the border, use the edging colour (blue) and join the thread into any corner space. Work 2 ch, 2 dc in the corner space, then work 1 dc into each corner space of each square across the edge to the next corner. Work 3 dc into the corner space and rep around the other three

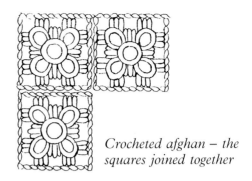

Crocheted afghan – the squares joined together

edges. Join with a ss in the second of the first 2 ch and fasten off. Darn in the loose end.

Wash the afghan gently and press on the wrong side, using the silk setting on your iron.

HOUSEWARES

DISHCLOTH OR FLANNEL *(Shown on page 186)*

This simple knitted square can be used in the dolls-house kitchen as a dishcloth or cleaning cloth, or in an old-fashioned bathroom as a flannel (facecloth). Isobel used an oddment of white cotton thread (DMC Fil à Dentelles 80 or similar) and 1mm knitting needles.
Cast on 20 sts. Work 40 rows in gs. Cast off loosely and use the thread end to work a small hanging-loop in buttonhole stitch. Darn in the loose ends.

POT HOLDER *(Shown on page 186)*

Crocheted pot holders were an essential item in the old-fashioned kitchen, where hot pans were lifted off the range, and they were usually hung on a hook by the fireplace. To make our pot holder, Isobel has used oddments of red or blue, and white cotton thread (DMC Fil à Dentelles or similar) but you can use any colour you wish. The pot holder is worked on a 0.60 crochet hook.
Work into the back of the loops throughout.
Using your chosen colour, make 5 ch and join into a ring with a ss.
Round 1: 3 ch, 2 tr into ring, (2 ch, 3 tr into ring) three times, 2 ch. Join with a ss into third of first 3 ch. Fasten off and cut thread. Using white, join into one of the 2 ch spaces.
Round 2: 3 ch, turn work so ws is facing you. Into first 2 ch space, work 2 tr, 2 ch, 3 tr, 1 ch, then into each of the next three 2 ch spaces, work 3 tr, 2 ch, 3 tr, 1 ch. Join with a ss to third of

first 3 ch. Fasten off and cut thread.
Round 3: Turn work so rs is facing you. Using colour, rejoin thread into any 2 ch space, work 1 ch, then work 1 dc, 3 ch, 1 dc into this same 2 ch space (this is a corner). ★ (1 dc into each of the next 3 tr, 1 dc into the 1 ch space, 1 dc into each of the next 3 tr. For the corner, work 1 dc, 3 ch, 1 dc into the next 2 ch space). Rep from ★ three times, but on the second rep work 8 ch for the hanging-loop instead of 3 ch at the corner. On the last rep, omit the corner and join with a ss into the beginning dc. Fasten off and darn in the loose threads.

SMALL STRING BAG *(Shown on page 131)*

The quaint little knitted string bag was inspired by a similar one found used as a sponge-tidy in an antique dolls' house, but we have used ours to hold aromatic herbs under the hot-water tap in the bathroom. The bag could also be hung on the Victorian dressing table as a hair-tidy, or could be used as a small reticule. Isobel has used an oddment of DMC Fil à Dentelles 80 cotton thread in ecru, 1mm knitting needles and a 0.75 crochet hook.
Cast on 15 sts and k 1 row.
Patt row 1: k, winding the yarn twice around the needle on each st.
Row 2: k, dropping the extra loops.
Rep these 2 rows four times and cast off.
Fold the work in half and oversew along the bottom and side seam. Turn right side out. Work a handle for the bag, about ¾ inch long, in crochet or buttonhole stitch.

Tuck a tiny piece of natural sponge, a sprig of herb or a few strands of hair into the bag.

ROUND TABLE CENTRE *(Shown on page 59)*

This crocheted table centre would look attractive in any dolls' house, from the early nineteenth century to the present day. The delicate pattern shows to the best advantage in white, placed over a dark wood table or coloured table cloth. Isobel has used Guterman Perivale silk thread and a 0.60 crochet hook.

Work into the back of the loops throughout.
Make 8 ch and join into a ring with a ss.
Round 1: 2 ch (counts as first dc) 15 dc into ring. Join with a ss to second of first 2 ch.
Round 2: 2 ch, 1 dc into ss, 2 dc into each dc. Join with a ss to second of first 2 ch.
Round 3: 2 ch, 1 dc into each dc. Join with a ss to second of first 2 ch.
Round 4: Rep round 3.
Round 5: (8 ch, miss 1 dc, 1 dc into next dc) fifteen times, 8 ch, join with a ss to the base of first 5 ch.
Round 6: ss to fourth ch of first loop, (5 ch, 1 dc into next loop) fifteen times, 5 ch, join with a ss to first ss.
Round 7: 2 ch, 4 dc into first loop, ★ (5 dc into next loop). Rep from ★ to end. Join with a ss to second of first 2 ch.
Round 8: 2 ch, 1 dc into next 3 dc, 2 dc into fourth dc, ★ (1 dc into each of next 4 dc, 2 dc into fifth dc). Rep from ★ to end. Join with a ss to second of first 2 ch (96 sts).
Round 9: Rep round 3.
Round 10: (8 ch, miss 3 dc, 1 dc into next dc) twenty-three times, 8 ch. Join with a ss to base of first 8 ch (24 loops).
Round 11: ★ 8 dc into loop. Rep from ★ to end. Join with a ss to beginning dc. Fasten off and darn in loose ends. Press on the wrong side using the silk setting on your iron.

SQUARE ANTIMACASSAR OR TABLE-MAT

(Shown on page 59)

No Victorian parlour is complete without antimacassars on every chair and sofa, and mats or doilies on every table. This lacy crocheted square can be used as either, or work a pair and use them to make an elegant cushion cover. Isobel has used Guterman Perivale silk thread in white and a 0.60 crochet hook.

Work into the back of the loops throughout.
Make 6 ch and join into a ring with a ss.
Round 1: 3 ch, 2 tr into ring, 3 ch, ★ 3 tr into ring, 3 ch. Rep from ★ twice, join with a ss into third of first 3 ch.

Round 2: 3 ch, 1 tr into each of next 2 tr, ★ 2 tr, 3 ch, 2 tr into corner loop, 1 tr into each of next 3 tr. Rep from ★ twice, then 2 tr, 3 ch, 2 tr into corner. Join with a ss to third of first 3 ch.
Round 3: 3 ch, 1 tr into each of next 4 tr, ★ 2 tr, 3 ch, 2 tr into corner loop, 1 tr into each of next 7 tr. Rep from ★ twice, then 2 tr, 3 ch, 2 tr into corner, 1 tr into each of next 2 tr, join with a ss to third of first 3 ch.
Round 4: ss into first tr, 5 ch, miss 2 tr, 1 dc into next tr, ★ 3 ch, 3 tr, 3 ch, 3 tr into corner, 3 ch, miss 2 tr, 1 dc into next tr, (5 ch, miss 2 tr, 1 dc into next tr) twice. Rep from ★ twice, then 3 ch, 3 tr, 3 ch, 3 tr into corner, 3 ch, miss 2 tr, 1 dc into next tr, 5 ch. Join with a ss to the first of the first 5 ch.
Round 5: (5 ch, 1 dc into next loop) twice. ★ 3 ch, 3 tr, 3 ch, 3 tr into corner loop, 3 ch, 1 dc into next loop, (5 ch, 1 dc into next loop) three times. Rep from ★ twice, then 3 ch, 3 tr, 3 ch, 3 tr into corner, 3 ch, 1 dc into next loop, 5 ch, 1 dc into next loop.
Round 6: Work 3 tr into each of next three loops, ★ 1 tr into each of next 3 tr, 2 tr, 3 ch, 2 tr into corner loop, 1 tr into each of next 3 tr, 3 tr into each of next five loops. Rep from ★ twice, then 1 tr into each of next 3 tr, 2 tr, 3 ch, 2 tr into corner loop, 1 tr into each of next 3 tr, 3 tr into each of next two loops, then join with a ss to top of beginning tr. Fasten off and darn in the loose ends. Press the antimacassar on the wrong side using the silk setting on your iron.

HOT-WATER BOTTLE COVER

(Shown on page 131)

Hot-water bottles are available from most dolls-house shops, or can be modelled in Fimo or a similar compound, but any hot-water bottle is much cosier with a knitted cover. You could make one in different colours for each member of the family. June has used half a skein of blue 1–1½-ply wool (yarn) and 1mm needles. The cover is fastened with two tiny buttons or beads.
Cast on 15 sts. Work 30 rows in ms, beg first row with k1.

Hot-water bottle cover

NEEDLEWORK AND GOSSIP
Crocheted afghan, dishcloth, pot holder, tea-cosy (Chapter 1), triangular shawl (Chapter 2), bless-this-house sampler (Chapter 3), curtains with rings, round tablecloth, braided-wool rug (Chapter 5), shawl, straw hat (Chapter 6), raffia basket, shopping basket (Chapter 8)

Row 31: ms6, cast off 3 sts (1 rem on needle), ms5.

Row 32: ms6, cast on 3 sts, ms6.

Work a further 30 rows in ms.

Next row: ms4, cast off 7 sts (1 rem on needle), ms3.

Work 4 rows ms on last 4 sts.

Next row: k1, p1, m1, p2 tog.

Next row: p1, k1, p1, k1. Cast off and cut yarn.

Rejoin yarn to inside edge of rem 4 sts. Work 4 rows in ms, beg first row with p1.

Next row: p1, k1, m1, k2 tog.

Next row: k1, p1, k1, p1. Cast off and cut yarn.

Darn in loose ends. Sew on buttons loosely to correspond with buttonholes. With right sides together, join the side seams and turn right side out.

BATH MAT *(Shown on page 131)*

This delightful knitted bath mat is perfect for any old-fashioned bathroom. June has used oddments of cream and blue 1–1½-ply wool (yarn), though you might choose other colours, and 1mm needles. (In cream) cast on 40 sts and work 7 rows in gs. Slip the first st of each row.

Beg the centre panel of ss as follows:

Next row: s1, k4, k next 30 sts, k5.

Next row: s1, k4, p next 30 sts, k5.

Rep last 2 rows, twice.

Beg letters, looping blue yarn behind cream on alt sts as follows:

Next row: s1, k4, k5. Join in blue yarn and follow the patt chart, k10.

Next row: s1, k4, p5, follow patt from row 2 of chart, p5, k5.

Continue, keeping 5 border sts at each end in gs, and 5 sts at each end of patt sts in ss, until row 7 of the letters patt has been worked. This completes the word BATH. Cut blue yarn leaving end to darn in.

Next row: s1, k4, p30, k5.

Next row: s1, k4, k30, k5.

Next row: s1, k4, p30, k5.

Rep last 2 rows once more. With ws of work facing, work 6 rows in gs. Cast off loosely on wrong side. Darn in blue yarn ends so that they do not show on right side and darn in cream yarn ends. Press the centre panel of the bath mat carefully so as not to flatten the border.

PURL ROWS   KNIT ROWS

			×	×	×			×	×		×	×	×	×	×		×		×		7
	6		×			×		×			×			×		×					
			×		×			×			×			×		×				5
	4		×	×			×	×	\	×		×			×	×	×	×			
			×		×		×			×			×		×				3
	2		×			×		×			×			×		×				
			×	×	×		×		×			×		×		×			1

Bath mat – chart for colour stitches

Knitted tea-cosy

TEA-COSY *(Shown on page 186)*

This irresistible knitted tea-cosy will fit any teapot approximately 1 inch high, and no kitchen should be without one. To make it, you will need an oddment of 1–1½-ply wool (yarn) – June has chosen rust colour – 1mm needles, and a small wooden bead or a pom-pom.

Cast on 25 sts.

Row 1: ★ k3, p2. Rep from ★ to end.

Row 2: ★ k2, p3. Rep from ★ to end.

Rep these 2 rows ten times (22 rows).

Next row: k1, k2 tog twice. Rep from ★ to end (15 sts).

Next row: ★ k2 tog, p1. Rep from ★ to end (10 sts).

Cut yarn and use a sewing needle to thread the end through remaining sts. Draw up, leaving yarn end to join seam. Make a second piece in the same way. With wrong sides together, join the side seams leaving ½ inch gaps at each side to accommodate the teapot handle and spout. Stitch the bead (or glue a pom-pom) to the top.

TABLE-MATS AND RUNNER *(Shown on page 59)*

This set of one large and two small knitted mats with a matching runner can be used on the dressing table or on a sideboard in the drawing room. June has used oddments of DMC 100 crochet cotton in ecru, but white or cream would also be suitable. The set is knitted on size 21 needles.

SMALL MAT

Cast on 13 sts. s1, p to end of row, working into back of sts, k1.

Patt row 2: (Right side) s1, k1, yf, s1, k1, psso, k5, k2 tog, yf, k2.

Row 3 and alt rows: s1, p to last st, k1.
Row 4: s1, k2, yf, s1, k1, psso, k3, k2 tog, yf, k3.
Row 6: s1, k3, yf, s1, k1, psso, k1, k2 tog, yf, k4.
Row 8: s1, k4, yf, s1, k2 tog, psso, yf, k5.
Row 10: s1, k3, k2 tog, yf, k1, yf, s1, k1, psso, k4.
Row 12: s1, k2, k2 tog, yf, k3, yf, s1, k1, psso, k3.
Row 14: s1, k1, k2 tog, yf, k5, yf, s1, k1, psso, k2.
Row 16: s1, k2 tog, yf, k7, yf, s1, k1, psso, k1.
Row 17: s1, p to last st, k1. Cast off on the rs p wise, loosely. Make the second small mat in the same way.

LARGE MAT

Work as for the small mat (above) until the first patt is complete. Rep the patt rows 2–17 four more times (5 patts in all). Cast off on the rs p wise, loosely.

RUNNER

Cast on 15 sts.
Patt row 1: k3, yf, s1, k1, psso, k5, k2 tog, yf, k3.
Row 2 and alt rows: s1, p to end, k1.
Row 3: k4, yf, s1, k1, psso, k3, k2 tog, yf, k4.
Row 5: k5, yf, s1, k1, psso, k1, k2 tog, yf, k5.
Row 7: k6, yf, s1, k2 tog, psso, yf, k6.
Row 9: k5, k2 tog, yf, k1, yf, s1, k1, psso, k5.
Row 11: k4, k2 tog, yf, k3, yf, s1, k1, psso, k4.
Row 13: k3, k2 tog, yf, k5, yf, s1, k1, psso, k3.
Row 15: k2, k2 tog, yf, k7, yf, s1, k1, psso, k2.
Row 16: s1, p to end, k1.
Rep the patt of 16 rows three times (64 rows). Cast off loosely and fasten off loose ends.

DRESSING-TABLE SET *(Shown on page 59)*

This dainty crocheted set of one large and two smaller mats would grace any lady's dressing table, and also makes an attractive set of doilies for the drawing room. Isobel has used Guterman Perivale silk thread in white, but cream or ecru would also be appropriate. The mats are worked with a 0.60 crochet hook.

LARGE MAT

Make 6 ch and join into a ring with a ss.
Round 1: 3 ch, 4 tr into ring. ⋆ 4 ch, 5 tr into ring. Rep from ⋆ two more times, ch 4, join with a ss to third ch of beginning 3 ch.
Round 2: ss into next tr, then 1 dc into next tr, ⋆ 3 ch, 4 tr, 3 ch, 4 tr into next 4 ch space, 3 ch, 1 dc into third tr of next group of 5 tr. Rep from ⋆ three more times, but in the third repeat, omit the last dc and ss to first st of beginning 3 ch instead.
Round 3: ss into next 2 ch. ⋆ 3 ch, 4 tr, 3 ch, 4 tr into next 3 ch space, 3 ch, 1 dc into last tr of next group of tr, 3 ch, 1 dc into first tr of next group of tr. Rep from ⋆ three more times, but omit last dc and ss to first ch of 3 ch instead. Fasten off.

SMALL MATS

Work as the large mat to the end of round 2 and fasten off. Darn in all loose ends and press the mats on the wrong side using the silk setting on your iron.

TOYS

KNITTED TEDDY
(Shown on page 43)

June's cuddly little teddy bear is knitted in garter stitch from an oddment of ecru crochet cotton yarn on 1mm needles.

PAWS: (Make four the same) Cast on 10 sts, work in gs for 16 rows. Cast off.

HEAD AND BODY: Cast on 10 sts, work in gs for 16 rows.
Next row: k.
Next row: p.
Work next two rows in gs.
Next row: k4, make a st by picking up yarn between 4th and 5th sts (pick-up inc), k2, pick-up inc, k4.

Next row: k5, pick-up inc, k2, pick-up inc, k5.
Next row: k6, pick-up inc, k2, pick-up inc, k6.
Next row: k7, pick-up inc, k2, pick-up inc, k7.
Next row: k8, pick-up inc, k2, pick-up inc, k8.
Next row: k (20 sts).
Next row: k5 (k2 tog) twice, k2, (k2 tog) twice, k5.
Next row: k3, (k2 tog) twice, k2, (k2 tog) twice, k3.
Next row: k3, k2 tog, k2, k2 tog, k3.
Work in gs for next 14 rows.
Next row: p.
Work in gs for next 16 rows. Cast off.

EARS: (Make two the same) Cast on 4 sts, work in gs for 2 rows.
Next row: (k2 tog) twice.
Next row: k2 tog. Cast off.
Working on the right side with small oversewing

stitches, join the long seams on each paw, and across one end. Stuff each paw with a tiny amount of kapok or polyester pushed in carefully to make plump, rounded limbs. Close the other end, leaving long yarn ends to sew limbs to body. Fold the head and body piece in half, and join the side seams. Stuff the body, and use a small knitting needle and your fingers to ease out the nose shaping. Stuff the head firmly, shaping as you go. Finish stuffing the body, and join the end seam. Stitch the paws to the body, and the ears to the head. Embroider the features in black thread. Tie a fine silk ribbon bow around the bear's neck.

CUDDLY DOLL

(Shown on page 43)

June's sweet old-fashioned doll is designed to be a little girl's best friend. She is knitted from leftover oddments of pink cotton yarn with knitted-in shoes in black, socks in white, and knickers in lilac yarn. Her removable dress is lilac – though you can, of

THE NURSERY

Cot blanket, cot cover, bedspread, soft ball (Chapter 1), layette jacket and bonnet (Chapter 2), flower vase sampler (Chapter 3), changing-mat and nappy bag (Chapter 4), sheets and frilled pillowcase, fur rug, lampshade (Chapter 5), baby gown, slippers, teddy bears and doll (Chapter 6), baby basket and nappies (Chapter 8)

course, use any leftover cotton yarns or choose any colours you prefer. You will need 1mm needles to make the doll.

ARMS: (Two the same) Cast on 10 sts and work 16 rows in ss.
LEGS: (Two the same) In black, cast on 10 sts and work 4 rows in ss. Join in white, and work 3 rows in ss and 1 row in gs. Join in pink, and work 8 rows in ss. Join in lilac, and work 2 rows in ss. Cast off in lilac, and cut black, white, pink, and lilac leaving short ends for making up.
HEAD AND BODY: In lilac, cast on 10 sts, work 6 rows in ss. Join in pink, work 10 rows in ss.

Next row: k3, (k2 tog) twice, k3.
Next row: s1, p6, k1.
Next row: k2, inc by working twice into next st, k2, inc again in next st, k2 (10 sts).
Continue in ss for next 22 rows.
Next row: s1, p1, p2 tog, p2, p2 tog, p1, k1.
Work 2 rows in ss on 8 sts.
Next row: k2, inc by working twice into next st, k2, inc again in next st, k2 (10 sts).
Work 10 rows in ss, beg with a p row. Join in lilac and work 6 rows in ss beg with a k row. Cast off in lilac and cut pink and lilac yarn leaving short ends for making up.
Working on the right side with small oversewing stitches, fold the arms lengthwise and join the long seam and one end. Fold the legs lengthwise and join the seams using matching threads for each colour. Stuff arms and legs carefully with kapok or polyester to make them plump and rounded. Close the opening on each limb. Fold the head and body piece lengthwise and join the side seam using matching thread on each colour. Stuff the head and body and close the lower end in matching thread. Sew on the arms and legs. (Make and dress the doll before working the hair and features.) Embroider the doll's features and make curly hair, in the colour of your choice, by covering the scalp with short stitches, then working loops of thread through the stitches all over the head.

DRESS: Front – Cast on 19 sts and work 8 rows ms.
Next row: k4, k2 tog, k1, k2 tog, k1, k2 tog, k1, k2 tog, k4 (15 sts).
Next row: s1, p13, k1.
Continue in ss, casting off 1 st at beg of next 2 rows (13 sts).
★ Work 5 rows ss beg with a k row.
Next row: s1, p3, turn and work 2 rows on these 4 sts. Cast off.
Rejoin yarn to rem 9 sts, cast off 5 sts (1 st rem on needle) p2, k1.
Work 2 rows on these 4 sts. Cast off.
Back – Work as for front until ★ row is completed.
Next row: s1, k6, turn and cast on 2 sts for overlap, s1, p7, k1.
Continue in ss and beg with a k row, work 8 rows. Cast off.

Rejoin yarn to rem 6 sts, cast on 2 sts for underlap, k8.
Beg with a p row, work 9 rows in ss. Cast off.
Join shoulder seams on ws and secure over and underlap neatly at waist on ws.
Sleeves (two the same) – With rs of work facing, join in yarn and pick up 13 sts evenly between cast-off underarm edges. Work 5 rows in ms and cast off loosely.
Join skirt and sleeve seams and fasten off any loose threads. Put the dress on the doll and close the back opening. If required, sew on a tiny button or bead at the closure.

SOFT BALL
(Shown on page 43)

This simple knitted ball is worked on 1mm needles from an oddment of cotton yarn. Isobel used DMC Fil à Dentelles cotton in random-dyed colour 109 and 1mm needles.
The ball is worked in gs (every row k) throughout.
Cast on 8 sts.
Patt rows 1, 3, 5 and 7: k.
Row 2: Inc in each st to end.
Row 4: (k1 inc). Rep to end.
Row 6: (k2 inc). Rep to end.
Row 8: (k3 inc). Rep to end.
Work 7 rows straight in gs, then dec thus:-
Row 1: (k3, k2 tog). Rep to end.
Rows 2, 4, 6 and 8: k.
Row 3: (k2, k2 tog). Rep to end.
Row 5: (k1, k2 tog). Rep to end.
Row 7: (k2 tog). Rep to end.
Cut yarn and thread through the rem sts, draw up and fasten off. Draw up the cast on sts and join the seam, stuffing the ball with a little kapok or polyester as you go. Roll the ball in your hands to shape.

Knitted toys

— CHAPTER TWO —

Knitted Clothes

The clothes in this chapter are designed to fit $\frac{1}{12}$ scale dolls-house dolls and they are all removable. The same tools and materials discussed in Chapter 1 are used for these patterns and the techniques and abbreviations are also the same, so rather than repeating them, we suggest you refer to Chapter 1 as necessary.

The main difference between knitting a blanket and knitting a garment is the fitting. As minor changes in tension, needles and yarn can make a considerable difference to the finished size of the work, it is not practical to give an accurate tension gauge – which does not matter if you are knitting a garment to hang on the back of the door or drape over a chair. However, if you are making a garment for a specific doll, it should be fitted on the doll. As dolls vary in size and shape, you may need to adjust the pattern by adding or subtracting a few stitches or rows. Sleeves especially may need lengthening or shortening. (For details of the dolls we have used as models in this chapter, see the Acknowledgements at the back of the book.)

CLOTHES FOR ADULTS

TRIANGULAR SHAWL *(Shown on page 27)*

This quick and simple knitted shawl is a good project for the beginner but any dolls-house lady would find it an attractive addition to her wardrobe. Knitted in white, it will make a good shawl for a baby. Isobel has used Guterman Perivale silk thread which drapes and hangs particularly well, and has chosen purple, but you can use any colour you please. You will need two spools of thread, 1.5mm knitting needles, a 2mm needle for casting off, and a fine crochet hook to make the fringe.
Cast on 3 sts. K one row.
Work 68 rows in gs, increasing one st at the beg of each row (71 sts). Cast off loosely, using a

2mm needle, and darn in the loose ends.

To make the fringe, cut two strips of card about 4 x 1 inches. Wind yarn around the cards about 70 or 80 times, then cut between the cards to make even strands of yarn. Use a crochet hook to knot single strands through the two shorter edges of the shawl.

Triangular shawl – making the fringe

LACY FRINGED SHAWL *(Shown on page 71)*

This exquisite shawl is knitted in silk thread, and can be made in any colour you please for a lady, and in white or pastel shades for a baby. Silk hangs beautifully so the shawl looks elegant when worn, and will also drape well over a chair, sofa, or piano. The pattern is appropriate for any house from the eighteenth century to the present day. To make the shawl, you will need two spools of Guterman Perivale silk thread (or similar). Isobel chose cream for the lady's shawl and white for the baby's version. You will also need a pair of 1mm knitting needles, a 1.5mm needle for casting off, and a fine crochet hook for knotting the fringe.
Cast on 71 sts. Work 4 rows in gs, slipping the first st on every row except the first. Then continue in patt.
Row 1: s1, k2, k2 tog, yf, ★ (k5, yf, s1, k2 tog,

Clothes for adults

psso, yf). Rep from * to last 8 sts, k5, yf, s1, k1, psso, k3.
Row 2 and alt rows: s1, k1, p to last 2 sts, k2.
Row 3: Rep row 1.
Row 5: s1, k4, * (yf, s1, k1, psso, k1, k2 tog, yf, k3). Rep from * to last 2 sts, k2.
Row 7: s1, k2, k2 tog, yf, * (k1, yf, s1, k2 tog, psso, yf). Rep from * to last 6 sts, k1, yf, s1, k1, psso, k3.
Rep these 8 patt rows another fourteen times. Work 4 rows gs. Cast off loosely using a 1.5mm needle, and darn in the loose ends.
Cut 2 inch strands of yarn (as above) and use a crochet hook to knot fringe around the four edges of the shawl. Pin out on an ironing board and press the shawl on the wrong side over a damp cloth.

BED JACKET AND SLIPPERS *(Shown on page 83)*

Any dolls-house lady who feels the cold will appreciate this cosy, knitted bed jacket with matching slippers – the perfect thing to wear for breakfast in bed on winter mornings. One skein of 1–1½-ply wool (yarn) will make bed jacket and slippers. June has used lilac, and you will need 1mm needles and a little narrow silk ribbon.

BED JACKET

Slip the first st on every row to make a neat, firm edge. The welts at waist and cuff are worked in double rib (2 sts k, 2 sts p, on each row). Cast on 32 sts. Work 2 rows in double rib.
Row 3: * s1, k1, m1, p2 tog. Rep from * to end.
Work another 3 rows in double rib.
Work next 8 rows in gs.
Cast on 8 sts at beg of next 2 rows (48 sts).
Work the next 27 rows in gs.
Next row: k20, cast off 8 sts (1 st rem on needle) k19.
Working on last 20 sts, k another 30 rows.
Next row: Cast off 8 sts at sleeve edge, k to end.
Work 8 rows on rem 12 sts.
Work 3 rows in double rib.
Next row: * s1, k1, m1, p2 tog. Rep from * to end.
Work next 2 rows in double rib. Cast off loosely.
Rejoin yarn to neck edge of other 20 sts.
Work 29 rows in gs.
Next row: Cast off 8 sts at sleeve edge, k to end.
Work 8 rows in gs.
Work 3 rows in double rib.
Next row: * s1, k1, m1, p2 tog. Rep from * to end.
Work another 2 rows in double rib. Cast off loosely. Choose one side of the work to be the right side, with rs facing, pick up and k 24 sts

evenly spaced along first sleeve edge. (Fold sleeve in half and mark halfway point with thread to gauge even spacing.)
Work 5 rows in double rib.
Next row: * s1, k1, p2 tog. Rep from * to end.
Work another 2 rows in double rib.
Make second sleeve edge (cuff) in the same way. Fasten off loose ends neatly at the neck. Use yarn ends to join the side seams. Thread fine silk ribbon through the waistline and cuffs.

SLIPPERS (both the same).
Cast on 19 sts, work 8 rows in gs.
Row 9: s1, k6, cast off 5, k7.
Working on last 7 sts, k 2 rows. Cast off and cut yarn. Rejoin yarn at inside edge to first 7 sts and k 2 rows. Cast off. Join long straight cast-on edge to form sole seam, join back edge. Darn in yarn ends at top edge. Make second slipper in the same way. Add tiny ribbon bows or pom-poms.

LACY CAPE

(Shown on page 27)

This lacy knitted cape is designed as a bed jacket, but it is pretty enough for daytime wear too. June used DMC 100 cotton in ecru, and 1mm needles, and tied the neck with narrow fine silk ribbon.
Patt row 1: k2, * k2 tog, yf, k1, yf, s1, k1, psso, k2. Rep from * to end.
Row 2: p.
Row 3: k1, * k2 tog, yf, k3, yf, s1, k1, psso. Rep from * to last st, k1.
Row 4: p.
Cast on 99 sts. K into backs of sts to make a firm edge.
Next row: s1, k2, work patt row 1 until 3 sts rem, k3.
Next row: s1, k2, work patt row 2 until 3 sts rem, k3.
Next row: s1, k2, work patt row 3 until 3 sts rem, k3.
Next row: s1, k2, work patt row 4 until 3 sts rem, k3.
Rep last 4 rows twelve times (53 rows from row 1).
Next row: s1, k2, k2 tog. (k2, k2 tog) twenty-three times, k3 (75 sts).
Next row: s1, k2, p to last 3 sts, k3.
Next row: s1, k2, k2 tog. (k1, k2 tog) twenty-two times, k4 (54 sts).
Next row: s1, k2, p to last 3 sts, k3.
Next row: s1, p to last st, k1.
Next row: s1, k1, * m1, k2 tog. Rep from * to last 2 sts, k2.
Next row: s1, k to end.
Cast off loosely. Darn in loose ends, and press carefully. Thread fine silk ribbon through the neckline, leaving long ends to tie in a bow.

DRESSING-GOWNS

(Shown on page 123)

Every gentleman resident of a ninteenth- or early twentieth-century dolls' house will want this splendid dressing-gown. It will hang beautifully on the back of the bedroom or bathroom door, or fit comfortably over the nightshirt on page 125. June has used a nice old-fashioned snuff colour for our gentleman's dressing-gown, but any sombre colour would be suitable and you will need four skeins of 1–1½-ply wool (yarn), 1mm needles and three tiny buttons or beads. The lady's version of the dressing-gown is similar, but smaller and shorter and June has used a rich blue-green colour, though you might choose a pastel shade. You will need two skeins of wool, 1mm needles, and one tiny button or bead for this version (shown on page 38).

GENTLEMAN'S DRESSING-GOWN

Knit into back of sts on all cast-on rows. Slip first st on every row unless otherwise stated.
BACK: Cast on 42 sts. Work 11 rows in gs. Work 24 rows in ss beg with a k row.
Next row: k2 tog at beg and end of row.
Work 11 rows in ss, beg with a p row.
Rep last 12 rows twice (36 sts).
Next row: k2 tog at beg and end of row.
Work 3 rows in ss beg with a p row.
*Armholes: Cast off 5 sts at beg of next 2 rows.
Work next 24 rows in ss.
Next row: Cast off 6 sts, k to end of row.
Next row: Cast off 6 sts, p to end of row.
Leave rem 12 sts on a safety pin.
RIGHT FRONT: Cast on 28 sts. Work 11 rows in gs.
Row 12: k.
Row 13: s1, p to last 10 sts, k 10.
Rep rows 12 and 13 eleven times (24 rows ss).
Row 36: k to last 2 sts, k2 tog.
Row 37: s1, p to last 10 sts, k10.
Keeping 10 border sts correct, work another 10 rows in ss then work dec row again, followed by 11 rows of ss. Rep dec row again, followed by another 11 rows of ss (25 sts).
Next row: k until 2 sts rem, k2 tog.
Work 4 rows in ss with 10 gs border sts as before.
*Next row: Cast off 5 sts (1 st rem on needle), p8, k10.
Work 16 rows in ss keeping 10 gs border sts as before.
Next row: Cast off 7 border sts for neck (1 st rem on needle), k2, k2 tog, k6.
Next row: s1, p6, turn (transfer 3 sts from front border on to a safety pin).
Next row: k2 tog, k5.
Work another 5 rows in ss on rem 6 sts. Cast off.
LEFT FRONT: Cast on 28 sts, work 11 rows gs.
Row 12: k.

Row 13: s1, k9, p to end.
Work rows 12 and 13 eleven times more (24 rows ss).
Next row: k2 tog, k to end.
Work 11 rows in ss keeping front border of 10 gs sts correct.
(Work dec row again, followed by 11 rows in ss) twice, keeping front gs border correct (25 sts).
Work dec row again, followed by 3 rows in ss with gs border of 10 sts.
*Next row: Cast off 5 sts, k to end.
Next row: s1, k9, p to end.
Next row: s1, k to last 5 sts, k2 tog, m1, k3.
Now work in ss with 10 gs border for 6 rows.
Next row: s1, k2, m1, k2 tog, k5, p to end.
Now work in ss with 10 gs border for 6 rows.
Next row: s1, k to last 5 sts, k2 tog, m1, k3.
Now work in ss with 10 gs border for 2 rows, ending at neck edge.
Next row: Cast off 7 sts for neck (1 st rem on needle) k2, k2 tog, k to end.
Next row: s1, p6 (transfer 3 border sts to a safety pin).
Next row: k2 tog, k to end.
Work 4 rows in ss, cast off. Join the shoulder seams.
COLLAR: With rs of work facing, transfer 3 border sts from right front safety pin on to needle. Join in yarn and pick up and k 8 sts up side of neck. Transfer and k 12 sts from pin at back of neck, pick up and k 8 sts down side of neck on left front. Transfer and k 3 sts from border sts on pin (34 sts).
K 2 rows in gs.
Next row: k8, inc in next st, k2, inc in next st, k10, inc in next st, k2, inc in next st, k8.
Next row: k.
Next row: k8, inc in next st, k4, inc in next st, k10, inc in next st, k4, inc in next st, k8.
Next row: k.
Next row: k8, inc in next st, k6, inc in next st, k10, inc in next st, k6, inc in next st, k8.
Work another 2 rows in gs. Cast off loosely k wise.
SLEEVES: (Both the same) With rs of work facing, pick up 29 sts beg at corner of armhole dec (to ensure even spacing, pick up 14 sts either side of shoulder seam and 1 st on seam).
Work 17 rows in ss beg with p row.
Next row: (Dec row) k2 tog at each end of row.
Work another 11 rows in ss beg with a p row.
Work dec row again.
Work 2 rows in ss beg with p row.
Work 11 rows in gs. Cast off k wise.
Press the work lightly, pinning out to shape to ensure gs borders do not pull up. Sew cast-off 5 sts at armholes of back and fronts to corresponding rows on sleeve edges. When these four seams are complete, join the sleeve and side seams. Darn in all loose ends and press seams lightly. Sew on buttons to correspond with

THE KNITTING LADY
Triangular shawl, lacy cape (Chapter 2), bless-this-house sampler, Turkoman rug (Chapter 3), hooded cloak, umbrella (Chapter 6), shopping basket (Chapter 8)

buttonholes. Make a small hanging-loop inside the back neckline with 5 ch crochet on a fine hook if required.

LADY'S DRESSING-GOWN

Slip the first st on every row and k into the back of sts on every cast-on edge.
BACK: Cast on 38 sts. Work 11 rows in gs. Work next 46 rows in ss beg with a k row.
Next row: s1, k3, k2 tog, k2, k2 tog, k18, k2 tog, k2, k2 tog, k4.

Work 3 rows in ss beg with a p row. Continue as for the gentleman's dressing-gown from ★ Armholes.
LEFT FRONT: Cast on 26 sts. Work 11 rows in gs.
Row 12: k.
Row 13: s1, k9, p16.
Rep the last 2 rows, twenty-two times.
Next row: s1, k3, k2 tog, k2, k2 tog, k to end.
Next row: As row 13.
Next row: As row 12.
Next row: As row 13.
Continue as for the gentleman's dressing-gown from ★ Armhole but making only one buttonhole at the neck.
RIGHT FRONT: Cast on 26 sts. Work 11 rows in gs.
Row 12: k.
Row 13: s1, p15, k10.
Rep the last 2 rows, twenty-two times.

Next row: s1, k15, k2 tog, k2, k2 tog, k4.
Next row: As row 13.
Next row: As row 12.
Next row: As row 13.
Next row: As row 12.
Continue as for gentleman's dressing-gown from
* Armhole. Join the shoulder seams and make the
collar as described above.
SLEEVES: (Both the same) With rs of work
facing, and beg at inside armhole edge, pick up
and k 29 sts (one st on seam, 14 either side of
seam).
Work 28 rows in ss beg with p row.
Work 10 rows in gs. Cast off k wise on ws of
work to make a neat edge.
Press and make up as for the gentleman's
dressing-gown. If you wish, the dressing-gown
might have a girdle made from ribbon, fine cord,
or plaited wool strands, which can be worn
through a couple of loops worked on each side
seam at the waistline.

LADY'S SWIMSUIT AND JACKET

(Shown on page 179)

When sunshine and seaside holidays became
fashionable in the 1920s, stylish beachwear was an
essential part of every lady's wardrobe and our
knitted swimsuit and matching short-sleeved jacket
would be appreciated by any lady living in a
between-the-wars dolls' house. You will need one
skein of 1–1½-ply wool (yarn) in the colour of your
choice for the swimsuit and two skeins for the
jacket, and an oddment of contrasting colour if you
wish to work the anchor motifs – June used cream
and emerald green. Both garments are knitted on
1mm needles, and you will also need two spare
1mm needles, and two tiny buttons or beads for the
fastening. This pattern is designed for more experienced knitters.

SWIMSUIT

If the anchor motif is not required, simply k in ss
throughout.
BACK: (Main body) Cast on 14 sts. Work 6 rows
in k1, p1 rib. Cut yarn and transfer sts to a spare
needle. Work the second leg the same way.
Next row: Rib 14, turn, cast on 2 sts, turn, rib 14
sts from the other needle (30 sts).
Work 3 rows k1, p1 rib. Work 4 rows ss beg with
k row.
K2 tog at each end of next and every 6th row
until 24 sts rem.
Work three rows ss.
Cut yarn and leave sts on spare needle.
SKIRT: Cast on 30 sts, work 2 rows k1, p1 rib.
Work 10 rows ss.

Lady's swimsuit and jacket

Continue in ss and k2 tog at each end of next
and every 6th row until 24 sts rem.
Work 3 rows.
Now join the two parts of the garment together.
With the skirt sts directly in front of the body sts,
k first st from the skirt together with first st from
the body. Ease the sts carefully along both needles
(be warned, if you drop a st you will find that it
is almost impossible to pick it up). Continue
knitting second st from skirt with second st from
body, etc until all sts have been worked and there
is one set of 24 sts on one needle. Ensure that
you have the skirt in front of (outside) the body.
P one row. K2 tog at each end of next row. P one
row. Work 4 rows in k1, p1 rib. Cast off.
FRONT: Work the main body piece as for the
back (above) and leave on spare needle while
working the skirt. If the motif is not required, cast
on 32 sts and work as for the back skirt until 24
sts rem.
P one row. K2 tog at each end of next row. P one
row. To knit the anchor motif, cast on 32 sts, and
work two rows in k1, p1 rib. Work 4 rows ss.
Then begin motif: k 20, join in colour, k3 from
first row of motif (wind yarn around M to avoid
holes), k9.
Work another 5 rows following motif pattern
while keeping ss correct.
Next row: k2 tog at each end of row while
following row 7 of motif from the chart.
Continue in ss (working last two rows of motif).
Dec 1 st at each end of every sixth row from last
dec until 26 sts rem. P one row. K2 tog at each
end of next row. P one row. Now join skirt and

main body together as for back. P one row. K2 tog at each end of next row. P one row. Work 6 rows k1, p1 rib. Work 4 rows ss.

Next row: s1, k6, inc in next st, k6, inc in next st, k7.

Next row: p.

Next row: s1, k7, inc in next st, k6, inc in next st, k7.

Continue in ss for next 7 rows.

Work 5 rows in k1, p1 rib.

Next row: Rib 9, cast off 8 sts (1 st rem on needle), rib 8. Working on last set of 9 sts, to make strap, and keeping k1, p1 rib correct, rib 9.

Next row: k2 tog, rib 7.

Work 22 rows in rib.

Next row: Rib 4, m1, p2 tog, rib 2.

Work three more rows in rib. Cast off.

Rejoin yarn to first set of 9 sts at inner neck edge work 1 row rib beg with a p st.

Next row: Rib 7, p2 tog.

Now finish to match first strap.

Press the work lightly under a slightly damp cloth. Stitch buttons at the back waist. With wrong sides facing, join the inside leg seams and side body seams. Turn body right side out, and join the skirt side seams. Press lightly under a dry linen cloth and gently pull the legs down so that they show under the skirt.

JACKET

If the anchor motif is not required, k throughout in ss.

Cast on 30 sts. Work in gs for 7 rows.

Work 20 rows in ss, k2 tog at each end of next and foll tenth row (26 sts), work 3 rows.

To knit the motif: k12 sts, join in colour and k2, k12 in M. Continue with motif, winding yarn around M to avoid holes, for next 5 rows (if not knitting motif work 6 rows). Either continuing in straight ss or following motif, cast on 2 sts at beg of next 2 rows for sleeve, then 5 sts at beg of foll 2 rows (40 sts). Either continue in straight ss for a further 13 rows, or work last 8 rows of motif, cut coloured yarn, and work another 5 rows in ss.

Next row: s1, p11, k16, p11, k1.

Next row: k.

Rep last 2 rows, twice.

Next row: s1, p11, k4, cast off 8 sts (1 st rem on needle), k3, p11, k1.

On last set of 16 sts, continue thus:-

Next row: s1, k to end.

Next row: s1, p11, k4.

Rep last 2 rows, three times, then first row again.

Next row: Cast on 5 sts, k9, p11, k1 (21 sts).

Next row: s1, k to end.

Next row: s1, k8, p11, k1.

Rep last 2 rows once more.

Next row: k.

Next row s1, k3, p to last st, k1.

Rep last 2 rows eight times.

Keeping 4 k sts border at front edge, cast off 5 sts at armhole edge at beg of next row.

Next row: s1, k3, p to last st, k1.

Next row: Cast off 2 sts at beg of row for armhole.

Next row: s1, k3, p to last st, k1 (14 sts).

Next row: s1, k to end.

Next row: s1, k3, p12, k1.

Rep last 2 rows four times.

Next row: s1, k to last st, inc in last st.

Next row: s1, k3, p10, k1.

Next row: s1, k to end.

Work the last 2 rows three times more.

Next row: s1, k to last st, inc in last st (16 sts).

Next row: s1, k3, p11, k1.

Next row: s1, k to end.

Work last 2 rows nine times more.

Work 8 rows in gs.

Cast off k wise on ws of work.

Rejoin yarn to rem set of 16 sts at neck edge and k all along the row.

Next row: s1, p11, k4.

Next row: k.

Rep last 2 rows three times, then first row once.

Cast on 5 sts at beg of next row, k all along row.

Next row: s1, p11, k9.

Next row: k.

Rep last 2 rows twice.

Next row: s1, p16, k4.

Next row: k.

Rep last 2 rows three times.

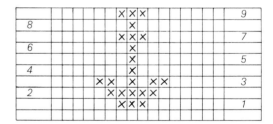

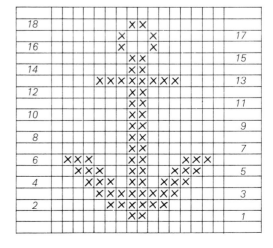

Lady's swimsuit and jacket – anchor motifs

Next row: Cast off 5 sts (1 st rem on needle), p11, k4.
Next row: k.
Next row: Cast off 2 sts (1 st rem on needle) p9, k4.
Next row: k.
Next row: s1, p9, k4.
Rep last 2 rows four times.
Next row: Inc in first st, k to end.
Next row: s1, p10, k4.
Next row: k.
Rep last 2 rows, three times, then first row again.
Next row: Inc in first st, k to end (16 sts).
Next row: s1, p11, k4.
Next row: k.
Rep last 2 rows nine times.
Work 8 rows in gs. Cast off on ws.
Sleeve edges: (Both the same) with rs of work facing, pick up and k 25 sts evenly along sleeve edge. Work 4 rows in gs and cast off k wise. Darn in loose ends of colour neatly behind the motif. Join the side seams and press the jacket under a dry cloth.

HIS AND HERS STRIPED SWEATERS

(Shown on page 111)

Our splendid knitted sweaters are designed to fit man and lady dolls but they might also be made to hang over the back of a chair or fold in a drawer. Both sweaters are knitted in 1–1½-ply wool (yarn) on 1mm needles and you will need one skein of each colour wool. Isobel has chosen navy and pale blue for the man's sweater and pink and red for the lady's version.

HIS SWEATER

BACK: Cast on 30 sts in navy. K 6 rows, knitting into the back of the stitches on the first row to make a neat edge.
Join in pale blue. Starting with a k row and working alternate 2 rows in pale blue and two rows in navy, work 20 rows in ss.
Mark each end of the next row with a coloured thread (armholes), then work a further 21 rows in ss stripes. Cut pale blue.
Work 4 rows gs in navy and cast off.
FRONT: Make a second piece in the same way for the front.
Join the back to the front for approximately ½ inch at the shoulder seams (checking that the neck will go over the doll's head).
SLEEVES: (Both the same) With rs of the work facing you, in navy, pick up and k 30 sts between the thread markers (armholes).
P one row.
Join in pale blue and, working alternate two-row

AN OLD-FASHIONED BATHROOM

*Knitted flannel, small string bag, hot-water bottle cover, bath
mat (Chapter 1), gentleman's dressing-gown (Chapter 2),
cross-stitch text (Chapter 3), towels (Chapter 5), nightshirt and
nightcap, slippers (Chapter 6), bead and button accessories,
bathroom accessories (Chapter 8)*

stripes as before, ss 30 rows. Dec each end of the 5th, 11th, 17th, 23rd and 29th rows (20 sts). Cut pale blue.

In navy, gs 4 rows. Dec each end of the first gs row. Cast off. Darn in the loose ends and join the side and sleeve seams.

HER SWEATER

BACK: Cast on 26 sts in red. K 6 rows, knitting into the back of the stitches on the first row to make a neat edge. Join in pink.

Starting with a k row and working alternate two rows in pink and two rows in red, work 18 rows in ss.

Mark each end of the next row with a coloured thread (armholes), then work a further 19 rows in ss. Cut pink.

Work 4 rows gs in red and cast off.

FRONT: Make a second piece in the same way for the front. Join the shoulder seams for approximately ¼ inch (checking the fit on the doll).

SLEEVES: (Both the same) With rs facing you, in pink, pick up and k 26 sts between the thread markers (armholes).

P one row.

Join in red and, working alternate two-row stripes, ss 28 rows. Dec each end of the 7th, 13th, 17th and 23rd rows (18 sts). Cut pink.

In red, gs 4 rows. Cast off. Darn in the loose ends and join the side and sleeve seams.

GENTLEMAN'S COMBINATIONS

(Shown on page 114)

The gentlemen residents of your dolls' house will not be able to resist these cosy combinations complete with buttoned 'trap door' at the back! Isobel's pattern is designed for advanced knitters, but the results are worth the effort. You will need two skeins of 1–1½-ply wool in cream as favoured by British gentlemen or red, which was more popular with Americans, ten tiny matching buttons, 1mm knitting needles, and a 0.75 crochet hook.

RIGHT FRONT LEG: Cast on 10 sts. Work 4 rows single rib.

Starting with a k row, work 40 rows in ss, inc each end of rows 15 and 25. Cut yarn and leave this leg on a safety pin.

LEFT FRONT LEG: Make a second leg as above, but do not cut yarn.

Next row: k across sts already on needle, then, with rs of leg facing, k across the 14 sts left on the safety pin (28 sts).

Starting with a p row, work 7 rows ss and mark each end of the 7th row with a coloured thread. *

LEFT FRONT: Next row: k 15, turn, leaving rem

13 sts on a safety pin. Work on these 15 sts for the left front as follows:-

Next row: k2, p to end.

Keeping the 2k st border at centre correct, work 6 rows ss.

Next row (buttonhole row): k to last 3 sts, k2 tog, yf, k1.

Continue in ss for 5 rows, remembering k st border, then work buttonhole row again.

Repeat these 6 rows twice more.

Next row: k2, p to end.

Next row (armhole row): Cast off 2 sts, k to end (13 sts).

Remembering k st border, work 3 rows ss, then work buttonhole row again.

Work another 10 rows in ss remembering the k st border, working a sixth buttonhole on the sixth of these 10 rows.

Next row (neck): Cast off 5 sts, p to end (8 sts).

Work 10 rows straight in ss. Cut yarn and leave these sts on a safety pin.

RIGHT FRONT: Transfer 13 sts from the safety pin to the needle with point facing to centre. With rs of work facing you, rejoin yarn at centre edge, cast on 2, k to end.

Starting with a p row, and keeping a 2 k st border on centre edge as before, work 26 rows ss on these 15 sts.

Next row (armhole): Cast off 2 sts, p to last 2, k2 (13 sts).

Starting with a k row, and keeping k st border correct, work 14 rows ss.

Next row (neck): Cast off 5 sts, k to end (8 sts).

Starting with a p row, work 10 rows ss.

Next row: p 8 sts already on needle, cast on 8 sts, then p on the 8sts of left shoulder from the safety pin (24 sts).

Starting with a k row, work 14 rows ss.

Armholes: Cast on 2 sts at beg of next 2 rows (28 sts).

Work 12 rows ss.

Work 4 rows rib. Cast off in rib.

SLEEVES: (Both the same) With rs of work facing, pick up and knit 25 sts round the armhole.

Starting with a p row, ss 33 rows. Dec each end of 10th, 18th, 26th and 32nd rows (17 sts).

Rib 4 rows. Cast off in rib.

BACK LEGS: Work as the front legs up to *.

Starting with a k row, work 16 rows ss.

Rib 2 rows.

Buttonhole row: Rib 3, yf, k2 tog, rib 5, yrn, p2 tog, rib 5, yf, k2 tog, rib 5, yrn, p2 tog, rib 2.

Rib one row. Cast off in rib.

Darn in loose ends. Catch down the two cast-on sts of right front border behind left front border to form a placket. Join sleeve and side seams in one. Join outside leg seams up to thread markers. Join inside leg seams. Using crochet hook, work a row of dc around the neck. Sew on buttons – six on front and four on back flap.

VICTORIAN BATHING COSTUMES

(Shown on page 34)

In the nineteenth century sea-bathing was a very modest affair and men and women wore voluminous knitted or flannel costumes which covered them from neck to ankles. Our patterns are typical of the period, and if the residents of your Victorian dolls' house are planning a holiday they will be delighted with such fashionable garments. The lady's costume will need three skeins of 1–1½-ply wool with oddments of a contrasting colour for the frills. June chose French navy trimmed with white. The gentleman's costume needs two skeins of wool in the main colour and oddments of three toning colours for the stripes. June used maroon striped with blue and light and dark grey. Both costumes are knitted on 1mm needles and fastened with tiny buttons, three for the lady's costume, two for the gentleman's version.

LADY'S COSTUME

FRONT: Cast on 10 sts. Work 8 rows in ss.
Inc 1 st at each end of next and every foll 8th row until there are 16 sts.
Work another 15 rows in ss. Cut yarn and transfer sts to a spare needle.
Make the second leg in the same way.
Next row: k across all 32 sts.

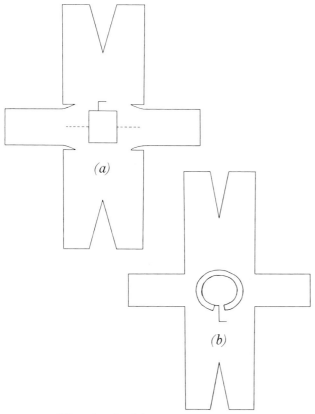

*Victorian bathing costumes – for a
a) gentleman and b) lady*

Work another 3 rows.
K2 tog at each end of the next and every foll 6th row until 22 sts remain.
★★ Work 3 rows.
Cast off 2 sts for armhole at beg of next 2 rows.
Next row: k5, inc in next st, k6, inc in next st, k5.
Next row: p.
Next row: k6, inc in next st, k6, inc in next st, k6 (22 sts).
Continue in ss for next 9 rows.
Neck: k7, cast off 8 sts, k7.
Working on last set of 7 sts, p one row.
Next row: k2 tog, k5.
Work another 3 rows on rem 6 sts. Cast off.
Rejoin yarn to first set of 7 sts at inner neck edge and p one row.
Next row: s1, k4, k2 tog.
Work another 3 rows on rem sts. Cast off.
BACK: Work as for the front up to ★★, p one row.
Begin the opening as follows:-
k11, turn, cast on 3 sts, k1, p12, k1.
To shape for the armhole, cast off 2 sts, k to end (12 sts).
Work 5 rows.
To make buttonhole, k2, m1, k2 tog, work to end.
Continue in ss, making two more buttonholes on following 6th and 12th rows.
Work two more rows.
Cast off 6 sts at beg of next row, p to end.
Work 2 more rows. Cast off.
Rejoin yarn to rem 11 sts, cast on 3 sts, k to end.
Cast off 2 sts for armhole at beg of next p row.
Work 20 rows.
Cast off 6 sts at beg of next row, k to end.
P one row. Cast off.
Press the work lightly under a damp cloth. Over- and underlap the button placket and stitch neatly at the base. Join the shoulder seams and sew buttons on to the placket to correspond with buttonholes.
SLEEVES: (Both the same) With rs facing, and beg at sts cast off for armhole, pick up and k 28 sts.
Work 11 rows, beg with a p row.
K2 tog at both ends of next and every foll 8th row until 20 sts rem.
Work 3 rows. Cut M and join in white to make the frill. K one row.
Next row: ★ k1, inc in next st. Rep from ★ to end.
Next row: k. Cast off.
NECK FRILL: In white, cast on 25 sts, k one row.
Next row: k1, inc in next 23 sts, k1.
K two rows.
Cast off loosely.
With right side of work facing, place the neck frill to neck, leaving the button placket free, and oversew neatly in place with matching yarn. With wrong sides facing, join the sleeve seams, then the inner leg seams and side seams.

GENTLEMAN'S COSTUME

FRONT: Cast on 14 sts. Work four rows in k1, p1 rib then work 6 rows ss.
Inc at each end of next and foll eighth row.
Work 23 rows ss beg with a p row. Cut yarn and transfer sts to a spare needle.
Work the second leg in the same way.
Work across all 36 sts. P one row.
Next row: s1, k15, k2 tog twice, k16.
Work 3 rows.
Next row: s1, k14, k2 tog twice, k15.
Work 5 rows.
K2 tog at both ends of next row.
Work 3 rows.
Cut M and join in first contrast colour. Work 4 rows. Cut first c and join in second c. Work 4 rows. Cut second c and join in third c. Work 4 rows. ★★ Rejoin M and work 4 rows.
Armholes: Cast off 3 sts at beg of next 2 rows.
Work 10 rows on rem 24 sts.
Next row: s1, k3, ★ k1, p1. Rep from ★ until 4 sts rem, k4.
Next row: s1, p3, ★ k1, p1. Rep from ★ until 4 sts rem, p3, k1.

Rep last 2 rows twice more.
Next row: s1, k3, k1, p1, k1, p1, cast off 8 sts in rib for the neck, k1, p1, k1, p1, p3, k1.
On last set of 8 sts, s1, p3, k1, p1, k1, p1.
Next row: k1, p1, k1, p1, k4.
Next row: s1, p3, k1, p1, k1, p1.
Rep last 2 rows once. Cast off. Rejoin yarn to inside neck edge of rem 8 sts, k1, p1, k1, p1, p3, k1.
Next row: s1, k3, k1, p1, k1, p1.
Next row: k1, p1, k1, p1, p3, k1.
Rep last 2 rows once. Cast off.
BACK: Work as for the front up to ★★. Rejoin M and work 2 rows.
Next row: To make back placket opening, s1, k14, turn, cast on 3 sts for placket underlap, turn, k1, p16, k1.
Cast off 3 sts for armhole at beg of next row.
Work 11 rows.
Next row: s1, k3, ★ k1, p1. Rep from ★ to last 2 sts, k2.

AN EARLY MORNING DIP
Victorian bathing costumes (Chapter 2)

Next row: s1, p1, * k1, p1. Rep from * to last 4 sts, p3, k1.

Rep last 2 rows three more times and first row once again. Cast off 7 sts at beg of next row (1 st rem on needle), p1, k1, p1, p3, k1.

Next row: s1, k3, k1, p1, k1, p1.

Next row: k1, p1, k1, p1, p3, k1. Cast off. Rejoin yarn to rem 15 sts at centre edge. Cast on 3 sts for placket overlap, k all across. Work 2 rows.

Next row: Cast off 3 sts for armhole, work to end. Work 6 rows in ss.

Next row: s1, k1, m1, k2 tog, work to end. Work another 3 rows in ss.

Next row: s1, * k1, p1. Rep from * to last 4 sts, k4.

Next row: s1, p3, * k1, p1. Rep from * to last st, k1.

Rep last 2 rows twice more.

Next row: s1, k1, m1, k2 tog, p1, k1, p1, k1, p1, k1, p1, k4.

Work another 3 rows, keeping rib patt correct.

Next row: Cast off 7 sts (1 st rem on needle), p1, k1, p1, k4.

Next row: s1, p3, k1, p1, k1, p1.

Next row: k1, p1, k1, p1, k4. Cast off.

Press the work lightly under a damp cloth. Align under- and overlaps on the placket, and stitch neatly at the base. Join the shoulder seams and sew buttons to the placket.

SLEEVES: (Both the same) Beg at inside corner of armhole edge, pick up and k 28 sts. Work 15 rows in ss beg with a p row.

Work 2 tog at each end of next and foll 8th row (24 sts).

Work 9 rows.

Work 6 rows in k1, p1 rib. Cast off in rib.

With wrong side of work facing, join sleeve heads to body at armhole edges, then join the sleeve seams. Join the inside leg seams, then the side seams, matching the contrasting stripes in the pattern and using matching yarns. Ease gently into shape and press carefully under a dry cloth.

CLOTHES FOR CHILDREN

HAT, SCARF AND MITTENS *(Shown on page 43)*

This simple set of accessories is so quick to knit, you could make them for every child in your dolls' house. Isobel has chosen red, but each child could have a set in a different colour. You will need one skein of 1–1½-ply wool (yarn) for each set, 1mm knitting needles, and a fine crochet hook for the scarf fringe.

HAT

Cast on 30 sts. Work 6 rows in k1, p1 rib. Starting with a k row, work 6 rows in ss. Decrease for the crown as follows:-

Dec row 1: (k3, k2 tog) six times.

Next and alt rows: p.

Dec row 2: (k2, k2 tog) six times.

Dec row 3: (k1, k2 tog) six times.

Cut yarn, leaving an end long enough to thread through remaining 12 sts. Fasten off, and with right sides together, stitch up back seam, sewing in the loose ends. Turn right side out. If required, glue a tiny pom-pom to the crown of the hat with fabric glue.

SCARF

Cast on 10 sts. Work 90 rows in k1, p1 rib, working into the back of k sts on the first row only to make a neat edge. Cast off in rib and darn in the loose ends. Using a fine crochet

hook, knot 2 inch lengths of yarn into each end of the scarf to make a fringe and trim the fringes to ½ inch.

MITTENS

To make each mitten, cast on 12 sts. Work 3 rows k1, p1, rib, knitting into the back of k sts only on the first row to make a neat edge.

Starting with a p row, work 8 rows ss.

Next row: (p2 tog) rep to end. Cut yarn, leaving an end long enough to thread through the remaining 6 sts, fasten off and with right sides together, stitch up the back seam, sewing in the loose ends. Turn right side out.

DRESS AND KNICKERS *(Shown on page 43)*

This charming little dress trimmed with a pattern of stars in a contrasting colour on the hem and sleeves, and matching knickers, are designed for a little girl about 3¼ inches tall. June knitted our dress and knickers in Mercer crochet cotton 100 in white, with oddments of scarlet for trimming, on 1mm needles. You will also need a tiny button or bead and a little fine ribbon.

DRESS

Patt: To make a star, p3 tog leaving sts on needle, yrn, then p the same 3 sts again.

Row 1: k.
Row 2: s1, p2, ★ make star in next 3 sts, p1. Rep from ★ to last 2 sts, p1, k1.
Row 3: k.
Row 4: s1, ★ make star in next 3 sts, p1. Rep from ★ to last 4 sts, make star, k1.
FRONT: Cast on 33 sts in M. K one row working into backs of sts.
Work first 2 rows of patt, join in contrast colour (C) and work rows 3 and 4 of patt in C.
Work first 2 rows of patt in M.
Work rows 3 and 4 of patt in C. C, then first 2 rows of pattern in M. Cut C.
Work 13 rows in ss beg with k row.
Next row: s1, p1, p2 tog, rep from ★ to last 2 sts, p1, k1 (23 sts).
Next row: s1, ★ yf, k2 tog. Rep from ★ to end.
Next row: s1, p to end, k1.
Armhole: Cast off 2 sts at beg of next 2 rows.
Next row: k2 tog at beg and end of row (17 sts). Work 7 rows in ss.
Next row: s1, p5, cast off next 5 sts, p5, k1.
Working on last 6 sts, s1, k3, k2 tog at neck edge. Work 3 rows beg with a p row on rem 5 sts. Cast off. Rejoin yarn to neck edge of first set of 6 sts.
Next row: k2 tog, k4.
Work 3 rows on 5 rem sts. Cast off.
BACK: Work as for front until both sets of 2 cast-off sts have been worked for armhole.
Next row: k2 tog, k8, turn (to make back opening), cast on 2 sts, p 10, k1.
Beg with k row, work 8 rows in ss on these 11 sts.
Next row: s1, k8, yf, k2 tog.
Next row: Cast off 6 sts at beg of next row, p to last st, k1.
Next row: Cast off rem 5 sts. Rejoin yarn at middle back to other 9 sts. Cast on 2 sts, k to last 2 sts, k2 tog (10 sts).
Beg with a p row, work 9 rows.
Next row: Cast off 5 sts, p4, k1. Cast off.
Press lightly. With wrong sides facing, join the shoulder seams and darn in loose ends. Stitch under- and overlaps of back opening, secured at the waist. Work a row of dc crochet around the neckline if required, to neaten. Sew on button.
SLEEVES: (Both the same) With rs of work facing, and beg at 2 cast-off sts at armhole edge, pick up and k 25 sts in M.
Next row: Work row 2 of patt. Join in C and work rows 3 and 4. Cut C and work rows 1 and 2.
Next row: s1, k2, k3 tog, k5, k3 tog, k5, k3 tog, k3 (19 sts). Cast off.
Join the sleeve and side seams, using yarn on pattern. Press dress and thread ribbon at waist.

KNICKERS

Cast on 22 sts. Work in k1, p1 rib for 4 rows.
Work in ss for next 12 rows.
Cast off 9 sts at beg of next 2 rows.
Work 4 rows ss on rem 4 sts.

Cast on 9 sts at beg of next 2 rows.
Work 11 rows in ss beg with k row.
Work 4 rows in k1, p1 rib. Cast off.
Press, and join the side seams. Thread doubled shirring elastic through the waist to fit the doll.

CLOAK OR CAPE
(Shown on page 43)

The pattern for this versatile knitted cloak is designed to fit a 3 inch child, but can easily be shortened, or lengthened for a taller child or a lady – simply knit fewer, or more, rows before working the decreasing rows. Isobel has used white DMC Fil à Dentelles 80 cotton thread trimmed with red, blue and yellow to make a beach cape, but the pattern might also be knitted in one plain colour as a child's or lady's cloak. Consider making an adult-size version to hang on the back of the kitchen door. To make the cape, you will need one ball of white yarn and oddments of red, blue and yellow, 1mm knitting needles, and a 0.60 crochet hook.
Using white (W) cast on 88 sts. Work one row in k1, p1, rib. Continue working a two-row patt as follows:-
Row 1: k.
Row 2: ★ k1, p1. Rep from ★ to the end.
Join in red (R), leaving W hanging. Work patt rows 1 and 2 in R. Cut R.
Work patt rows 1 and 2 in W. Join in blue (B) leaving W hanging.
Work patt rows 1 and 2 in B. Cut B.
Work patt rows 1 and 2 in W. Join in yellow (Y) leaving W hanging.
Work patt rows 1 and 2 in Y. Cut Y. Continue in W.
Next row: k.
Next row: k3, p to last 3 sts, k3.
Rep these 2 rows six more times. (Lengthen the patt here if required.)
Dec row 1: k5, (k8, k2 tog) seven times, k13.
Starting with a p row, work 5 rows ss keeping a k3 border at each end.
Dec row 2: k5, (k7, k2 tog) seven times, k13.
Starting with a p row, work 3 rows ss keeping a k3 border at each end.
Dec row 3: k5 (k3, k2 tog) twelve times, k9.
Starting with a p row, work 3 rows ss keeping a k3 border at each end.
Dec row 4: k5 (k2, k2 tog) thirteen times, k5.
Next row: k3, p to last 3 sts, k3.
Eyelet row: k1, ★ (yf, k2 tog). Rep from ★ to the end.
K two rows. Cast off and darn in loose ends.
Crochet a chain 110 ch in length to make a drawstring for the cape – or use fine ribbon.
Press the cape and thread the drawstring through the eyelet holes.

CHILDREN'S SWIMSUITS

(Shown on page 43)

SWEATER AND SHORTS *(Shown on page 43)*

These sweet little swimsuits are suitable for children living in a twentieth-century dolls' house, and the pattern is given in two sizes, for a 2½ inch toddler, and a 3 inch child. If your children don't go to the seaside, they could wear their swimsuits to play in the garden. Isobel has used red and blue 1–1½-ply wool (yarn), but almost any colour would be suitable and you will need one skein for each swimsuit. They are knitted on 1mm needles.

TODDLER SIZE

Cast on 18 sts. Work 2 rows single rib, working into the back of k sts on the first row only.
Work 6 rows ss.
Continuing in ss, dec at each end of the next 8 rows (2 sts).
Work 2 rows ss.
Continuing in ss, inc at each end of the next 8 rows (18 sts).
Work 6 rows ss.
Work 2 rows single rib.
Next row: Cast off 5 sts, k to last 5 sts, cast off these rem 5 sts. Cut yarn.
For the bib: Rejoin the yarn to ws of centre 8 sts.
Row 1: k2, p4, k2.
Row 2: k.
Rep row 1 again, then k 2 rows.
Next row: k2, cast off 4, k2.
Work 16 rows gs on first 2 sts for the strap, then fasten off. Rejoin yarn to the other 2 sts and work the second strap to match. To make up, darn in the loose ends and with right sides facing, sew up the side seams. Turn right side out, cross the straps at the back, and stitch to the waist edge at centre back.

CHILD SIZE

Cast on 20 sts, work 2 rows single rib as above.
Work 8 rows ss.
Dec each end of the next 8 rows (4 sts). Work 2 rows ss.
Inc each end of next 8 rows (20 sts).
Work 8 rows ss.
Work 2 rows single rib.
Next row: Cast off 5 sts, k to last 5 sts, cast off remaining 5 sts. Cut yarn.
For the bib: Rejoin yarn to ws of centre 10 sts.
Row 1: k3, p4, k3.
Row 2: k.
Rep these two rows once then row 1 again.
K two rows.
Next row: k3, cast off 4, k3.
Work 26 rows gs on each set of 3 sts for the straps. Make up as above.

Our stylish sweater and shorts are designed to fit a little boy or girl about 3¼ inches tall. You will need a skein of 1–1½-ply wool (yarn) for each garment – June has used scarlet for the sweater and grey for the shorts. Both are worked on 1mm needles.

SWEATER

FRONT: Cast on 26 sts.
Patt row 1: s1, p3, k2, p2, k2, p2, k2, p2, k2, p2, k2, p3, k1.
Row 2: k4, p2, k2, p2, k2, p2, k2, p2, k2, p2, k4.
Row 3: s1, p3, work mock cable into next 2 sts thus:- k into front of second st on needle, then k first st, slipping both sts off needle at same time (c2f). p2, k2, p2, c2f, p2, k2, p2, c2f, p3, k1.
Row 4: As row 2.
Rep these 4 patt rows twice more (12 rows). Keeping patt correct, cast off 2 sts for underarm on next two rows (22 sts). Work 11 rows in patt noting that patt will now begin with s1, p1 and end with p1, k1 on the 1st and 3rd rows, and k2 at beg and end of the 2nd and 4th rows.
Next row: k2, p2, k2, turn and work 2 rows in patt on first 6 sts. Cast off. Transfer the next 10 sts to a safety pin, rejoin yarn to last 6 sts and work 3 rows in patt. Cast off.
BACK: Work as for the front until 11 rows in patt have been completed, to the top of the shoulder.
Next row: Work 6 sts in patt, turn and work another row in patt. Cast off. Transfer next 10 sts to a safety pin, rejoin yarn to last 6 sts, work 2 rows in patt. Cast off. With wrong side of work facing, join the right shoulder seam.
Neck: With rs of work facing, pick up 5 sts down left side of front, transfer 10 sts from safety pin to needle, pick up 5 sts up right side of front, pick up 3 sts from right side of back neck edge, transfer 10 sts from pin to needle and pick up 3 sts up back of neck (36 sts). The transferred sts are already in k2, p2 rib from the body patt, so adjust your k2, p2 rib for the neck to correspond, noting that the rib patt will begin with a spare st thus:-
Row 1: p1, k2, p2, (k2, p2 along 10 sts transferred) k2, p2, k2, p2 (k2, p2 along 10 sts transferred), k2, p1.
Row 2: k1, * p2, k2, rep from * to last st, k1.
Rep rows 1 and 2, then row 1 again. Cast off very loosely in k2, p2 rib to correspond with sts. With wrong side of work facing, join the left shoulder seam.
SLEEVES: (Both the same) With rs of work facing, and beg at inside, cast off underarm edge, pick up and k 22 sts.
Row 1: s1, p1, k2, p2, k2, p2, c2f, p2, k2, p2, k2, p1, k1.

LISTEN WITH MOTHER

Small lacy blanket, table-mats and runner, cuddly doll (Chapter 1), lacy cape, lady's dressing-gown, child's dress and knickers (Chapter 2), diamond eiderdown and bedspread (Chapter 4), curtains with frill, braided-wool rug, lampshade on bead-base lamp (Chapter 5), French knickers and petticoat, handbag, slippers (Chapter 6), dressing-table stool, ottoman (Chapter 7), bead and button accessories, nightdress case, laundry bin (Chapter 8)

Row 2: s1, k1, ★ p2, k2. Rep from ★ to end.
Row 3: s1, p1, ★ k2, p2. Rep from ★ to end.
Row 4: As row 2.
Rep last 4 rows.
Row 9: k2 tog, k2, p2, k2, p2, c2f, p2, k2, p2, k2, k2 tog.
Row 10: s1, ★ p2, k2. Rep from ★ to last 3 sts, p2, k1.
Row 11: s1, ★ k2, p2. Rep from ★ to last 3 sts, k3.
Row 12: As row 10.
Rep last four rows.
Row 17: k2 tog, k1, p2, k2, p2, c2f, p2, k2, p2, k1, k2 tog.
Row 18: s1, p1, ★ k2, p2. Rep from ★ to end.
Row 19: s1, k1, ★ p2, k2. Rep from ★ to end.
Row 20: As row 18. Cast off loosely. With the wrong side of the work facing, join the sleeve and side seams.

SHORTS

Back and front the same. Cast on 30 sts. Work 4 rows in single rib (k1, p1).
Rows 5 and 6: Keeping rib patt correct, cast off 1 st at beg of each row.
Row 7: k2 tog at beg and end of row.
Continue in single rib for next 9 rows. Cast off loosely in single rib. Knit second piece in the same way.
Join the two pieces together at centre front and back, waist to crotch seams, then join inside leg seams. Thread doubled shirring elastic through the waist to fit the doll.

CROCHETED SUN HAT *(Shown on page 43)*

Isobel has made our crocheted sun hat in white DMC Fil à Dentelles cotton thread trimmed with red, yellow and blue to match the beach cape. If you prefer, it can be worked in one colour – perhaps cream or ecru – and trimmed with ribbons and flowers to make a hat for a little girl or a lady. You will need long oddments of thread and a 0.60 crochet hook.
Work into the back of the loops throughout.
To work the crown: In yellow (Y), 5 ch. Join with a ss to make a ring.
Round 1: Work 6 dc into ring.
Round 2: Work 2 dc into each dc (12 dc). Cut Y and join in white (W). Work the next two rounds in W.
Round 3: ★ 1 dc into next dc, 2 dc into next dc. Rep from ★ to the end.
Round 4: ★ 1 dc into each of the next 2 dc, 2 dc into next dc. Rep from ★ to the end. Leave W hanging and join in blue (B). Work next two rounds in B.
Round 5: ★ 1 dc into each of next 3 dc, 2 dc into next dc. Rep from ★ to the end.
Round 6: ★ 1 dc into each of the next 4 dc, 2 dc into next dc. Rep from ★ to the end. Cut B and work next two rounds in W.
Round 7: ★ 1 dc into each of the next 5 dc, 2 dc into next dc. Rep from ★ to the end.
Round 8: 1 dc into each dc to the end. Leave W hanging and join in red (R). Work next two rounds in R.
Round 9 and 10: Rep round 8. Cut R and work next two rounds in W.
Round 11 and 12: Rep round 8.
To work the brim:
Round 1: (In W) ★ 1 dc into each of next 2 dc, 2 dc into next dc. Rep from ★ to the end. Leave W hanging and join in Y.
Round 2: (In Y) ★ 1 dc into each of the next 3 dc, 2 dc into next dc. Rep from ★ to the end. Cut Y.
Round 3: (In W) ★ 1 dc into each of next 4 dc, 2 dc into next dc. Rep from ★ to the end. Leave W hanging and join in B.
Round 4: (In B) ★ 1 dc into each of next 5 dc, 2 dc into next dc. Rep from ★ to the end. Cut B.
Round 5: (In W) ★ 1 dc into each of next 6 dc, 2 dc into next dc. Rep from ★ to the end. Cut W and join in R.
Round 6: (In R) ★ 1 dc into each of next 7 dc, 2 dc into next dc. Rep from ★ to the end.
Join with a ss, fasten off and darn in loose ends.

CLOTHES FOR BABIES

PRAM SET *(Shown on page 43)*

This delightful little pram set of knitted jacket, bonnet, and leggings will fit a baby boy or girl about 2¼ inches tall. The pattern is designed for more experienced knitters, and Isobel has chosen white but pastel colours would also be suitable. It is knitted in 1-ply wool (yarn) and ½oz will be more than enough to make the set. You will also need two tiny buttons or beads, about 8 inches of fine silk ribbon, and a little shirring elastic. The pram set is knitted on 1mm needles and you will need a 0.75 crochet hook for finishing.

JACKET

BACK: Cast on 31 sts, k one row.
Patt row 1: k2, ★ (yf, s1, k2 tog, psso, yf, k1).

Rep from ★ to last st, k1.
Rows 2 and 4: p.
Row 3: k1, k2 tog, yf, k1, ★ (yf, s1, k2 tog, psso, yf, k1). Rep from ★ to last 3 sts, yf, s1, k1, psso, k1.
Work these four patt rows twice in all. Then, starting with a k row, ss 6 rows.
Dec row: k1, ★ (k2 tog). Rep from ★ to end (16 sts). K one row.
Armholes: Continuing in gs, k2 tog at each end of next 2 rows (12 sts).
K 9 rows.
Shoulders: Cast off 3 sts at the beg of next 2 rows.
Cast off rem 6 sts.
LEFT FRONT: Cast on 19 sts, k 1 row.
Work 4 patt rows (as above) twice, then ss 6 rows.
Dec row: (k2 tog) four times, k3 tog, (k2 tog) 4 times.
★★On 9 sts, k 1 row.
Armholes: Continue in gs, k2 tog at beg of next row and end of foll row (7 sts).
K 7 rows.
Neck edge: Cast off 4 sts beg of next row, work 3 rows gs, cast off.
RIGHT FRONT: Work as left front (above) up to ★★.
Buttonhole row: k to last 3 sts, k2 tog, yf, k1.
Armholes: Continue in gs, k2 tog at end of next row and beg of foll row (7 sts).
K 6 rows, working a second buttonhole at end of row 6.
Neck edge: Cast off 4 sts at beg of next row.
K 4 rows. Cast off.
SLEEVES: (Both the same) Join shoulder seams. With rs of work facing, pick up and k 16 sts evenly around the armhole.
Starting with a p row, ss 10 rows, dec 1 st at each end of 6th and 8th rows (12 sts).
Rib 2 rows. Cast off.
Darn in the loose ends. Join side and sleeve seams. Work a row of dc crochet around the neck and fasten off. Sew on two buttons to the left front to correspond with the buttonholes on the right front.

BONNET

Cast on 23 sts, k 1 row.
Work 4 patt rows (as above) once.
Starting with a k row, ss 6 rows.
To shape the crown:-
Row 1: (k2, k2 tog). Rep to last 3 sts, k3.
Row 2 and alt rows: p.
Row 3: (k1, k2 tog). Rep to end.
Row 5: (k2 tog) Rep to end. Cut the yarn, leaving a long enough end to allow you to thread through the 6 sts rem on the needle. Fasten off and join the back seam as far as beg of crown shaping.
Crochet a row of dc around the face edge.

Thread the ribbon through the spaces formed by the row of dc.

LEGGINGS (both legs the same)

Cast on 18 sts, rib 2 rows.
Ss 14 rows.
Cast off 2 sts at beg of next 2 rows. K2 tog at beg of next 2 rows (12 sts).
Ss 12 rows. Cast off.
Fold each leg in half and join toe and leg seams. Join centre front and back seams. Thread shirring elastic through the waistline to fit the baby.

LAYETTE *(Shown on page 43)*

The exquisite dress, matinee jacket, bonnet, knickers, and bootees in this layette will fit babies about 2¼ inches tall. Isobel has designed the pattern for experienced knitters, and uses DMC Fil à Dentelles 80 cotton thread in white or pastel shades. One ball of yarn will make the layette, and you will need three tiny buttons or beads, ½ yard of fine silk ribbon, and a little shirring elastic. The layette is knitted on 1mm needles, with a 0.75 crochet hook for finishing.

DRESS

BACK: Cast on 33 sts, k one row.
Patt row 1: k2, ★ (p1, yon, s1, k2 tog, psso, yrn). Rep from ★ to last 3 sts, p1, k2.
Row 2: p2, ★ (k1, p3). Rep from ★ to last 3 sts, p1, k2.
Row 3: k2 ★ (p1, k3). Rep from ★ to last 3 sts, p1, k2.
Row 4: Rep row 2.
Work these 4 patt rows twice in all, then starting with a k row, ss 16 rows.

Clothes for babies

Dec row: k1, ★ (k2 tog). Rep from ★ to end (17 sts). ★★ continue in gs.
Next row: k8, leave these 8 sts on a small safety pin, k to end.
Work on these 9 sts for the *RIGHT BACK:* dec 1 st at armhole edge of next 2 rows (7 sts).
K 6 rows.
Buttonhole row: k to last 3 sts, k2 tog, yf, k1.
Next row: Cast off 4, k to end.
K 3 rows straight. Cast off.
LEFT BACK: With rs of work facing, rejoin yarn to inside edge of rem 8 sts. Cast on 3, k to last 2 sts, k2 tog.
Dec at beg of next row, k to end (9 sts).
K 8 rows.
Next row: Cast off 6, k to end. K 2 rows straight. Cast off.
FRONT: Work as for back (above) as far as ★★.
K one row.
Continue in gs, dec 1 st at each end of next 2 rows (13 sts).
K 6 rows.
Next row: k3, leave these sts on a safety pin. Cast off 7, k to end.
On last 3 sts, k 4 rows. Cast off. With rs of work facing, rejoin yarn to inside edge of rem 3 sts and k 4 rows. Cast off.
SLEEVES: (Both the same) Join shoulder seams. With rs of work facing, pick up and k 16 sts evenly around the armhole.
Beg with a p row, work 3 rows ss, then 2 rows single rib. Cast off.
Darn in loose ends. Catch down the 3 cast-on sts of left back behind the right back to form a placket. Join the side and sleeve seams in one. Crochet a row of dc around the neck edge. Sew button to the left back to correspond with buttonhole.

MATINÉE JACKET

BACK: Cast on 33 sts, work 4 patt rows (as for dress) twice, then starting with a k row, work 6 rows ss.
Dec row: k1, k3 tog, (k2 tog) thirteen times, k3 tog (16 sts).
K one row.
Armholes: Continue in gs, k2 tog at each end of next 2 rows (12 sts).
K 9 rows.
Shoulders: Cast off 3 sts at beg of next 2 rows. Cast off rem 6 sts.
LEFT FRONT: Cast on 21 sts. K 1 row.
Work 4 patt rows (as for dress) twice, then ss 6 rows.
Dec row: (k2 tog) three times, (k3 tog) three times, (k2 tog) three times. ★★
On 9 sts, k 1 row.
Armholes: Continue in gs, k2 tog at beg of next row and end of foll row (7 sts).
K 7 rows.

Neck edge: Cast off 4 sts at beg of next row. Work 3 rows gs. Cast off.
RIGHT FRONT: Work as left front to ★★.
Buttonhole row: k to last 3 sts, k2 tog, yf, k1.
Armholes: Continue in gs, k2 tog at end of next row and beg of foll row. On 7 sts, k 6 rows working a second buttonhole at end of row 6.
Neck edge: Cast off 4 sts at beg of next row, work 4 rows gs. Cast off.
SLEEVES: (Both the same) Join shoulder seams. With rs of work facing, pick up and k 16 sts evenly around the armhole.
Starting with a p row, ss 10 rows. Dec 1 st at each end of 6th and 8th rows (12 sts).
Rib 2 rows. Cast off.
Darn in loose ends. Join side and sleeve seams in one. Work a row of dc crochet around the neck edge and fasten off. Sew two buttons to the left front to correspond with the buttonholes.

BONNET

Cast on 40 sts.
Row 1: k.
Row 2: s1, k to last 2 sts, turn.
Row 3: As row 2.
Row 4 and 5: s1, k to last 4 sts, turn.
Row 6: s1, k to last 6 sts, turn.
Row 7: s1, k to end.
Row 8: k6, ★ k2 tog. Rep from ★ to last 6 sts, k6 (26 sts).
K 16 rows.
Crown row 1: ★ (k2 tog, k4). Rep from ★ to end.
Rows 2, 4, 6 and 8: k.
Row 3: ★ (k2 tog, k3). Rep from ★ to end.
Row 5: ★ (k2 tog, k2). Rep from ★ to end.
Row 7: ★ (k2 tog, k1). Rep from ★ to end.
Row 9: ★ (k2 tog). Rep from ★ to end. Cut yarn, leaving enough to thread through 4 sts rem on needle. Fasten off and join back seam of bonnet to crown shaping. Stitch ribbon ties to either side of bonnet.

KNICKERS

Cast on 20 sts, work 2 rows single rib, then 6 rows ss.
Dec 1 st each end of next 8 rows.
Work 2 rows ss.
Inc 1 st at each end of next 8 rows.
Work 6 rows ss, then 2 rows single rib. Cast off.
Join the side seams and thread shirring elastic through the waistline to fit the baby.

BOOTEES (both the same)

Cast on 17 sts. Work 4 rows gs.
Dec row 1: k6, s1, k1, psso, k1, k2 tog, k6.
Dec row 2: k5, s1, k1, psso, k1, k2 tog, k5.
Rib 3 rows. Cast off loosely, using a 1.5mm needle. Fold and join sole and back seams.

THE CHILDREN'S COLLECTION
1 Soft ball, 2 knitted teddy, 3 cuddly doll (Chapter 1), 4 hat, scarf and mittens, 5 cloak or cape, 6 crocheted sun hat, 7 swimsuit, 8 sweater and shorts, 9 dress and knickers, 10 pram set, 11 layette (Chapter 2), 12 changing-mat and nappy bag (Chapter 4), 13 baby gown, 14 teddy bear and doll (Chapter 6), 15 nappies (Chapter 8)

CHAPTER THREE
Needlepoint and Embroidery

The tools, materials and techniques used in miniature needlepoint and embroidery are virtually the same as those used in full-size work. If you have a basic knowledge of the craft, and enjoy working in small scale, you should have no difficulties with the patterns in this chapter.

You will need the smallest needles, for the needlepoint projects this will usually be size 26 tapestry needles and for embroidery and cross stitch, size 10-12 crewel needles. Embroidery and needlepoint are both easier to work with the fabric or canvas in a hoop or frame to keep it taut. Commercial embroidery hoops are widely available, the sizes required ranging from 4 inch diameter for cushions and pictures, 6 inch for larger projects to 10 inch for bedspreads. Commercial tapestry frames, however, are too large for most miniature needlepoint rugs and carpets, and as embroidery hoops will not accept canvas, we recommend making your own frame in inexpensive ¾ inch square section timber from the local do-it-yourself shop. Simply glue and nail, or screw, lengths of wood together to make a frame 2 inches larger all round than the finished size of the project you are working on. Use masking tape to bind the edge of the canvas and pin it taut on to the frame with drawing pins (thumb tacks). Using a frame keeps the work clean, helps to prevent distortion, and makes you use a 'stab' stitch rather than a sewing action which frays the thread. We recommend using a well-fitting metal thimble and small, sharp-pointed scissors are essential.

Needlepoint rugs and carpets are worked on canvas with 22 holes (21 threads) to the inch, or on 23-count coin net. Smaller needlepoint projects such as cushions are worked on evenweave linen or cotton with a count of 30 threads per inch. Cross-stitch projects are worked on Hardanger 22/23 threads per inch. Most of the embroidery projects are stitched on fine silk (Habotai or similar) which should always be backed with cotton lawn (or batiste). The two layers of fabric are placed together so that they are both on the straight grain when put into the hoop, and worked together as one piece.

The most suitable thread for miniature work is stranded cotton (floss) from Anchor (MEZ) or DMC or similar, which is supplied in skeins in a vast range of colours, though experienced embroiderers may like to use pure silk thread. Most projects use only one or two strands of thread, and the larger carpets use three or four strands. Separate the strands by cutting a length approximately one yard (metre) at a time, fanning the individual threads and holding one end firmly in one hand while you pull one strand at a time upward and out with the other hand. Separate the required number of threads individually and then reassemble them before use. This adds bulk to the threads so that they cover the canvas better and lie flatter when worked. Gold thread has been used in several projects, and we recommend Madeira size 40 or Krienik Japan threads which are produced for machine embroidery. These have a tendency to fray, so we suggest using a slightly larger needle. The materials required for each project are detailed throughout the chapter.

Designs for embroidery can be traced directly from the book on to light-coloured silk by taping the silk over the page with surgical tape (from chemist shops/drugstores) and tracing the pattern with a well-sharpened B pencil. If you prefer, the pattern can be traced on to paper, mounted on a sheet of glass, and the silk taped to the glass which can be held to the light to transfer the pattern. Fabrics which fray easily, such as silk, can be sealed around the edges with Fraycheck or a similar product before working the embroidery or before making up.

All the tools and materials discussed are available from the haberdashery (notions) department in large stores, and from needlework suppliers including the UK and US stockists listed at the back of the book. The stitches used in this chapter are the simple embroidery stitches illustrated on page 45.

As an alternative to real embroidery or needlepoint, the 'tapestry' in our Tudor bedchamber is colour laser printed on to linen from a catalogue illustration. This 'cheats' method can be used to produce effective samplers, pictures, wall hangings, and rugs – very simply. Just choose the picture you want to copy (which can be enlarged or reduced in the process) and take it to a photocopying bureau that does colour laser printing on T-shirts. The process is most effective on natural fabrics, such as fine linen or cotton for cushions, bedspreads, etc, and cotton velveteen for rugs. The machine can print up to A4 size which is large enough for a carpet in most dolls' houses.

Embroidery stitches

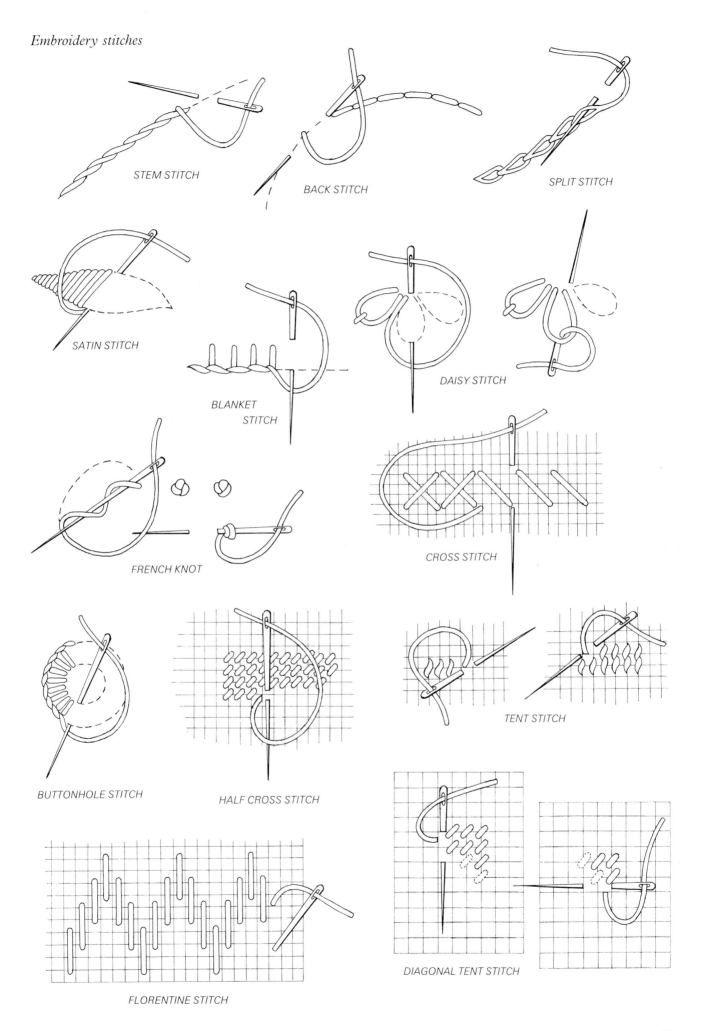

STEM STITCH

BACK STITCH

SPLIT STITCH

SATIN STITCH

BLANKET STITCH

DAISY STITCH

FRENCH KNOT

CROSS STITCH

BUTTONHOLE STITCH

HALF CROSS STITCH

TENT STITCH

FLORENTINE STITCH

DIAGONAL TENT STITCH

CUSHIONS

TUDOR ROSE CUSHION *(Shown on page 11)*

This traditional *petit point* design would be appropriate for any dolls' house from the Tudor period to the present day. Dora has used Anchor stranded cotton (embroidery floss) in shades of pink, gold, and green on a cream background. The cushion front is worked on evenweave linen in a 4 inch hoop and backed with matching cotton fabric.

Work the pattern in half cross stitch using two strands of thread. Begin at the centre and work outward. When the pattern is complete, trim the fabric evenly to ten threads outside the work all round. Turn in and tack (baste) this seam allowance, mitring the corners. Cut a 2 inch square of backing fabric and turn in and tack a similar seam allowance with mitred corners. With wrong sides facing, slip stitch the two pieces together around three sides, stuff the cushion lightly with a little kapok or polyester and slip stitch the fourth side.

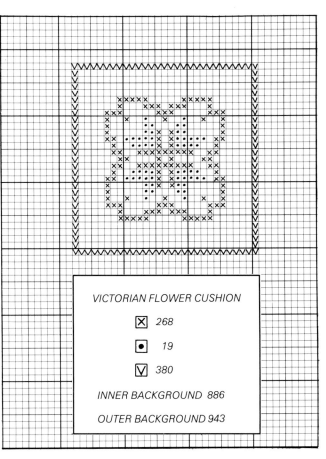

VICTORIAN FLOWER CUSHION

☒ 268

⦿ 19

☑ 380

INNER BACKGROUND 886

OUTER BACKGROUND 943

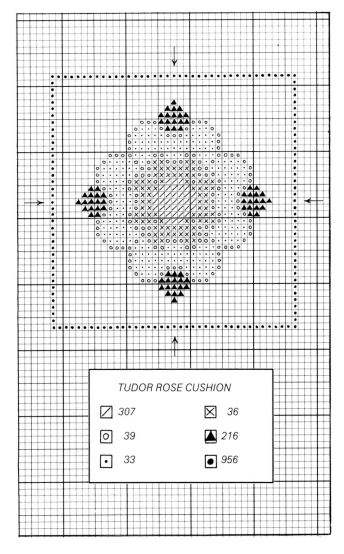

TUDOR ROSE CUSHION

⧄ 307	☒ 36
⦿ 39	▲ 216
• 33	⦿ 956

VICTORIAN FLOWER CUSHION

(Shown on page 11)

The design and colours of this petit point cushion are typical of the Berlin woolwork patterns which were so fashionable in the nineteenth century. Isobel used Anchor stranded cotton (embroidery floss) in green, red, and brown on a gold background and worked the cushion front on 23 threads per inch coin net, backed with felt.

Begin at the centre of the pattern and work outward, using three strands of thread throughout. The pattern is worked in tent stitch, and the background is filled in diagonal tent stitch. When the pattern is complete, dampen the piece slightly and ease it into shape. Trim the coin net evenly to $\frac{1}{2}$ inch outside the work all round and fold this $\frac{1}{2}$ inch to the wrong side, mitring the corners. Using three strands of brown thread, whipstitch (overcast) all round the edge of the piece. Trim the coin net $\frac{1}{4}$ inch from the bound edge. Cut a piece of felt to fit for the backing and with one strand of thread, and small oversewing stitches, sew the back to the front on three sides. Stuff the cushion lightly with a little kapok or polyester and slip stitch the fourth side.

SPRAY OF BERRIES CUSHION *(Shown on page 11)*

Dora's pretty embroidered cushion with its delicate berry spray pattern is made in pale blue silk over lawn worked in Anchor stranded cotton (embroidery floss) in crimson and green (13, 876) in a 4 inch hoop.

Trace the pattern on to the silk. Stitch the embroidery with one strand of thread using stem stitch for the stems and satin stitch for the leaves in green. Work the berries in crimson in satin stitch. When the embroidery is complete, trim the silk and lawn to the cutting line shown on the pattern. Cut a second piece of silk to back the cushion, and with right sides facing, stitch the two pieces together around three sides. Trim the seams and corners and turn through. Stuff the cushion lightly and turn in and slip stitch the fourth side closed.

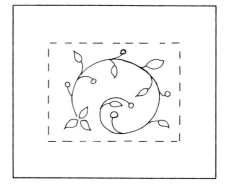

Spray of berries cushion

TUDOR FOOT CUSHION *(Shown on page 11)*

This rich purple cushion, embroidered in gold, makes an excellent foot cushion for any house from the Tudor period to the nineteenth century. Dora has used silk over lawn worked with Madeira gold thread in a 4 inch hoop.

Trace the pattern on to the silk. Work the embroidery in stem stitch, except for the shaded areas which are satin stitch. Cut both layers of fabric on the cutting line, then trim the lawn backing to the seam line. Turn in and tack (baste) the silk seam allowance. Cut a backing for the cushion in silk and lawn to match, trim and turn in the seam allowance on the backing. Cut a strip of silk, $6\frac{1}{2}$ x $\frac{3}{4}$ inch to make the cushion side. Turn in both long edges to meet and tack to hold in place. Slip stitch the side to the cushion top around four edges. Slip stitch the side to the cushion back around three edges, stuff the cushion firmly, retaining the flat square shape, and slip stitch the fourth side closed.

Tudor foot cushion

GEORGIAN CUSHION *(Shown on page 11)*

The stylized flower motif embroidered on this cushion is typical of the formal patterns of the eighteenth century. Dora worked the embroidery in pinks and blue-greens on cream silk over lawn in a 4 inch hoop.

Trace the pattern on to the silk. Work the pattern in one strand of thread (floss) using stem stitch and satin stitch as shown. When the embroidery is complete, trim the silk and lawn on the cutting line.

Satin Stitch
921
921
969
970
920

Georgian cushion

Cut a back for the cushion to match. With right sides facing, stitch the two pieces together around three sides. Trim the edges and corners and turn through. Stuff the cushion lightly, turn in and slip stitch the fourth side closed. Trim the cushion with a fine cord, glued with fabric glue or whip stitched (overcast), around the four sides on the seam line. We used a fine cream cord made by pulling apart a piece of commercial silky lampshade trimming. If you prefer, you can make cord by twisting two strands of embroidery thread tightly until the twist springs back on itself to form the cord.

INDIAN CUSHION
(Shown on page 11)

This Indian-style cushion with its embroidery and 'mirror' sequins would be appropriate for any late nineteenth- or twentieth-century house. The cushion should be made in bright colours and Dora has chosen scarlet silk over lawn with a pattern in black, white, scarlet, green, and yellow. The tiny mirror sequins are cut from large sequins with a paper-hole punch. Work the cushion in a 4 inch hoop.

Trace the pattern on to the silk. Using one strand of thread (floss), work the green and yellow diamonds in satin stitch and outline them in black, making one stitch from each point. Work the two border lines in split stitch in black. Outline the

◈ GREEN   ◇ YELLOW

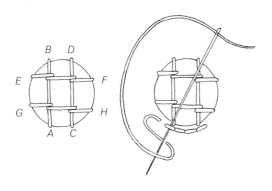

Indian cushion

TUDOR LOZENGE PANEL			
SQUIRREL	ACORN	STRAWBERRY	SNAIL
▣ 352	▣ 846	▣ 42	· 393
· 349	✕ 843	✕ 40	◉ 391
✕ 307	· 905	· 216	✕ 853
	◉ 903		▢ 856
BIRD	OWL	THISTLE	CORNFLOWER
▣ 401	▣ 381	▣ 110	▣ 123
· 400	· 379	✕ 108	◉ 121
✕ 307	✕ 307	· 218	✕ 307
▲ 403	▲ 403	◉ 216	· 218
CARNATION	DEER		
▣ 1023	▣ 352	⬤ 94 OCTAGON	
· 216	· 349	◻ 880 BACKGROUND	

circles with small back stitches in scarlet. Apply a spot of glue (Pritt or similar) to the back of the sequins, stick them into the circles and leave to dry. Work buttonhole stitch over a lattice, in scarlet, around the sequins to hold them in place (as if working an eyelet hole) as shown. Work the triangles in satin stitch in white. When the embroidery is complete, trim the silk and lawn to the cutting line and trim the lawn to the stitching line. Cut a back for the cushion to match in silk. Turn in the seam allowance on front and back, and tack (baste) to hold. Slip stitch the two pieces together around three sides, stuff the cushion lightly and slip stitch the fourth side.

TUDOR LOZENGE PANEL *(Shown on page 11)*

This traditional *petit point* pattern, with motifs of stylized animals, birds, and flowers in octagonal lozenges, can be used for a variety of projects. Four lozenges will make a cushion, or six a fire screen, and eighteen will make a rug, choosing whichever motifs and colours you prefer. Dora has used a pattern of ten motifs with the needlepoint panel mounted on a purple silk over lawn cushion for the bed in our Tudor room. The needlepoint is worked on evenweave linen 30 threads per inch in Anchor stranded cotton (embroidery floss).

For convenience, each motif on the chart has its own key (so you can choose the motifs you want) and for clarity, only the outer row of the back-

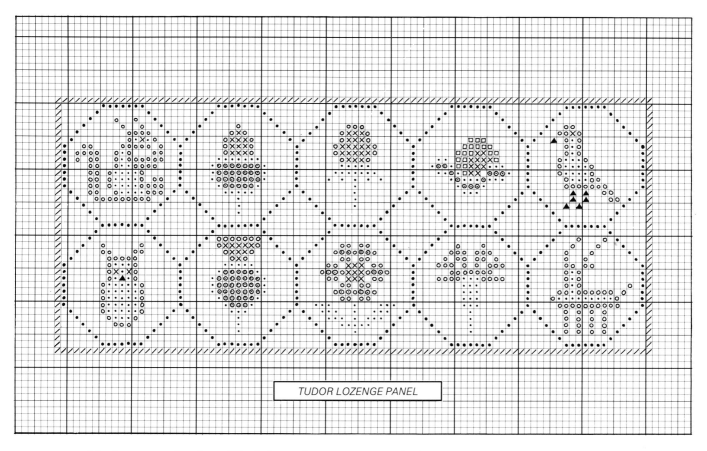

TUDOR LOZENGE PANEL

ground is shown on the chart. Work from the centre outward. The octagons and the motifs are worked in cross stitch, using one strand of thread. The background is filled in half cross stitch using two strands of thread. When the work is complete, trim the fabric to four threads from the outside edge of the panel.

To make the cushion, mount the silk over lawn in a 6 inch hoop. Tack (baste) the panel squarely on to the centre of the silk. Place matching silk ribbon over the raw edge (four threads) of the panel and slip stitch the ribbon to the panel and to the silk, mitring the corners (or cut four strips of ribbon and tuck the raw ends in). Mark a line 1 inch outside the ribbon-edged panel and cut the silk and lawn on this line. Trim the lawn to leave ½ inch seam allowance on the silk. Cut a back for the cushion in silk to match. Turn in and tack (baste) the seam allowance on cushion front and back. Slip stitch the two pieces together around three sides, stuff the cushion lightly and slip stitch the fourth side.

If you use motifs to make a small cushion, see the needlepoint cushions for instructions on finishing; for a fire screen, see the fire screens on page 58. If you are making a rug, follow the instructions given on page 69 for rugs.

PICTURES AND SAMPLERS

CROSS-STITCH TEXT *(Shown on page 55)*

Isobel's simple cross-stitch text adds an amusing touch to an old-fashioned bathroom, but would be equally appropriate in a Victorian bedroom or kitchen. Patterns are given for both 'GOD IS LOVE' and 'GOD SEES ALL' – the method is the same for both. The text is worked on Hardanger cloth, 22/23 threads per inch in one colour of stranded cotton (embroidery floss).

Use one strand of thread and start in the centre. Work the words of the text first, and then the border in cross stitch. When the work is complete, press lightly on the wrong side so that the cross-stitch text is completely square and trim to ½ inch outside the border.

FRAMING

To frame the text you will need dolls-house picture-frame moulding, stained or painted as you wish, a small mitre box, a small saw, and wood glue. Glue the text on to thin, stiff cardboard (posterboard) using a light coat of fabric glue on the card, allow to dry slightly until it becomes tacky. Smooth the cloth squarely on to the glued card and allow to dry. Trim the fabric-covered card squarely to the required size. Cut the picture-frame moulding to fit with mitred corners, and assemble the frame around the

THE TUDOR BEDCHAMBER
Tudor rose cushion, Tudor foot cushion, Tudor lozenge panel, book with embroidered cover, scroll bedspread and hangings, table carpet (Chapter 3), towels (Chapter 5), bead accessories (Chapter 8)

card. Glue thin paper (or use a self-adhesive paper label) over the back of the frame and card, trimming the outside edge.

FLOWER VASE SAMPLER *(Shown on page 55)*

This traditional sampler has a design of stylized flowers in a classical vase and is worked on Hardanger, 22/23 threads per inch in stranded embroidery cotton (floss). Isobel has chosen light and dark rose-pinks with pale gold centres for the flowers, and light and dark sage-green leaves, in a beige vase with dark brown lettering. You may prefer other colours, and you will wish to work your own initials and date into the design. The finished sampler is approximately $1\frac{1}{2}$ x 2 inches.

Start at the centre of the pattern and using one strand of thread, work the flowers and vase in cross stitch. Work the letters and numbers in back stitch, then work the remainder of the pattern and border in cross stitch. When the work is complete, trim the Hardanger, mount on card, and frame as described for the cross-stitch text.

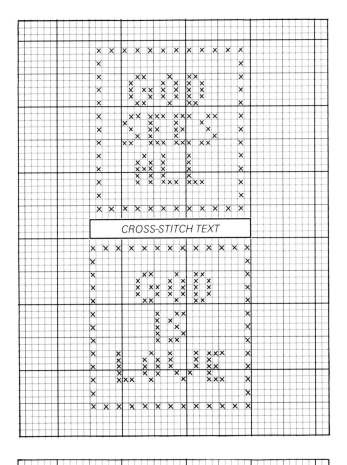

CROSS-STITCH TEXT

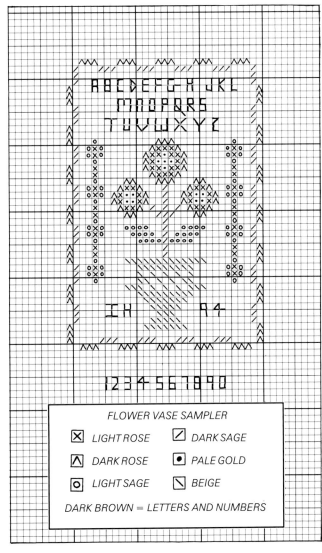

FLOWER VASE SAMPLER

- ☒ LIGHT ROSE
- ☑ DARK SAGE
- ⊼ DARK ROSE
- ⊡ PALE GOLD
- ⊙ LIGHT SAGE
- ⊠ BEIGE

DARK BROWN = LETTERS AND NUMBERS

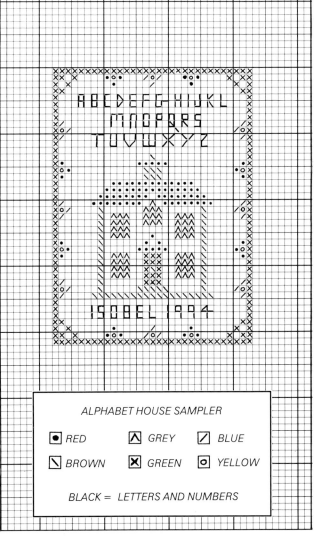

ALPHABET HOUSE SAMPLER

- ⊡ RED
- ⊼ GREY
- ☑ BLUE
- ⊠ BROWN
- ☒ GREEN
- ⊙ YELLOW

BLACK = LETTERS AND NUMBERS

ALPHABET HOUSE SAMPLER *(Shown on page 55)*

Isobel's second sampler has a traditional house and alphabet design worked on Hardanger 22/23 threads per inch in stranded cotton (embroidery floss). Our house has a red roof, brown walls, grey windows, and a green front door. The alphabet is worked in black and the border flowers have yellow centres. You may prefer other colours, and will wish to work your own name into the design. The finished sampler is approximately 1½ x 2 inches.

Work from the centre outward, using one strand of thread. Begin with the house in cross stitch, then work the letters and numbers in back stitch. When the work is complete, trim the Hardanger, mount on card and frame the sampler as described for the cross-stitch text.

PARROT PICTURE

(Shown on page 55)

Dora's needlework picture, showing a parrot and cat in lifelike detail, is reminiscent of the Berlin woolwork patterns which were so fashionable in the nineteenth century. The picture is worked on evenweave linen with 30 threads per inch, in Anchor stranded cotton (embroidery floss) in a 4 inch hoop. Our parrot is green, blue, and red and the cat is black and white with green eyes. The bird stand is grey and the flowers and foliage are in shades of green and pink in a blue archway. The finished picture is approximately 1¼ x 2 inches.

Begin at the centre and work outwards. Either use one strand of thread and work the animals, bird stand, flowers, and foliage in cross stitch, then, with two strands of thread, fill in the background in tent stitch, or work the complete design in tent stitch using two strands of thread throughout. When the work is complete, trim the fabric to eight threads from the pattern and mount, trim and frame the picture as described for the cross-stitch text.

BLESS-THIS-HOUSE SAMPLER *(Shown on page 55)*

Sue's very fine little sampler is worked on evenweave linen or cotton with 30 threads per inch in stranded cotton (embroidery floss) and is approximately 1¼ inches square. The traditional design has a house with trees, flowers, and the motto 'BLESS THIS HOUSE' within a scrolled border and is shown in two colourways. Choose colours which best complement your own decorating scheme.

With one strand of thread, work the scrolled border in cross stitch. Work the house, trees, and

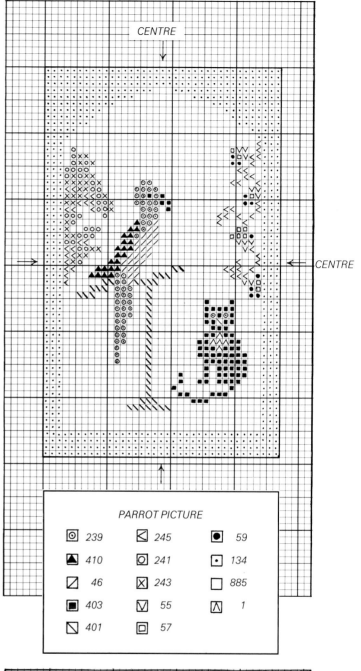

PARROT PICTURE

◉ 239	◲ 245	● 59
▲ 410	⊡ 241	· 134
◪ 46	⊠ 243	□ 885
■ 403	▽ 55	⋀ 1
� 401	▣ 57	

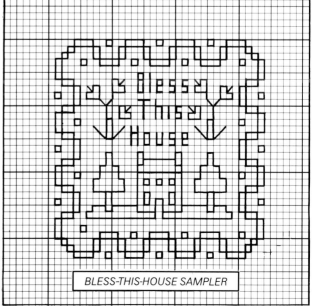

BLESS-THIS-HOUSE SAMPLER

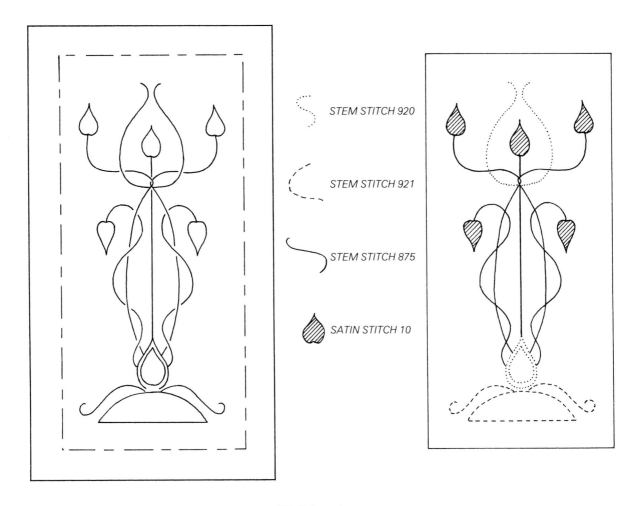

STEM STITCH 920

STEM STITCH 921

STEM STITCH 875

SATIN STITCH 10

Wall hanging

flowers in cross stitch and the motto in back stitch. When the work is complete, secure the edges of the sampler by machine stitching three times around on the proposed cutting line, with the smallest stitch. Trim the fabric as close as possible to the machine-stitched line. Mount the sampler on a piece of card, trim the card and frame as described for the cross-stitch text.

 # WALL HANGING
(Shown on page 55)

This elegant wall hanging in the art-nouveau style is embroidered on silk over lawn in stranded cotton (embroidery floss), worked in a 6 inch hoop. Dora has used shades of grey and grey-green with apricot Anchor thread on a rich blue background but you may prefer other colours to complement the decorating scheme in your own house. The embroidered panel is hung from fine dowelling by a twisted-thread cord and when completed this delightful design will adorn any wall, and measures approximately 4 x 2 inches.

First trace the pattern on to the silk. Then with one strand of thread, work the design in stem stitch and satin stitch as shown. When the embroidery is complete, cut out the panel on the cutting line. Cut a lining in lawn to the same size. Trim the lawn backing of the embroidered panel to the seam line shown. Turn in and tack (baste) the silk seam allowance on both long sides, then the bottom end, with mitred corners. Turn the silk seam allowance at the top end of the panel over a 2½ inch length of fine dowelling, and make a line of tiny running stitches as close as possible to the dowelling to secure it in place. Turn in and press the seam allowance around four edges of the lawn lining piece. With wrong sides together, place lining to panel, tack (baste), then slip stitch the two pieces together. Remove the tacking and press the panel lightly.

To make the hanging cord, cut three 24 inch strands of thread. Knot the strands of thread together at both ends, and then twist them until they spring back on themselves to form a realistic hanging cord. Stitch the cord to the back of your art-nouveau wall hanging just below the dowelling at either side, adjusting the length as required, and trim the ends.

THE PICTURE COLLECTION

1 cross-stitch text, 2 flower vase sampler, 3 alphabet house sampler, 4 parrot picture, 5 bless-this-house sampler, 6 wall hanging, 7 printed tapestry (Chapter 3), 8 ship and cottage pictures, 9 rabbit pictures (Chapter 4)

FURNISHINGS

BUTTON FOOTSTOOL

(Shown on page 59)

Dora's ingenious little footstool is worked on evenware linen, 30 threads per inch in Anchor stranded cotton (embroidery floss), over a $\frac{3}{4}$ inch covered-button form which is glued into a large coat button. Our stool is worked in shades of pink and cream, but it could be in any colours you prefer. The coat button should be as large as possible, in black or brown, with a central well $\frac{3}{4}$ inch in diameter and a rim about $\frac{1}{8}$ inch deep.

Working with the fabric in a 4 inch hoop, mark a circle $1\frac{1}{2}$ inches in diameter on the fabric. Begin in the centre and work the motif in cross stitch with one strand of thread. Fill the background in half cross stitch with two strands of thread. Note that for clarity, only the outer row of the background is shown on the chart. When the embroidery is complete, make a line of gathering stitches just inside the marked circle, and a second line $\frac{1}{8}$ inch from the edge of the marked circle, leaving ends on both threads. Remove the work from the hoop, and trim the fabric on the marked line. (Remove the shank if necessary from the covered-button form) place the button form in the centre of the fabric and pull up the gathering stitches tightly, distributing the fullness evenly, and fasten off. Push the fabric into the teeth of the button form so that it is held securely. Apply glue to the back of the covered button and position it in the coat button.

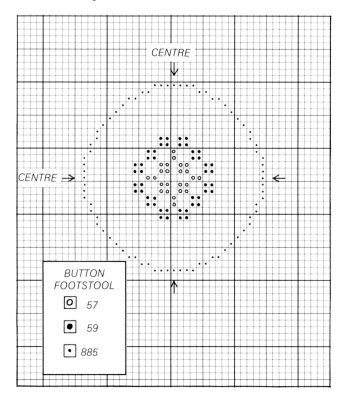

WORK UP TO 3 MORE PAIRS OF FLOWERS

BELL PULL AND STOOL SEAT			
● 893		V 213	
X 895		╱ 859	
⊡ 861			

BELL PULL AND STOOL SEAT

(Shown on page 59)

Isobel's pretty cross-stitch bell pull and matching stool seat cover are worked on Hardanger, 22/23 threads per inch with a rosebud motif in Anchor shades of pink and green stranded thread (floss). The length of the bell pull can be adjusted to suit the ceiling height of your own room, and when completed it is backed with soft iron-on interfacing

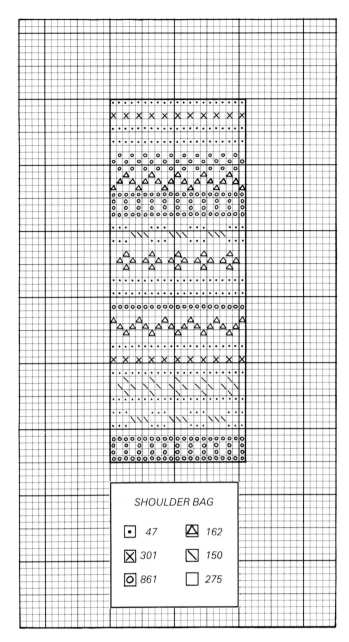

SHOULDER BAG

•	47	△	162
☒	301	◨	150
◎	861	□	275

the ring to the top edge. Make a small tassel in mid-green thread and stitch it to the bottom point.

STOOL SEAT COVER

Cut a piece of Hardanger 5 x 3 inches. Using one strand of thread and cross stitch throughout, begin with the central motif. Work the rosebuds as described above, then work the border. Press the work on the wrong side. Cut the Hardanger to fit the stool seat, and cover as described on page 140.

SHOULDER BAG

(Shown on page 119)

Dora's elegant little shoulder bag is worked in cross stitch on evenweave linen, 30 threads per inch in Anchor stranded cotton (embroidery floss). The traditional Greek pattern is in shades of red, green, blue, and yellow on a cream background.

With the fabric in a 4 inch hoop, work in cross stitch with one strand of thread throughout. Begin the pattern at the top edge and work downward. When the embroidery is complete, trim the fabric to leave a border of 12 threads all round. Apply narrow strips of Bondaweb (or similar) to the borders on both long sides, turn and press these borders to the wrong side using a hot iron over a damp cloth. Turn in the borders on both short sides and slip stitch to secure in place. Fold the bag with wrong sides together and slip stitch both side seams. To make the strap, cut three 18 inch strands of cream thread, knot both ends together, and twist the strands until they spring back on themselves to form a cord. (Or use a length of fine cord or ribbon.) Stitch the cord securely to each side of the bag at the top of the side seams, to make a strap $2\frac{1}{2}$ inches long, and trim the ends to leave $\frac{1}{4}$ inch long fringed 'tassels'.

EMBROIDERED FIRE SCREEN

(Shown on page 59)

This stylized flower spray pattern can be used to make a square panel for most commercial fire screens, or fire screen kits. It can also be used as a cushion cover. Dora worked the floral spray in a 4 inch hoop on cream silk over lawn, using Anchor stranded cotton (embroidery floss) with touches of gold thread.

Trace the pattern on to the silk. Work the embroidery with one strand of thread throughout in satin stitch and stem stitch as shown. Add the French knots in gold thread. When the embroidery is complete, press lightly. To make a fire screen panel, cut a piece of firm thin card fractionally

(Vilene, Pellon or similar) and hung from a $\frac{3}{8}$ inch diameter jump ring. The seat cover will fit the longer version of the dressing-table stool on page 137, and the pattern can easily be adjusted to fit the shorter version of the stool if required.

BELL PULL

Cut a piece of Hardanger $2\frac{3}{4}$ x 9 inches. Using one strand of thread and cross stitch throughout, begin 1 inch from the top of the fabric, and in the centre. Work (up to) twelve rosebuds with light pink centres and dark pink outer petals, then dark pink centres and light pink outer petals alternately. Work the stems and leaves in dark green. Note that the rosebuds face left and right alternately. Work the inner border line in pale green and the outer border line in mid-green. When the work is complete, trim the fabric to $\frac{1}{4}$ inch outside the border all round. Turn this $\frac{1}{4}$ inch allowance under, mitring the corners, and press. Cut a backing in interfacing to fit, and iron it on to the back of the bell pull. Stitch

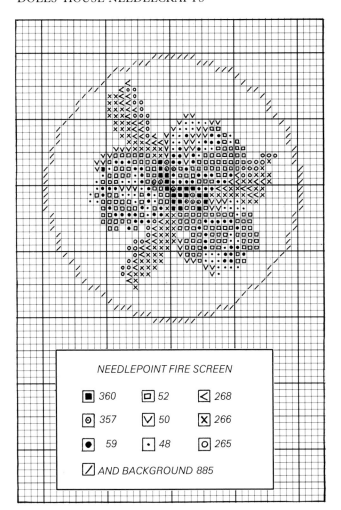

NEEDLEPOINT FIRE SCREEN

■ 360	▣ 52	◩ 268
◉ 357	☑ 50	⊠ 266
● 59	⊡ 48	⊙ 265
⧄ AND BACKGROUND 885		

necessary. With the fabric in the hoop, mark the centre lines with tacking (basting) threads. Begin at the centre and work outward. Work the roses and leaves in cross stitch with one strand of thread. Fill the background in tent stitch with two strands of thread or, if you prefer, work the whole pattern in tent stitch with two strands of thread throughout. When the work is complete, press lightly and cut the fabric to ½ inch outside the embroidery. Cut a card panel to fit loosely into the recess in the screen, centre the panel on the back of the work, held in place with a little fabric glue. Clip the curved edge around the fabric, and fold and glue the edge to the back of the card. Allow the glue to dry, then glue the covered panel into the recess in the screen.

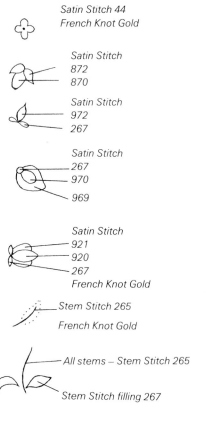

Satin Stitch 44
French Knot Gold

Satin Stitch
872
870

Satin Stitch
972
267

Satin Stitch
267
970
969

Satin Stitch
921
920
267
French Knot Gold

Stem Stitch 265
French Knot Gold

All stems – Stem Stitch 265

Stem Stitch filling 267

Embroidered fire screen

smaller than the panel recess in your fire screen. Trace the outline of the card on to the back of the embroidered piece and cut both layers of fabric ½ inch outside this line. Trim the lawn backing to the marked line. Centre the card on the back of the embroidery, fold the silk seam allowance at top and bottom and glue to the back of the card. Allow to dry, then fold and glue the side seam allowances to the back of the card, mitring the corners neatly. Glue the panel into the recess in the fire screen. To make a cushion, follow the instructions for the Georgian cushion on page 47.

 NEEDLEPOINT FIRE SCREEN *(Shown on page 59)*

This pattern can be used to make a round panel for most commercial fire screens or kits and would also be appropriate for a footstool – see the cotton-reel stools on page 136. Dora's design of pink roses and green leaves on a cream or black background is typically Victorian. It is worked on evenweave linen with 30 threads per inch in Anchor stranded cotton (embroidery floss) in a 4 inch hoop.

The pattern given will fit a 1⅝ inch diameter panel, so check the size of your own screen, make a paper template if necessary to transfer the outline to the fabric and add or subtract background as

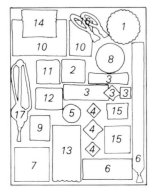

THE FURNISHINGS COLLECTION

1 Round table centre, 2 square antimacassar or table-mat, 3 table-mats and runner, 4 dressing-table set (Chapter 1), 5 button footstool, 6 bell pull and stool seat, 7 embroidered fire screen, 8 needlepoint fire screen, 9 book with embroidered cover (Chapter 3), 10 antimacassars (Chapter 4), 11 beadwork cushion, 12 beaded footstool, 13 cushion and antimacassar, 14 nightdress case, 15 workbox and glove-box, 16 macramé curtain tie-backs, 17 macramé plant-pot hanger (Chapter 8)

Book with embroidered cover

down the centre of the fabric. Secure the cards squarely to the fabric with small pieces of double-sided tape. Fold and glue the seam allowance of silk over the edges of the cards at top and bottom, smooth in place and allow to dry, then fold and glue the silk seam allowance at both ends to the cards with neatly mitred corners and allow to dry. Place the assembled pages on the cover and glue the outside of the first and last pages to the inside of the cover. Place the book, embroidered-side down, on a padded surface and press under a weight as the glue dries. If required, make a clasp by bending a small brass strap-hinge to fit and glue it to the back cover of the book.

BOOK WITH EMBROIDERED COVER *(Shown on page 59)*

This impressive book, with its embroidered cover worked in gold thread on rich crimson silk, might be an ancient family bible, or a Victorian album. Dora used Madeira thread and Habotai silk over lawn worked in a 4 inch hoop for the cover and typing-paper pages bound with thin, stiff card for the book. You will need a sharp craft knife and a steel ruler for cutting, and a tacky craft glue.

Using the craft knife and metal ruler, cut twelve pieces of typing paper $1\frac{7}{8}$ x $1\frac{1}{8}$ inches. Fold each piece in half and crease sharply on the fold. With a fine line of glue along the fold of one piece of paper, stick the second piece squarely to it. Repeat with each piece so that all twelve folded pieces are glued together, and leave them to dry pressed under a weight. Cut two pieces of card $1\frac{1}{4}$ x 1 inch.

Trace the pattern on to the silk. Work the embroidery using satin stitch for the flowers and leaves and stem stitch for the scrolling lines. When the embroidery is complete, cut both layers on the cutting line, then trim the lawn to the seam line. Place the embroidered cover right-side down and fit the card pieces at each end to leave a $\frac{1}{8}$ inch gap

PILLOWCASE *(Shown on page 83)*

This dainty embroidered pillowcase will fit the pillow on page 109, and is suitable for any standard-size bed – you will need two for a double bed. Dora worked the pattern in white stranded cotton (embroidery floss) on white cotton lawn but it would also be very pretty in pastel colours.

Trace the pattern on to the fabric, but do not cut out the pillowcase until the embroidery is completed. With one strand of thread, work the scalloped edge in close buttonhole stitch. Work the scrolls in stem stitch and the flowers in daisy stitch (detached chain stitch). Make a French knot at the centre of each flower. Press the work lightly and paint a fine line of Fraycheck (or similar) around the scallops and angles, and the cutting line on both long sides. Allow to dry. Cut out the pillowcase with small sharp scissors, trimming carefully around the scallops. Make a $\frac{1}{8}$ inch hem on the short straight end (flap). Fold in the seam allowance on both long sides, and tack (baste) to hold in place. Fold the flap (wrong sides together) and slip stitch both side edges in place. With wrong sides facing, fold the pillowcase and slip stitch the side seams so that the scalloped edge overhangs the flap fold slightly.

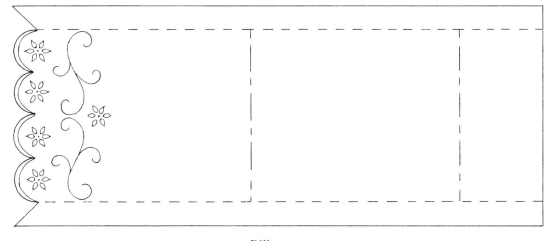

Pillowcase

Screen panels

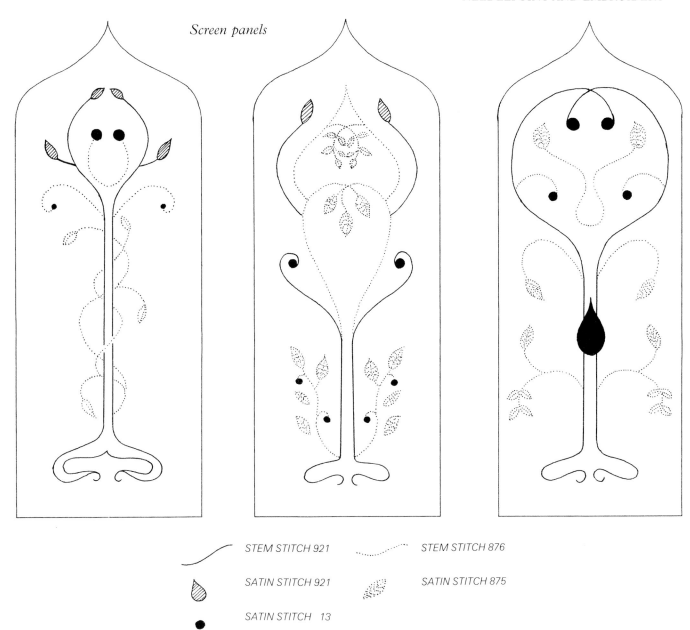

STEM STITCH 921	STEM STITCH 876
SATIN STITCH 921	SATIN STITCH 875
SATIN STITCH 13	

SCREEN PANELS
(Shown on page 167)

Dora has used these art-nouveau style panels to cover a Gothic screen made from a kit, but they can also be used to cover the screen in Chapter 7. Simply work the embroidery as described here, then cut the panels and make up the screen as described on page 141. Our panels are made in pale grey silk over lawn embroidered in Anchor stranded cotton (embroidery floss) in shades of grey-blue, grey-green, and rusty red worked in a 6 inch hoop, but you may wish to use your own colours.

Trace each pattern on to an 8 inch square of silk over lawn. Work the pattern(s) in stem stitch and satin stitch as shown. Either work three panels for the front of the screen, and cut three panels in plain matching fabric for the back, or work six panels to cover the front and back of the screen. When the

embroidery is complete, press lightly and make up the screen as described. If you are using a similar kit, the screen is covered in the same way, but the panels are hinged with small, commercial brass hinges fixed with Superglue and pins, rather than hinged with silk ribbon.

FLORAL BEDSPREAD AND BOLSTER *(Shown on page 62)*

This beautiful crewel-work bedspread and matching bolster with its delicate pattern of stylized flowers would be suitable for almost any period bedroom. Dora has used soft, natural colours on cream silk over lawn to create a very pretty effect, but consider working the design in pale colours, or gold on a rich, dark background, for a more

THE TOILETTE

Bell pull and stool seat, floral bedspread and bolster, rose-garland rug, flower-trellis rug (Chapter 3), drapes with shaped pelmet, pleated bed hangings and tester (Chapter 5), straw hat, walking-stick (Chapter 6), dressing-table stool (Chapter 7), dummy board (Chapter 8)

Floral bedspread

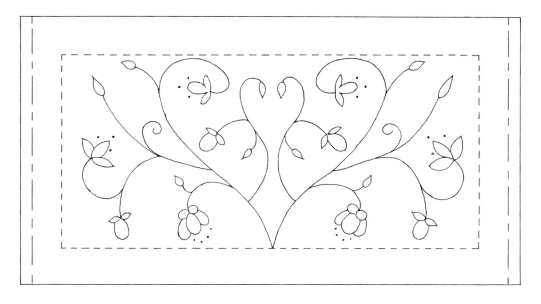

Floral bolster

dramatic effect. To make the bedspread and bolster you will need ¼ yard (metre) of fine silk and lawn, Anchor stranded cotton (embroidery floss), and Madeira metallic gold thread – or fabrics and colours of your choice. You will also need 10 inch and 6 inch embroidery hoops.

BEDSPREAD

Trace the pattern on to the silk. Using one strand of thread, work the embroidery through both silk and lawn using satin stitch for the flowers, buds, and leaves and stem stitch for the stems and scrolls following the colour guide if required. Add small French knots in gold thread to define the flower stamens. When the embroidery is complete, remove the fabric from the hoop and press lightly on the underside. Cut out the bedspread and cut a lining to fit in lawn. With right sides facing, stitch the bedspread to the lining on the marked seam line, leaving a small opening at the top edge to turn through. Clip the corners, trim the seam allowance to ½ inch evenly all round, turn through, and slip stitch the opening closed. Press lightly on the underside to make crisp edges.

BOLSTER

Trace the pattern on to the silk. Work the embroidery using one strand of thread and following the colours and stitches used for the bedspread. Remove from the hoop and press on the underside. Trim the lawn backing to the marked seam line. Apply Bondaweb (or similar) to a scrap of lawn and cut out a piece 4½ x 2 inches. Iron this piece on to the wrong side of the embroidery. Trim the silk to the cutting line. Turn in and tack (baste) the seam allowance on both long edges. Turn in the seam allowance on both short edges and work gathering stitches at each end, leaving thread ends. Slip stitch the long sides together (working on the right side) and remove tacking. Pull up the gathering tightly at one end and fasten off. Stuff the bolster firmly with wadding (batting), then pull up the gathering at the other end and fasten off. To make the 'buttons', bond card on to lawn, and cut two ½ inch circles. Bond lawn on to silk and cut two 1 inch circles. Bond the card circles to the centre of the silk circles on the lawn side. Gather around the edges and pull up tightly on the wrong side. Slip stitch one button to each end of the bolster to cover the gathering.

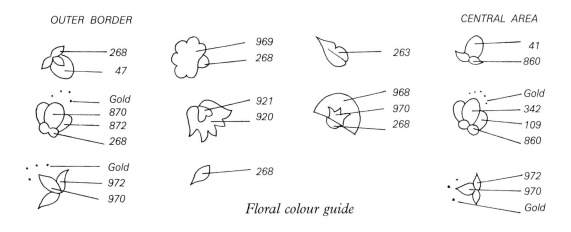

Floral colour guide

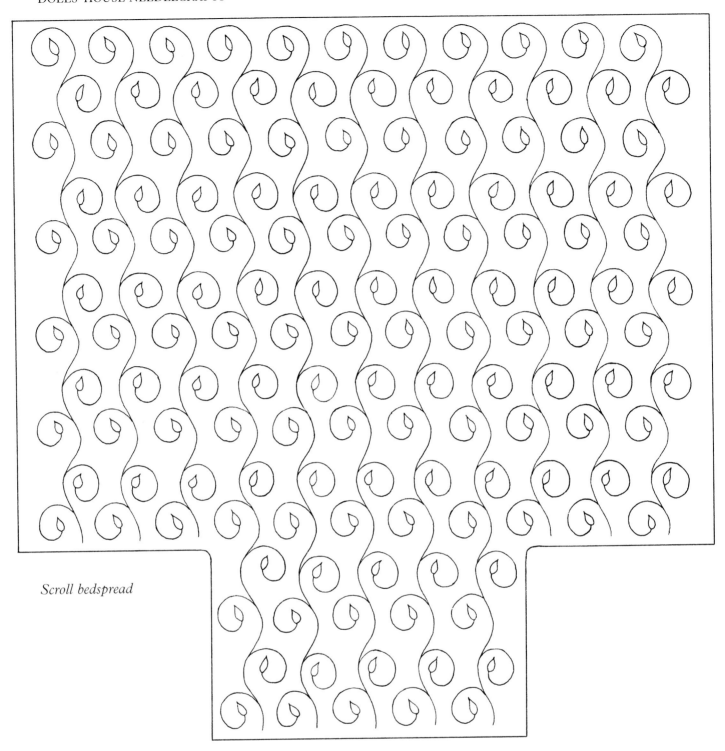

Scroll bedspread

 # SCROLL BEDSPREAD AND HANGINGS

(Shown on page 50)

This sumptuous bedspread with matching canopy and hangings has an embroidered pattern of formal scrolls and leaves. It is particularly suitable for a Tudor bed-chamber, embroidered in black and gold thread (floss) on white silk over lawn or it could equally well be made in other colours and other fabrics for any period house. Dora made our set to fit an oak four-poster bed supplied as a kit

and you may need to make minor adaptions to the size of the pattern to fit your own bed. The full set of bedspread and hangings requires ½ yard (metre) of silk and lawn, 24 inches of black double-picot braid, and 1 yard (metre) of gold satin ribbon ⅜ inch wide. You will also need a 10 inch hoop to work the embroidery.

BEDSPREAD

Trace the pattern on to the silk. With one strand of black thread (floss), work the scrolling lines in stem stitch. Work the leaves in gold in satin stitch. Cut out the bedspread with a ½ inch seam allowance all round. Cut a lining to fit in cotton lawn or silk. With right sides facing, stitch the two pieces together, leaving an opening at the top edge to turn through. Trim the seams, clip the corners, turn through, and slip stitch the opening closed. Press lightly. Cut lengths of satin ribbon to fit both side edges and the bottom edge of the bedspread with ¼ inch allowance at both ends of each piece. Cut off the selvedge along one side of each piece of ribbon and pull threads to make a deep fringe. Seal the short ends of each piece with Fraycheck (or similar), and allow to dry. Slip stitch the ribbon fringes to the bottom edge of both sides and the bottom of the bedspread, tucking the sealed ends to the wrong side.

BACK HANGING

Trace the pattern on to the silk. Embroider the scrolled lines in black and the leaves in gold as for

the bedspread. Cut out the hanging with a seam allowance of ½ inch all round. Cut a lining to fit in lawn. With right sides facing, stitch the two pieces together leaving an opening at the top edge to turn through. Trim the seams, clip the corners, turn through, and slip stitch the opening closed. Press lightly with an iron.

TESTER

The tester should fit exactly on to the top of the bed, so adjust the pattern as necessary. Bond two pieces of silk together with Bondaweb, Heat 'n Bond, or a similar iron-on adhesive material. Trace the pattern on to the silk and cut out the tester. Fold the edges as shown and crease sharply. Glue the tester to the top of the bed so that the corners of the folded edges meet neatly. Slip stitch or glue the top edge of the back hanging to the folded edge at the back of the tester.

Scroll back hanging

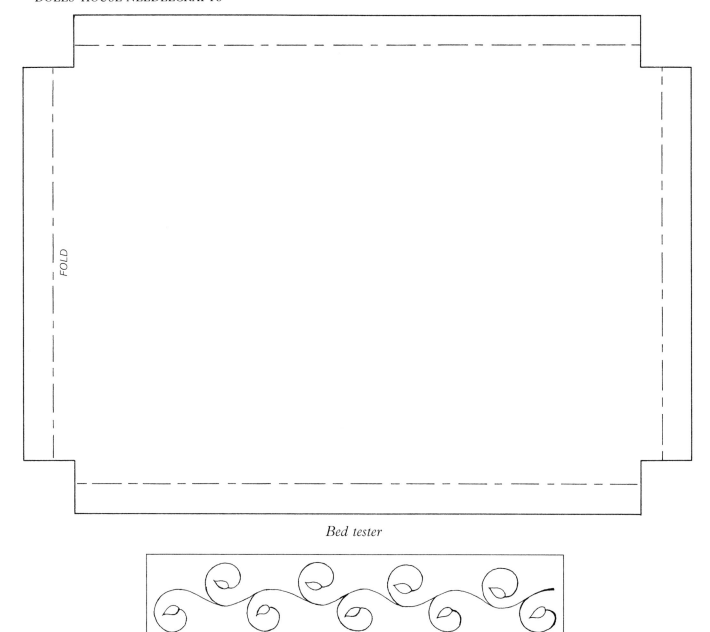

FOLD

Bed tester

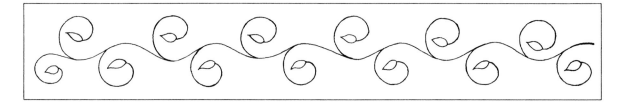

Tester valance panels

The tester valance is made in three panels to fit the sides and bottom of the bed. For each panel, trace the pattern on to the silk and work the embroidery as described above. Cut out the valance panels with a ½ inch seam allowance all round. Cut a lining to fit in lawn. With right sides facing, stitch the two pieces together leaving an opening at the top edge to turn through. Trim the seams, clip the corners, turn through, and slip stitch the opening closed. Press lightly. Cut and fray ribbon fringes and slip stitch them to the lower edge of each valance panel as described for the bedspread. Slip stitch or glue the valance panels to the folded edge of the tester at the sides and bottom of the bed so that they meet edge-to-edge at the corners. Apply a fine line of fabric glue to the double-picot braid and glue it in place to cover the join between the valance panels and back hanging and the tester.

RUGS AND CARPETS

RANDOM-STRIPE RUG *(Shown on page 146)*

This little needlepoint rug is so easy to make it does not need a chart. Isobel's clever use of random-striped embroidery threads (floss) in reds, bronzes, yellows, greens, blues, and violets, with a plain terracotta border, gives the effect of a traditional 'rag' rug. (Anchor colours 1202, 1218, 1243, 1216, 1211, 1209 and 10 – one skein of each.) It is worked on coin net, 23 threads per inch, and though our rug is approximately 4½ x 6½ inches, you can make it any size you wish by simply changing the number of stitches in the border.

Use three strands of thread approximately 18 inches long throughout. For the border, in plain colour, outline a rectangle 52 stitches wide by 104 stitches long in tent stitch or half cross stitch as you prefer. Fill in the centre of the rug in tent stitch or half cross stitch working from one end to the other in random-striped threads following the order of colours listed above. If you finish one thread on a pale shade of the colour, begin with the pale shade of the next colour and vice versa, so that the colours blend into each other without abrupt changes of

shade. When the work is complete, wash it gently in a mild soap solution, squeeze out excess water and gently pull to shape from edge to edge – not diagonally. Leave to dry on paper towels on a wire cake rack (or similar), then press on the wrong side with a hot iron to set the shape. Trim the coin net to leave a ½ inch allowance outside the border. Fold this allowance to the underside, mitring the corners. Bind the edge of the rug in plain colour with whipping or oversewing (overcasting) stitches. Trim the allowance to ¼ inch, close to the binding stitches, and press again on the wrong side. Secure the allowance if necessary with a little fabric glue, applied sparingly.

SMALL FRINGED RUG *(Shown on page 90)*

This delightful little needlepoint rug, worked in colours to suit your decorating scheme, would find a place by the hearth or beside the bed in any dolls' house. Isobel has used Anchor shades of pale blue and cream on a chestnut-brown background to make a striking art-deco effect, but the traditional

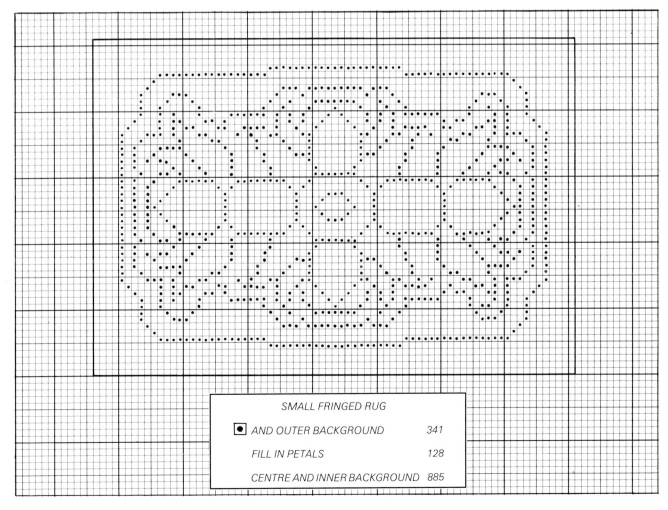

SMALL FRINGED RUG	
⊡ AND OUTER BACKGROUND	341
FILL IN PETALS	128
CENTRE AND INNER BACKGROUND	885

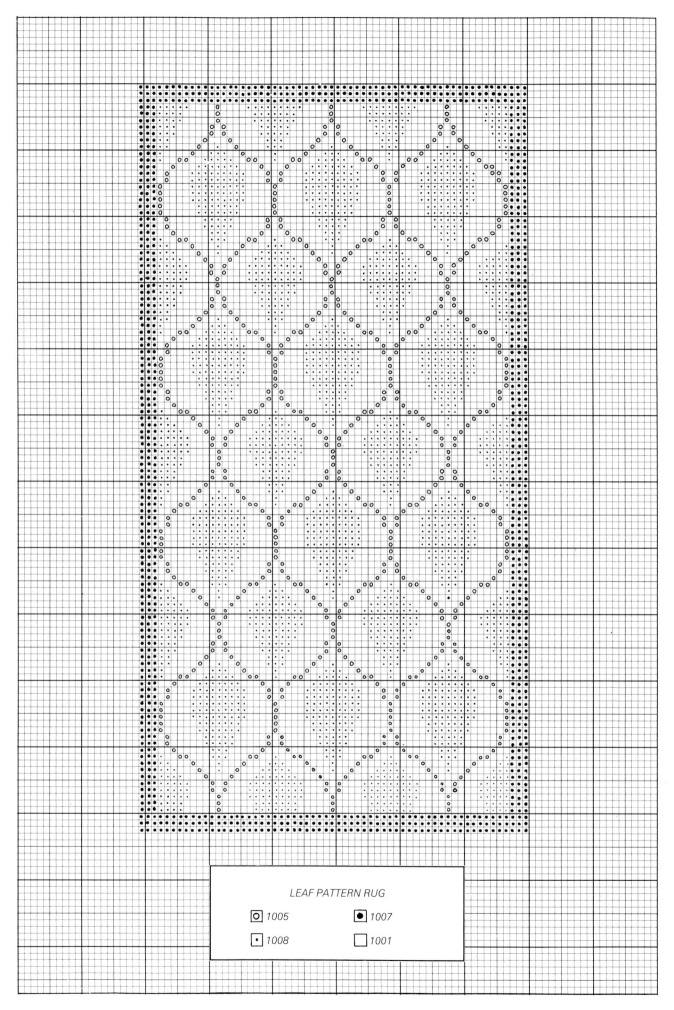

LEAF PATTERN RUG

☐ 1005		⬤ 1007	
・ 1008		☐ 1001	

THE FIRST VISITOR

*Lacy fringed shawl (Chapter 2), button footstool,
embroidered pillowcase, Florentine medallion carpet
(Chapter 3), sheets, pillows and pillowcases, lace
bedspread (Chapter 5), nightgown and mobcap
(Chapter 6), Louis armchair (Chapter 7)*

pattern will work equally well in pastel or strong
colours for a wide range of periods from Georgian
to the present day. The rug is worked on coin net, 23
threads per inch in stranded cotton (embroidery
floss) and is approximately 3½ x 2½ inches.

Using three strands of thread throughout, work
the pattern in tent stitch and fill the background in
diagonal tent stitch. Begin in the centre of the
pattern (in brown), and work the outline of the
design first as shown on the chart. Then (in blue),
work the small central lozenge and fill the petal
shapes. Work the outer central lozenge (in cream)
and fill the inner part of the background. Fill the
outer part of the background. When complete,
wash, shape, and iron the rug as described for the
random-stripe rug, and trim and bind the edges in

the same way. Using six strands of thread (in
brown) and a small crochet hook, knot fringes into
both short ends of the rug and trim the fringes
neatly to ½ inch long.

LEAF PATTERN RUG *(Shown in colour on page 83)*

This versatile needlepoint rug has a simple formal
pattern of leaves in ogee shapes worked in four
shades of colour. Dora has used four shades of blue
Anchor thread, but you can, of course, use any
colour or colours you prefer. Our rug is worked on
coin net with 23 threads per inch in stranded cotton
(embroidery floss) in a 9 inch square frame. The
finished rug is approximately 5 x 2½ inches, and is
suitable for use in several different rooms.

Working with a piece of coin net 9 x 4½ inches in
the frame, begin ¾ inch from the top of the coin net
and work downward. Work the pattern of ogees in
cross stitch with one strand of thread to give strong
definition to the shapes. Work the leaves and

71

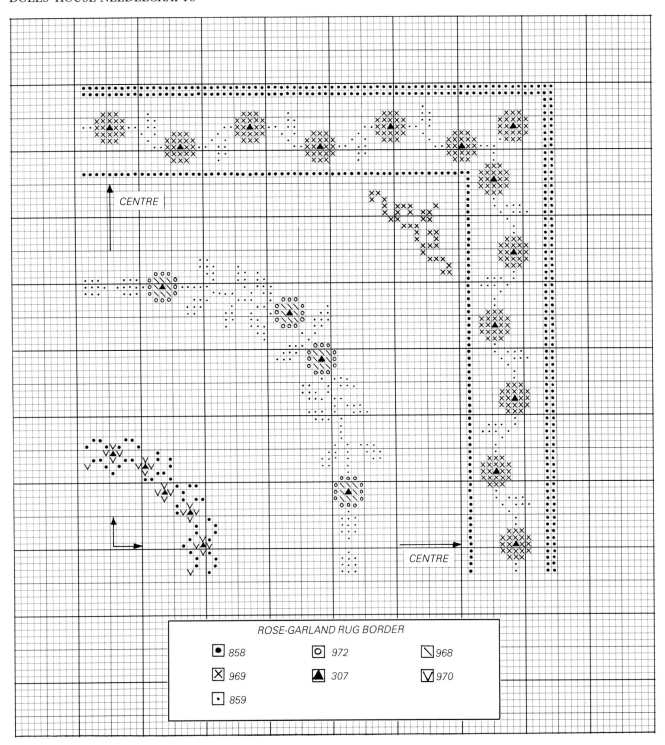

ROSE-GARLAND RUG BORDER

Symbol	No.	Symbol	No.	Symbol	No.
⊡	858	⊙	972	◩	968
☒	969	▲	307	◩	970
⊡	859				

background and the border in half cross stitch with two strands of thread. Trim the coin net to eight threads from the outside edge of the border. Turn under this allowance with mitred corners and slip stitch the edge of the coin net to the back of the rug. Press the rug on the wrong side.

ROSE-GARLAND RUG *(Shown on page 62)*

This pretty, square needlepoint rug is patterned with garlands of pink roses and green leaves on a pale cream background. Dora has used Anchor stranded cotton (embroidery floss), one skein of each colour and five skeins for the background, on coin net with 23 threads per inch worked in a 12 inch square frame.

Work in half cross stitch with three strands of thread throughout. Begin with the outer border in greens and pinks, then work the central garland and the outer garland, then the corner motifs. When these are complete, fill in the background in cream. When the work is complete, trim the coin net to ten threads outside the border. Turn this allowance to the underside, mitring the corners for neatness, and slip stitch the edge of the coin net to the back of the rug. Press the finished rose-garland rug lightly on the wrong side.

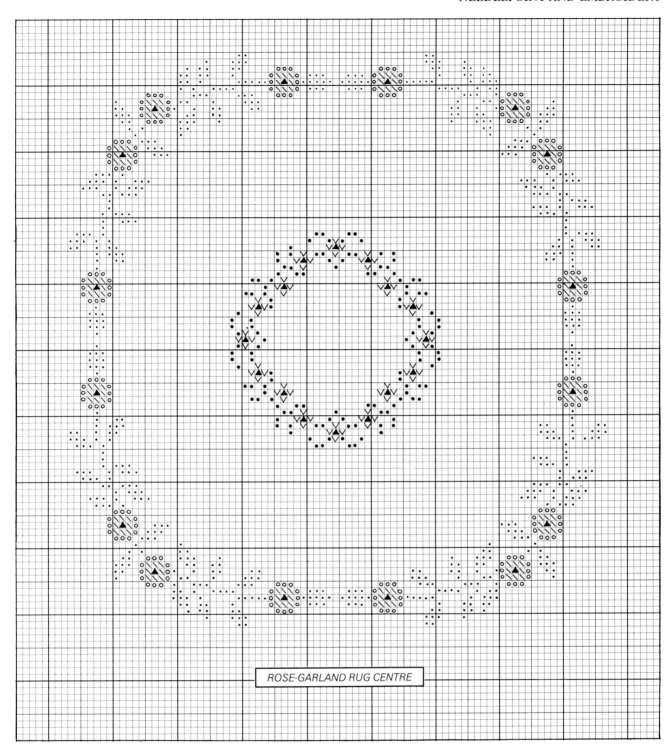

ROSE-GARLAND RUG CENTRE

VELVET AND NEEDLEPOINT CARPET *(Shown on page 111)*

Dora's clever carpet has a plain velvet centre panel with a needlepoint border worked on coin net with 23 threads per inch. Our carpet has a cream centre to match the border, which is worked in shades of peach and green on a cream background in Anchor stranded cotton (embroidery floss). The method is most effective if the velvet matches one of the colours used in the border. The carpet is made in a 12 inch square frame.

The chart shows one quarter of the pattern. With a piece of coin net $11\frac{1}{2}$ inches square in the frame, begin with the outer border, and work in half cross stitch – to make a flatter surface on the underside – with three strands of thread. Follow the chart to work the whole of the border except the innermost row – this is completed after the velvet panel.

Measure and cut a paper template to fit the central, unworked part of the carpet leaving a margin of one thread all around. Iron Bondaweb, Heat 'n Bond or a similar iron-on adhesive material on to the back of a piece of velvet and allow to cool. Using the paper template as a pattern, cut out the velvet central panel. Working with the frame over a raised object – such as a book covered with a folded

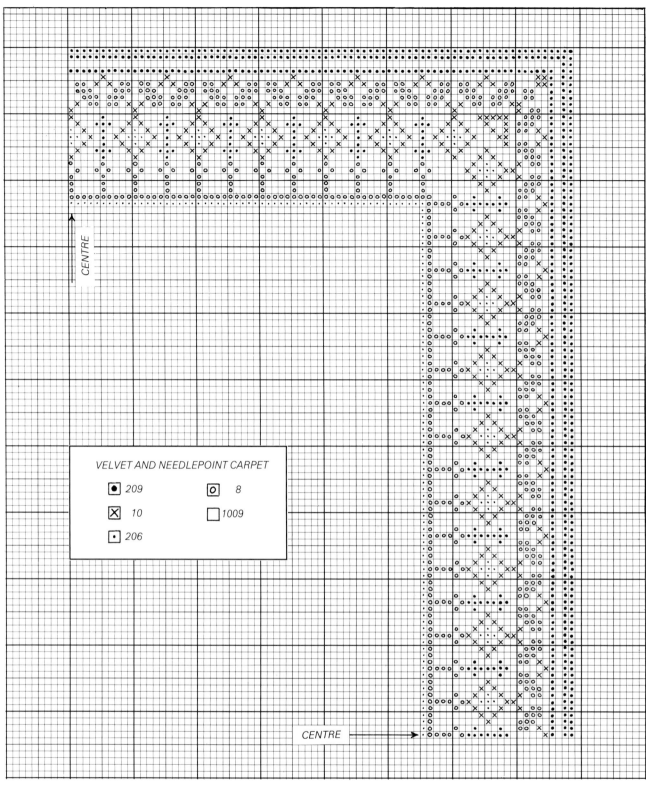

VELVET AND NEEDLEPOINT CARPET

● 209	◉ 8
☒ 10	☐ 1009
⊡ 206	

CENTRE

CENTRE ⟶

tea towel (dishtowel) so that the carpet lies flat – iron the velvet panel in place in the centre of the worked border with a hot iron over a damp cloth, and leave to cool. Work the innermost row of the border in half cross stitch with three strands of thread as the rest of the border, so that it meets the edge of the velvet panel. Trim the outer edge of the coin net to ten threads from the border. Turn this allowance under with mitred corners and slip stitch the edge to the underside of the carpet. Press the carpet, and raise the flattened pile of the velvet by stroking it firmly with the edge of a ruler.

TABLE CARPET

(Shown on page 50)

In the sixteenth and seventeenth centuries, carpets were far too expensive to walk on, and were used as table covers. Dora's table carpet has a central panel of needlepoint designed to fit the top of a refectory table, mounted on a velvet cloth cut to hang down the sides of the table. The needlepoint panel can also be used to make a beautiful rug for a dolls' house of a later period, following the making-up

TABLE CARPET

● 879	☒ 871	◉ 873
⊙ 45	▲ 216	☐ 956
• METALLIC GOLD		

instructions given for the rugs above. Our table carpet is worked in Anchor thread in rich, dark shades of purple, green, and gold on a beige background with an edging of narrow gold soutache braid on a dark green velvet cloth. The needlepoint is worked on coin net with 23 threads per inch in a 9 inch square frame and you will also need a 12 inch hoop to mount the panel on the velvet cloth.

With a 9 inch square of coin net in the frame, work the diamond shapes in cross stitch with the gold thread doubled in the needle. Work the remainder of the pattern in half cross stitch with three strands of thread. Begin with the outermost border (in dark green) to match the velvet, and work the pattern as shown on the chart. When the work is complete, trim the cross-stitched coin net to four threads outside the border.

With a 12 inch square of velvet in the hoop, position the needlepoint panel squarely in the centre and tack (baste) in place. Position soutache braid over the four-thread allowance and stitch the inside edge of the braid to the outermost row of the border and to the velvet. Stitch the outer edge of the braid to the velvet along each side of the panel and tuck in the raw ends of braid. Measure and trim the velvet so that the cloth hangs evenly on all sides of the table, sealing the raw edge on the inside with Fraycheck (or similar).

FLORENTINE CARPET *(Shown on page 78)*

This large rug, or small carpet, has an all-over pattern of ogee-shaped trellis worked in Florentine stitch within a plain border. The pattern is suitable for most houses from the early nineteenth century onward, and can be adapted to make a carpet of any size you wish simply by working a larger or smaller area. Our carpet is approximately $6\frac{1}{4}$ x $8\frac{1}{2}$ inches worked on 22-count canvas, and Sue has used three skeins of brown and gold and one skein of crimson DMC stranded cotton (embroidery floss) (838, 729 and 221), though you can of course use any colours you prefer. Work the carpet on a 9 x 12 inch canvas in a frame.

Leaving a margin of about 2 inches all round, with four strands of thread throughout, begin with a waste knot. Work the central panel first in Florentine stitch over four threads (five holes) of canvas, dropping the next stitch(es) by two threads. Work the trellis pattern (in brown) first from left to right, then from right to left, working the top of the ogee shape on one row and the lower part of the ogee shape on the return row, before moving down to the next row. When the (brown) trellis is complete, work the inner ogee shapes inside each (in gold) leaving spaces for the (crimson) rose shapes in the centre of each. Work the (crimson)

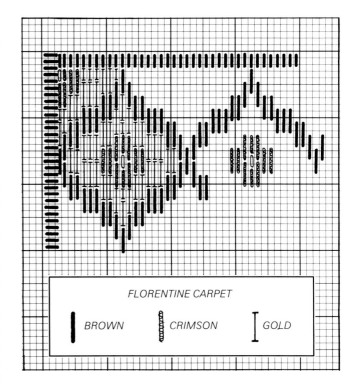

FLORENTINE CARPET

| BROWN | CRIMSON | GOLD |

roses and (gold) centres in the middle of each ogee. When the central panel is complete, work a small border around it in satin stitch (in brown). Remove the work from the frame, count eight holes (or more if you wish to make a wider border) from the central panel and fold the canvas under along a line of holes. Trim the canvas edge to meet the underside of the narrow border already worked. Matching the holes, bind the outside edge of the carpet by working satin stitch (in brown) over three holes of canvas to enclose the folded edge. Work the border in satin stitch (in gold), through both layers of canvas, enclosing the raw edge on the underside. Work back stitch (in crimson), over two threads of canvas to outline between the borders. Press the carpet on the wrong side between two clean cloths, but do not wash it.

FLORENTINE MEDALLION CARPET *(Shown on page 71)*

This elegant carpet has an all-over pattern of small diamonds with a central floral medallion within a plain border. The pattern is classical in style and will fit into most houses from the eighteenth century to the present day. Our carpet is $10\frac{1}{2}$ x 8 inches worked on 22-count canvas but it can easily be enlarged or reduced by working a larger or smaller area. Sue has used pale blue (four skeins), ecru (three skeins), pink and green (one skein each) DMC stranded cotton (embroidery floss) (932, 3033, 224 and 3053) but you can use any colours you wish. Work the carpet on a 12 x 15 (+) inch canvas in a frame.

FLORENTINE MEDALLION CARPET

EVENING DUTIES

Small rug or throw, square table-mat, small string bag, dressing-table set (Chapter 1), alphabet house sampler, Florentine carpet (Chapter 3), quilted cushion, square eiderdown, bedspread and bolster (Chapter 4), chemise and drawers, corset, nightgown and mobcap, straw hat, gloves, parasol (Chapter 6), chaise-longue (Chapter 7), beadwork cushion, beaded footstool, glove box, macramé curtain tie-backs (Chapter 8)

The pattern is virtually the same as the Florentine carpet above in that it is worked in a trellis pattern of ogees, but as these are all in the same colour (blue) it is not so apparent. Leaving a margin of 2 inches (or more) all round and using four strands of thread throughout, work the central panel first. Begin with a waste knot and work Florentine stitch over four threads (five holes), dropping the next stitch(es) by two threads. (The stitches share the hole at top and bottom.) Work from right to left, then left to right, (in blue), stitching the upper part of the ogee pattern on one row and the lower part on the return row before moving down to the next row. Complete the whole of the (blue) trellis outline, leaving the central medallion. When this is complete, work a small border in satin stitch (in blue) around the central panel. Fill the rest of the (blue) area inside each ogee, before working the (ecru) diamonds with (pink) centres in each. Run the thread ends through the back of the stitches to keep the work neat. When the central panel is complete, work the medallion, beginning with the (ecru) outline, then the (blue) inner line. Work the background ogee trellis (in ecru), then work the diamonds and flowers inside the ogees (in pink, green, and blue). Remove the work from the frame. Count eight rows from the border, fold the canvas on this line and trim the edge of the canvas to meet the border on the underside. Bind the folded edge by working satin stitch (in blue), over three holes, matching the holes. Working through both layers of canvas, work the border in satin stitch (in ecru), between the two narrow (blue) borders, enclosing the raw edge of canvas on the underside. Outline between the borders with back stitch over two threads of canvas (in pink). Press the carpet between two clean cloths, but do not wash it.

TIGER-SKIN RUG *(Shown on page 167)*

Dora's amusing needlepoint tiger-skin rug is perfect for the study or drawing room of a Victorian house. One can just imagine the tenant claiming that he 'shot it in Poonah'! You will need coin net with 23 threads per inch, Anchor stranded cotton (embroidery floss) in tan, white, and black, and a 9 inch square frame.

Work in half cross stitch with three strands of thread throughout. Begin by working one row of the pattern all the way round the outside edge to define the outline of the tiger. Work the white areas, then the light tan areas. Work the black stripes, then fill in the dark tan background.

There are several possible methods for finishing the rug, so choose whichever you prefer. EITHER: Cut out the tiger shape, ½ inch from the edge of the work, cut small strips of Bondaweb (or similar) ½

inch wide and apply them to the back of the worked outline all round. OR: Use fabric glue, ensuring that it is applied sparingly so that it does not seep to the right side. Working a little at a time, snip the allowance to the underside so that it lies flat, using the point of the iron to hold it in place. When the allowance is secured on the underside all round, press the rug with a hot iron over a damp cloth. OR: Cut out the rug as a rectangle, leaving six threads of coin net from the edge of the outline at the widest point. Cut a piece of Bondaweb (or similar) and apply to the back of the rug. Bond the backed rug on to a piece of black cotton fabric and allow to cool. Cut out the tiger shape, two threads outside the outline, with pinking shears and colour the bare threads with a black felt-tipped marker pen so that they blend in with backing fabric.

FLOWER-TRELLIS RUG *(Shown on page 135)*

The delicate flower-trellis pattern of Sue's *petit point* rug, designed for more experienced needlewomen, is based on traditional designs and can be worked in a wide variety of colours to suit any room. Our rug is in natural flower colours, softly shaded on a light background to make a pretty feminine effect, but the same pattern in light colours on a dark ground would look equally good and Indian carpets of this type are often worked in shades of gold and brown on a rich red background. The completed rug is 4¼ x 6½ inches worked on canvas with 22 threads per inch. Our rug is worked in DMC stranded cotton (embroidery floss) in ecru (3033 – two skeins) for the background, and gold, yellow, blue, red, pale green, and grey for the trellis and details. To achieve the subtle shaded effect in the flowers and leaves, they are stitched in three strands of mixed colours: dark gold (680) one strand, and (420) two strands. Pale pink (223) two strands, and (224) one strand. Medium pink (3372) two strands, and (223) one strand. Medium green (3347) two strands, and (3052) one strand. Red (356), pale green (3347), and grey (646) are used as supplied. Work the rug on 8 x 10 inch canvas in a frame.

Using three strands of thread throughout, work the trellis and flowers in half cross stitch and the background in diagonal tent stitch. Note that if you use continental tent stitch, the work will twist and would need stretching when completed. Begin with a waste knot and finish off all threads by running the needle through the back of the stitches. Begin at the centre and work outward. Plot the trellis of the centre panel first, then work the details and the background. Complete the whole of the central area before beginning the border.

When the centre of the rug is complete, remove the work from the frame, count the number of

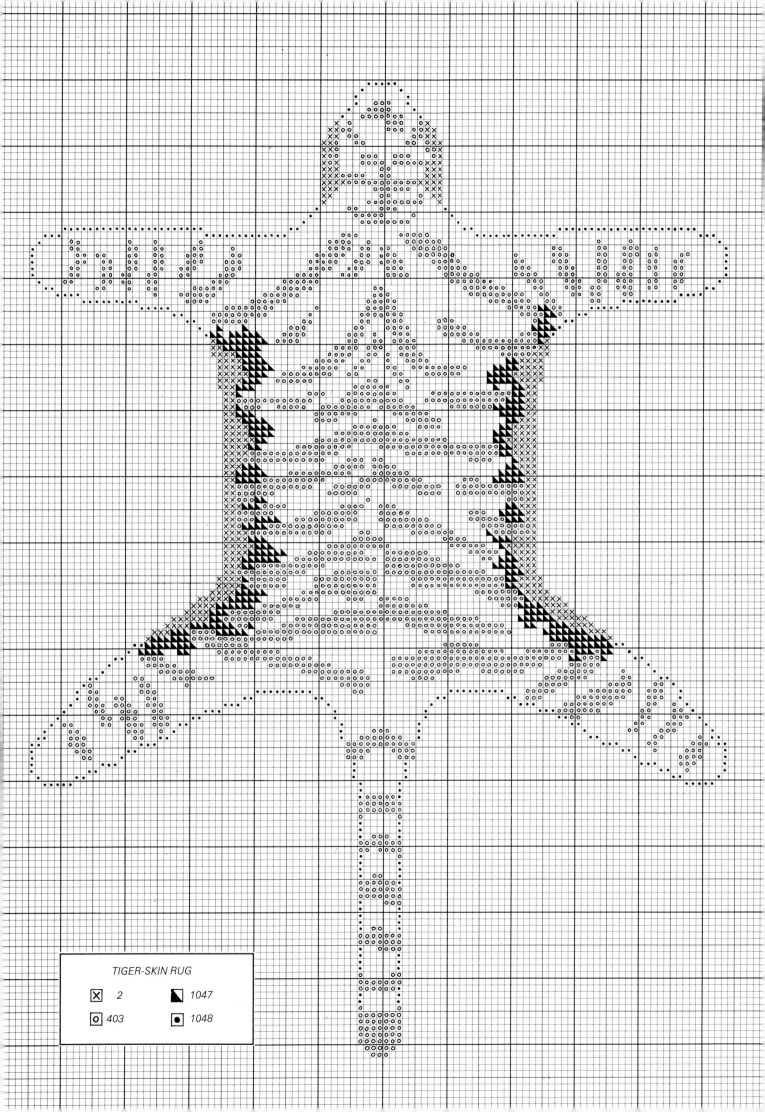

TIGER-SKIN RUG

☒	2	◣	1047
⊙	403	⊡	1048

FLOWER-TRELLIS RUG

◉	DARK GOLD	כ	RED
◪	YELLOW	◪	PALE GREEN
⊞	BLUE	◨	MEDIUM GREEN
⊠	PALE PINK	■	GREY
⊙	MEDIUM PINK	☐	ECRU

stitches/holes required for the border, and fold the outside edge of the canvas to the underside, lining up the holes, and trim the excess canvas in line with the inner edge of the border. Bind the outside (folded) edge around the rug with satin stitch and work the pattern and background of the border through both layers of canvas. When the work is complete, press the rug on the underside between two clean cloths, but do not wash it.

 # TURKOMAN RUG

(Shown on page 27)

This exquisite *petit point* rug is worked in an ancient traditional 'gul' pattern which was particularly popular in the nineteenth century. Sue's pattern is designed for experienced needlewomen and will make a rug approximately 4½ x 7 inches worked on 22-thread canvas. Our rug is stitched in DMC stranded cotton (embroidery floss) in black, blue, gold, and white on a red background and you may prefer to use brighter shades (3371, 336, 3045, 3033 and 3777) to represent a new rug, or faded colours (3371, 3750, 3045, 3033 and 632) for an 'old' rug. If you choose different colours, you may find it helpful to colour the chart on the bottom 'gul' pattern which has been left without

BREAKFAST IN BED

Simple blanket, square table-mat, hot-water bottle cover (Chapter 1), bed jacket and slippers (Chapter 2), embroidered pillowcase, leaf pattern rug (Chapter 3), shell pattern tea-cosy, squares quilt (Chapter 4), sheets and pillows (Chapter 5), art-nouveau lamp (Chapter 8)

symbols for this purpose. Work the rug on a 8 x 10 inch canvas in a frame.

Using three strands of thread throughout, begin at the centre of the pattern and work outward. Work the details of the central panel first in half cross stitch, then work the background in diagonal tent stitch.

When the central panel is complete, remove the work from the frame, count the number of holes/stitches required for the border, and fold the canvas under at the outside edge, lining up the holes and trimming the canvas edge to meet the inner edge of the border on the underside. Bind the folded edge of the rug with satin stitch and work the border through both layers of canvas using half cross stitch for the detail and diagonal tent stitch for the background as for the central panel. Make fringes at both short ends of the rug with Surrey stitch or simple knots. Press the rug between two clean cloths, but do not wash it.

TURKOMAN RUG

■ BLACK   ☒ GOLD

□ RED   ⊡ WHITE

◪ BLUE

— CHAPTER FOUR —
Patchwork, Quilting and Appliqué

Of the three needlecrafts in this chapter, quilting has the longest history. Examples of quilted garments exist from before the first century AD, so it is appropriate for dolls' houses of any period. Patchwork has been used for hundreds of years, first as a practical necessity when fabrics were so expensive that even scraps could not be wasted, then, when printed cottons became widely available at the end of the eighteenth century, as a decorative craft. Appliqué was used, with embroidery, to decorate hangings and bedcovers in grand houses in the sixteenth century. The three crafts have much in common and often the techniques are used together, for example in quilt making.

The tools, materials and methods are much the same whether you are working in lifesize or in miniature, but you will need the smallest needles you can comfortably work with to make the finest stitches, and fabrics should be natural silks and cottons in the lightest weight. Our small quilted projects are worked on Habotai (or similar) silk over lawn and we recommend silk wadding (batting) rather than polyester for the best results. Liberty Tana lawn is strongly recommended as the best fabric for patchwork. It can be bought by the yard (metre) in plain colours and tiny prints, but it is also available as bias binding, which can be a very economical way to acquire a range of patterns and colours. Tana lawn can be used on the 'wrong' side if you wish to make an item look older or faded.

Other fine cottons are also perfectly suitable for patchwork and appliqué and you will usually find a wide choice in shops which supply tools and fabrics for lifesize patchwork. Several projects, including appliqué, require iron-on bonding fabrics. These are sold under brand names such as 'Bondaweb' and 'Heat 'n Bond' and are available in several weights from department stores and needlework suppliers. You will need the lightweight variety which is suitable for miniature work.

The best thread for quilting is a fine polyester machine thread to complement the sheen of the silk. For patchwork, use a cotton thread to match the fabric. Commercial templates for $\frac{1}{4}$ inch patchwork hexagons are widely available, though the cutting-template supplied might be over-large. Trim it to $\frac{1}{2}$ inch with a craft knife for neater results. Typing paper is recommended for cutting the paper patches and a stitch ripper is useful for hooking the papers out of completed patchwork. We recommend wearing a well-fitting thimble to protect your middle finger and you will find small sharp-pointed scissors essential. Transfer patterns on to silk fabrics for quilting with a well-sharpened dressmakers' pencil or a Fadeaway or similar marker pen with ink which vanishes after a few hours. These tools and materials are all available from needlework suppliers or haberdashery (notions) departments in stores. See the UK and US suppliers listed at the back of the book.

CUSHIONS

 ## QUILTED CUSHION
(Shown on page 11)

This elegant cushion in Italian quilting would fit happily into almost any house. Dora has used gold silk over lawn, quilted in matching thread, but you might use any colour you prefer. You will also need about 18 inches of matching tapestry wool yarn in a crewel needle to raise the quilting.

Trace the pattern on to the silk, and tack (baste) silk and lawn together around the outside. Use tiny back stitches to work the lines of the pattern

Quilted cushion

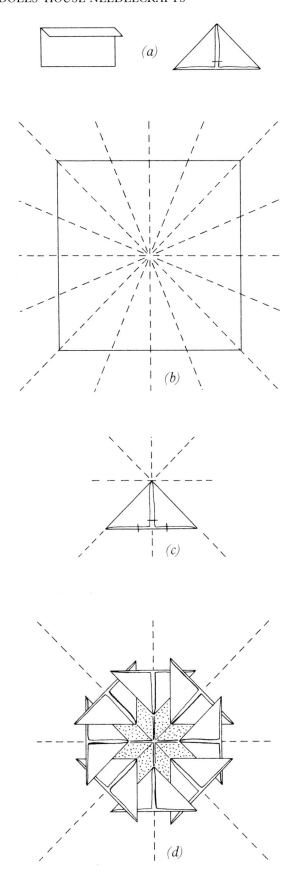

Folded-star cushion

through both layers of fabric. Thread the yarn through the channel between the fabrics, bringing the needle out and re-inserting it through the lawn backing at each corner of the pattern. Cut out the cushion front, and trim the lawn backing to leave a $\frac{1}{4}$ inch allowance on the silk. Cut a back for the cushion to fit in matching silk. Turn in the allowance on the front piece and tack (baste). Turn in a similar allowance on the back and tack (baste). With wrong sides facing, slip stitch the two pieces together around three sides. Stuff the quilted cushion lightly, slip stitch the fourth side and remove the tacking (basting).

 FOLDED-STAR CUSHION *(Shown on page 11)*

This impressive round cushion is made in folded-star patchwork in two patterned and two plain fabrics – Dora has used Tana lawn in pinks, cream, and pale green. You will also need a 4 inch embroidery hoop.

To prepare the pieces : Cut a strip $3\frac{1}{2}$ x $\frac{1}{2}$ inch in the first patterned fabric (A). Cut a strip 7 x $\frac{1}{2}$ inch in the second patterned fabric (C). Cut a strip 7 x $\frac{1}{2}$ inch in the first plain fabric (B) and two strips in the second plain fabric (D). Turn in $\frac{1}{8}$ inch along one side of each strip and press. Cut each strip into $\frac{7}{8}$ inch lengths. Fold each piece to mark the centre, then fold each piece sides-to-middle to form a triangle. Secure each triangle with a small back stitch and press (a).

Transfer the pattern (b) on to a 6 inch square of white cotton lawn in pencil, and place the fabric in the hoop. Place the first triangle (fabric A) with point to centre on the marked pattern. Stitch through the lawn backing, through the point of the triangle, and either side of the fold at the base of the triangle to secure it in place (c). Place and stitch the other three triangles in fabric A in the same way to complete the first round. With eight triangles in fabric B, place the point $\frac{1}{8}$ inch from the centre, lined up on the marked pattern lines, and secure the points and bases in the same way as the first round. Over- and underlap the base corners evenly all the way round as shown. Place and secure eight triangles in fabric C in the same way. Place and secure sixteen triangles in fabric D in the same way working outward from the centre by $\frac{1}{8}$ inch on each round (d). When all triangles are secured, cut a $1\frac{1}{2}$ inch circle of paper, mark the centre point, and tack (baste) the paper template over the work to define the outside edge. Make a row of small running stitches around the edge of the template, through all layers of fabric. Remove the template and take the work out of the hoop. Apply Bondaweb (or similar) to a scrap of white cotton lawn and cut a $1\frac{1}{2}$ inch circle. Bond this circle to the back of the patchwork inside the line of running stitches. Trim the work to

¹⁄₁₆ inch outside the line of running stitches.

Cut a back for the cushion to fit in fabric D, and cut a bias strip 5½ x ¾ inches in fabric B. With wrong sides facing, place the cushion front and back together and tack. Bind the outside edge of the cushion with bias strip, pushing a little stuffing into the cushion before completing the binding.

LOG-CABIN CUSHION *(Shown on page 11)*

This attractive little square cushion is made in log-cabin patchwork in two plain and two patterned fabrics on a white lawn backing. Dora has used soft shades of pink and blue Tana lawn.

On a 4 inch square piece of white lawn, trace a 1½ inch square in the centre and mark the horizontal and vertical centre lines of the square with a dressmakers' pencil. Cut a ¾ inch square in one plain fabric and tack (baste) it to the centre with a cross. Cut a strip of patterned fabric ½ x ¾ inch. Place this face down over the centre square, and, lining up the edges, stitch across one side, ³⁄₁₆ inch from the edge. Open out the patterned strip and press flat. Cut a second piece of patterned fabric ½ inch wide to fit the plain centre square plus one side of the patterned strip. Place this face down over the centre, matching edges, and stitch it to the second side of the centre square and edge of the patterned strip. Turn back and press. Repeat for the third and fourth sides of the square, noting that the fourth strip should be cut to fit the centre square and two strip side edges. Cut strips of the second patterned fabric ½ inch wide to fit and stitch them on to the

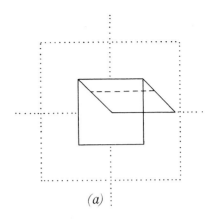

(a)

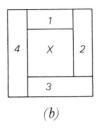

(b)

Log-cabin cushion

first patterned fabric, working around the square in the same way. Cut strips in the second plain fabric, ⅝ inch wide, and stitch them to the patterned fabric, working around the square in the same way. Trim the backing until it is even with the outside edge of the work.

Cut a back for the cushion to match in the second plain fabric. Turn in and tack a small allowance around both pieces. With wrong sides facing, slip stitch pieces together round three sides, stuff the cushion and slip stitch fourth side.

FURNISHINGS

SHIP AND COTTAGE PICTURES *(Shown on page 55)*

These simple little appliqué pictures are made from scraps of lightweight cotton fabric and framed with

Ship and cottage pictures

fine woodstrip. Use a touch of fabric glue to secure the pieces as you work, and fine-point fibre-tipped pens to add the details.

Select scraps of fabric in the appropriate colours and patterns to complete the picture and iron lightweight bonding (Bondaweb, Heat 'n Bond or similar) to the back of each scrap. Draw the outline of each piece on the fabric with a well-sharpened dressmakers' pencil or Fadeaway pen and cut out with small sharp-pointed scissors.

SHIP

Trace the outline of the picture on to plain pale blue fabric (sky). Cut the boat hull in red (or red-striped) fabric and place ⅓ of the way up from the bottom, slightly angled. Cut the sails in white and place above the hull. Cut the pennant in green and place above the sails. Cut the sea in blue-speckled print and place over the lower edge of the hull. Press carefully with a hot iron over a damp cloth to bond the fabrics together, and allow to cool. Draw the mast between the sails and the birds in the sky with black pen.

COTTAGE

Trace the outline of the picture on to plain pale blue fabric (sky). Cut the hill in plain dark green and place over the background. Cut the garden in tiny flower print, the top edge with pinking shears, and place over the hill, lining up with the bottom edge of the outline. Cut the cottage in beige and place over the garden. Cut the thatched roof in gold, the lower edge with pinking shears, and place over the cottage. Cut the chimney in beige and place on the roof. Cut the door in green and place in the centre of the cottage. Press to bond the fabric pieces together and allow to cool. Work small cross stitches across the roof to suggest decorative thatching. Draw the bird in the sky with black pen, and the smoke above the chimney with white. Draw the windows with brown pen and colour the panes with gold. Mark the doorknob with a black dot.

When the picture is complete, trim squarely on the marked outline. Cut a piece of thin stiff card ¼ inch larger all round and spread fabric glue over the card. Allow to dry a little until it becomes tacky. Smooth the appliqué on to the centre of the card and allow to dry. Cut fine woodstrip, (stained or painted as required) with mitred corners and glue to the card squarely around the outline of the picture with craft glue (UHU or similar) and allow to dry. Trim the card around the woodstrip frame with a craft knife and metal ruler.

Rabbit pictures

and place over the background. Cut the front hill in dark green print and place over the back hill. Cut the moon in white and place over the sky. Cut the rabbit in beige and place over the front hill, slightly to one side. Cut the toadstool stem in beige and place to the side of the rabbit, and the toadstool top in white-on-red spot print over the base. Press carefully with a hot iron over a damp cloth to bond the fabrics together, and allow to cool. Glue the pom-pom tail on to the rabbit.

SUN-RISE RABBITS

Trace the outline of the picture on to pale blue fabric (sky). Cut the sun in gold and place in the centre of the background. Cut the back hill in green and place over the sun. Cut the front hill in tiny flower print and place over the back hill. Cut the rabbits in beige and place over the front hill. Press to bond the fabrics together and allow to cool. Work the sun rays in gold in back stitch (or draw in with fibre-tipped pen). Glue the pom-pom tails on to each of the rabbits.

Mount and frame the pictures as described for the ship and cottage pictures.

RABBIT PICTURES

(Shown on page 55)

These two appliqué pictures are designed as a pair. They are made from scraps of fabric, framed with narrow woodstrip. The patterns could also be used to decorate a cot (crib) cover or bedspread for a child, or used to decorate a screen made from the pattern on page 141. The technique is very simple and can be used to make pictures to your own ideas. Often a particular scrap of fabric will suggest a subject – as with the 'moon-gazing rabbit' suggested by the dark blue cotton printed with tiny stars. I have used tiny cotton pom-poms for the rabbits' tails.

The method is the same as for the ship and cottage pictures above.

MOON-GAZING RABBIT

Trace the outline of the picture on to dark blue star print fabric (sky). Cut the back hill in dark green

CHANGING-MAT AND NAPPY BAG

(Shown on page 43)

This simple quilted changing-mat with a matching bag for nappies (diapers) make perfect accessories for a modern nursery. Isobel has used a lightweight printed cotton in shades of pink, but you could choose any plain colour or print.

Cut the patterns against the fold, on the straight grain of the fabric.

CHANGING-MAT

Cut a piece of thin wadding (batting) from the pattern. Fold and tack (baste) a small hem on both short edges of the fabric and press. Fold the fabric

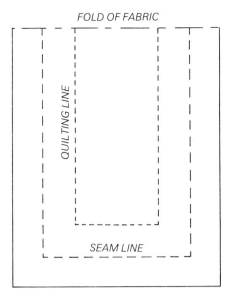

Changing-mat and nappy bag

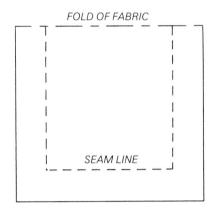

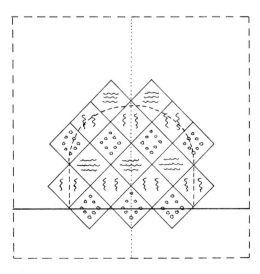

Ribbon-patch tea-cosy

in half with right sides facing, and place the wadding on top, tucked under the folded edge. Stitch through fabric and wadding (batting) down both side edges, clip the corners and turn through. Oversew the folded fabric edges together with small stitches. Quilt through all layers with machine stitches or tiny running stitches, close to the edge, then again on the inner line marked on the pattern. Do not press the changing-mat.

NAPPY BAG

Fold and stitch a small hem on both short edges of the fabric. Stitch small loops of narrow ribbon to the inside of the hems as shown for the bag handles. With right sides facing, stitch the side seams, clip the corners, turn through and press.

RIBBON-PATCH TEA-COSY *(Shown on page 186)*

This 'patchwork' tea-cosy is made by bonding squares of ribbon (or fabric) on to a backing of fine cotton lawn. Dora has used scraps of 7mm wide silk ribbon in pale shades of blue, green, and peach, but the method will work equally well with lightweight cotton fabrics – Tana lawn bias binding is especially good. This technique can also be used to make delightful cushion covers, a cosy cot (crib) cover or a bedspread.

Cut two $2\frac{1}{2}$ inch squares of cotton lawn for backings, and crease to define the vertical centre line on each piece. Mark a line $\frac{1}{2}$ inch from the bottom edge of each piece. Cut 3 inch strips of ribbon and iron Bondaweb (or similar) on to the back of each strip. (Or iron Bondaweb on to the back of cotton fabric, allow to cool and cut strips.) Cut the ribbons into 7mm squares. Working on one backing piece, place the first ribbon square on the centre line as shown, and bond it to the fabric with a warm iron. Place and bond the other ribbon squares to form the pattern, ensuring that the grain line on each patch runs in the same direction. Apply ribbon patches to the second backing in the same way. Press both pieces with a hot iron over a damp cloth and allow to cool. Make a paper template, and cut out the tea-cosy back and front, carefully lining up the pattern at the centre and lower edge. Cut two $5\frac{1}{2}$ inch pieces of ribbon for binding, fold and press along the length. Open out the ribbon, and applying fabric glue sparingly, glue one side of the ribbon around the outside edge of each piece of the tea-cosy easing carefully around the curve, then fold and glue the other edge of ribbon to the inside so that the fold defines the outer edge on each piece. When the glued ribbon binding is dry, place the two pieces together, wrong sides facing, and slip stitch the outside edges together to complete the tea-cosy.

SHELL PATTERN TEA-COSY *(Shown on page 186)*

Dora's quilted tea-cosy is made in pale blue silk over lawn, padded with silk wadding (batting) and quilted in a simple but attractive shell pattern with matching silk thread.

Cut two 3 inch squares in silk, wadding (batting), and lawn for the tea-cosy back and front. Trace the

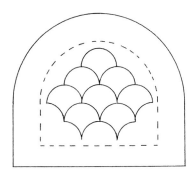

Shell pattern tea-cosy

CHRISTMAS TOMORROW
Set of cushions (Chapter 1), sweater and shorts (Chapter 2), small fringed rug (Chapter 3), antimacassar (Chapter 4), lampshade (Chapter 5), square stool (Chapter 7)

pattern on to both pieces of silk. Peel the wadding apart to halve the thickness and remove the 'skin' on each piece. Place wadding over lawn and silk over wadding and tack (baste) the three layers together. With small stitches, tack around the outline of the tea-cosy. With tiny running stitches, quilt the pattern on each piece.

Cut out the tea-cosy back and front. Lifting the silk aside, trim the lawn lining and wadding to the tacked outline on both pieces. Paint a line of Fraycheck around the edge of the silk and allow to dry. Fold the silk allowance in and tack to hold. Slip stitch the edge of the allowance to the lining, ensuring that the stitches do not show on the right side. Remove the tacking, and with wrong sides facing, slip stitch the two pieces together around the outside edge.

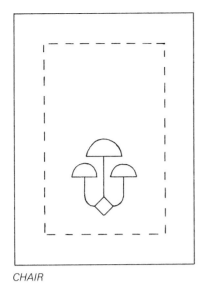

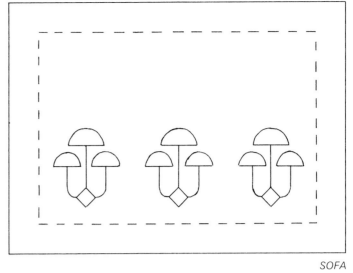

CHAIR　　　　　　　　　　　　　　　　　　　　　　　　SOFA

Antimacassars

 # ANTIMACASSARS

(Shown on page 59)

This charming set of appliquéd antimacassars in the art-deco style is particularly suitable for an early twentieth-century house. Dora has used Tana lawn in cream lined with white and worked the motifs with pale blue appliqué 'mushrooms' and dark brown embroidery. Patterns are given for antimacassars for an armchair and sofa (couch), the method is the same for both.

Trace the pattern on to a piece of cream fabric, backed with the same or white fabric (lining), a little larger than the pattern and tack (baste) the two pieces together. Apply Bondaweb (or similar) to a scrap of blue fabric and cut out the 'mushroom' motifs. Bond the motifs on to the cream fabric as shown and allow to cool. With one strand of matching thread, work tiny back stitches to outline around the motifs, through both layers of fabric. With one strand of dark brown thread, embroider the lines of the motif in stem stitch and the diamond in satin stitch, beginning in the centre and working outward through both layers of fabric. Press lightly if necessary. Cut out the antimacassar and trim the lining fabric by $\frac{1}{4}$ inch all round. Paint a line of Fraycheck (or similar) around the edge of the cream fabric and allow to dry. Turn the allowance on cream fabric to the back, mitring the corners and slip stitch the edge to the lining, ensuring that the stitches do not show on the right side.

BEDCOVERS

 # HEXAGON BEDSPREAD

(Shown on page 146)

This pretty bedspread is made in hexagon patchwork appliquéd on to a plain background. Hexagon patchwork in this scale is very time-consuming and to make the whole quilt in hexagons would be a real labour of love, but Dora's ingenious method is a much quicker alternative. Our quilt is cream, with patches in four different prints and a toning plain colour, all in Tana lawn. The bedspread is most easily worked in a 10 inch embroidery hoop.

Cut a 12 inch square in plain-colour lawn and trace the cutting and seam lines squarely on to the right side of the fabric in dressmakers' pencil. Tack (baste) the grid of dotted lines shown on the pattern as a guide for positioning the patchwork. Cut 71 patches in typing paper using a $\frac{1}{4}$ inch template, and 71 fabric patches as shown using a $\frac{1}{2}$ inch template. Make up the patches. Assemble the central block of patches as shown, then assemble the border by stitching the patches together, right sides facing, with tiny oversewing stitches in matching thread. Press both sets of patches well and remove the tacking and papers.

Working with the fabric in the hoop, position the central block of patches following the tacked guidelines, and tack in place. Using the smallest stitches and matching thread, bring the needle up through the fabric and down through the edge of the patch, to sew the patchwork block in place around the edge. Position the patchwork border, following the tacked guidelines, and tack, then stitch the border in place. Remove the work from the hoop. Remove all tacking and press. Trim the bedspread on the cutting line, and cut a lining to fit. EITHER: Turn in and tack a seam allowance around both pieces so that the lining is fractionally

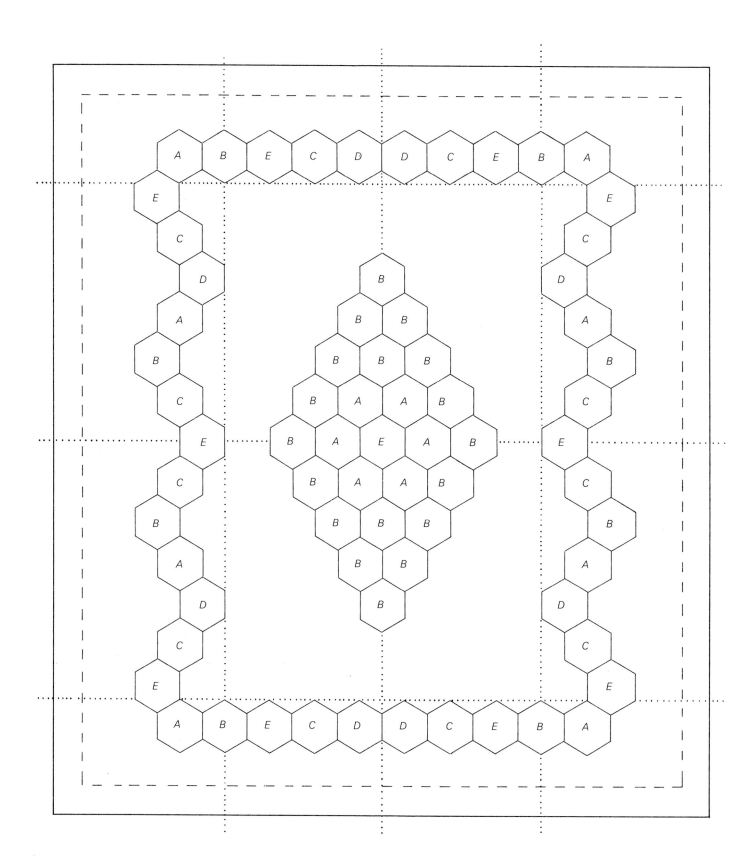

....TACKING LINES

Hexagon bedspread

smaller than the bedspread. With wrong sides facing, tack, then slip stitch the two pieces together around the edge. OR: With right sides facing, stitch the two pieces together leaving an opening at the top to turn through. Trim seams, clip corners, turn through and slip stitch the opening closed. Press to make crisp edges.

DIAMOND EIDERDOWN AND BEDSPREAD

(Shown on page 38)

This simple quilted eiderdown (comforter) with a matching bedspread is suitable for most nineteenth- or twentieth-century houses. The eiderdown and bedspread can be made in any lightweight silk or cotton fabric, in matching or toning plain colours or small prints. I have used rose-pink silk and lined the bedspread with cotton lawn. The bedspread pattern will fit most standard-size double beds which do not have footposts, including the divan on page 143, but check the measurements on your own bed and adjust as necessary. The method can easily be adapted to fit a single-size bed.

EIDERDOWN

Cut a piece of fabric 10 x 6 inches. Centre the pattern on the piece and trace the quilting lines on to the right side of the fabric with a Fadeaway marker pen or dressmakers' pencil and ruler. With right sides facing, stitch the two short edges of the piece together and press the seam open. With this seam to the centre, stitch across the top and bottom edges, leaving a 3 inch opening to turn through. Turn through, and press the seamed edges if necessary. Cut a piece of silk or polyester wadding (batting) 5 x 4½ inches and slip this inside the eiderdown case. Slip stitch the opening closed. Tack (baste) through all layers, vertically and horizontally through the centre, and around the edge to hold the wadding in place. Using the smallest machine stitch or tiny back stitches, quilt the pattern on the marked lines, beginning with the central diamond and working outward. Remove the tacking. Do not press.

BEDSPREAD

Cut one piece in fabric and one in lining, 9 x 9½ inches (or to fit your bed). With right sides facing, pin the pieces together, fold down the centre to match the edges, and trim the lower corners

Diamond eiderdown

rounded. Stitch the two pieces together, leaving a small opening at the top edge to turn through. Trim the seams, clip the corners, turn through and slip stitch the opening closed. Press the bedspread to make crisp edges.

STAR QUILT

(Shown on page 95)

This simple but effective quilt has appliquéd star motifs centred in each of the quilted squares. Dora has used scraps of nine different small prints on a plain cream background, but a variety of different colours and prints would be equally attractive. For example you might make the quilt in a plain dark or pale colour and use one toning dark or pale print for all the stars. Alternatively, you could make the quilt in a print and the stars in one or several toning plain colours. You will need lightweight cotton fabrics and wadding (batting) – ideally, silk wadding. This quilt will fit most standard-size beds including the divan beds on page 143.

The pattern is for a single-bed size quilt, for a double-bed size simply add one row of squares (so that the quilt is six squares across). Cut two pieces of fabric and one of wadding 10 inches square (double-bed size 10 x 12 inches). Peel apart the wadding to halve the thickness and remove the 'skin'. Make a template for the star in thin stiff card (postcard). Iron Bondaweb (or similar) on to the back of the printed fabric(s), allow to cool, and cut out 25 stars for the single or 30 for the double quilt.

Trace the quilting lines on to one piece of fabric in dressmakers' pencil or Fadeaway pen. Position one star in the first square, lining up carefully as shown, and secure in place with a warm iron. Position and secure each star in the same way. Press with a hot iron over a damp cloth and allow to cool. Place the wadding over lining and the appliquéd fabric over wadding and tack (baste) the three layers together. With tiny running stitches, quilt along the marked lines beginning at either side of the centre and working outward to keep the wadding evenly distributed. Work the vertical lines first, then the horizontal lines in the same way. Remove tacking, and cut out the quilt (through all three layers). Turn in and tack a seam allowance around the edge of the quilt top. Trim the wadding to just inside the folded edge. Turn in and tack a corresponding seam allowance on the lining. Tack through all three layers to hold the edges evenly together. With the quilt top uppermost, quilt $\frac{1}{16}$ inch from the edge with tiny running stitches and remove the tacking.

SQUARE EIDERDOWN, BEDSPREAD AND BOLSTER *(Shown on page 78)*

Dora's matching set of eiderdown (comforter), bedspread and bolster is designed to fit a standard-size double bed with posts and footboard. In our

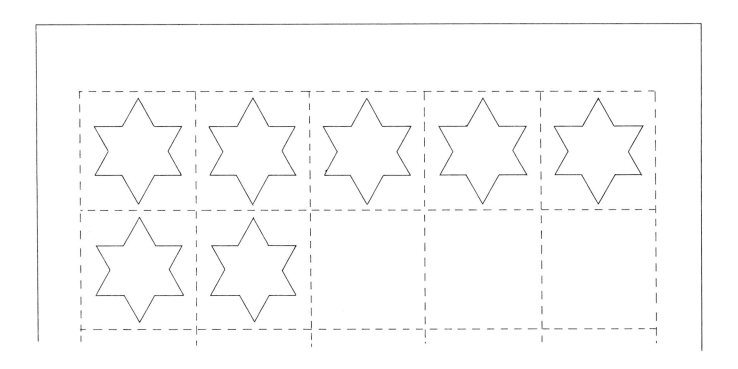

Star quilt

Victorian bedroom, the set is shown in crimson silk lined and trimmed with gold silk and picot braid, though you can of course use any colour(s) you prefer. (For the tester and back hanging on this bed see the instructions on page 66 for the scroll bedspread and hangings.)

EIDERDOWN

Cut two $5\frac{1}{2}$ inch squares in fabric and one in silk wadding (batting). Trace the pattern on to one square of fabric marking the seam line and quilting lines on the right side with a pencil and ruler. With right sides facing, place the two fabric pieces together and the wadding on top and tack (baste) the three pieces together. Machine stitch a $\frac{1}{2}$ inch seam around the outside through the three layers, leaving a small opening to turn through. Trim the wadding, clip the corners, turn through and slip stitch the opening closed. With matching thread and tiny running stitches, quilt on the marked lines. Stitch picot braid around the four edges to complete the eiderdown.

BEDSPREAD

Cut one piece each in (silk) fabric and lawn (interlining) 10 x $8\frac{1}{2}$ inches. Trace the pattern on to

LONELY NIGHTS

Baby blanket, dressing-table set (Chapter 1), bless-this-house sampler (Chapter 3), log-cabin cushion, star quilt (Chapter 4), rag rug (Chapter 5), lady's dressing-gown, nightgown and mobcap slippers, linen bag (Chapter 6)

the right side of the fabric, marking the cutting line, seam line and scalloped line and tack (baste) the two pieces together. Working through both layers, stitch picot braid on the marked scallop line. Trim the interlining to the marked seam line. Turn in and tack the fabric seam allowance. Cut a lining in silk $8\frac{3}{4}$ x $7\frac{1}{4}$ inches, turn in a seam allowance and tack so that the lining is fractionally smaller than the bedspread. With wrong sides facing, tack, then slip stitch the two pieces together.

BOLSTER

Cut a piece of fabric 5 x 4 inches. Fold the piece lengthwise, stitch the long edges together with a $\frac{1}{2}$ inch seam, and press the seam open. With the seam to centre, stitch across one short edge. Clip the corners and turn through. Stuff the bolster, then turn in and slip stitch the open end closed. Stitch picot braid around the four edges.

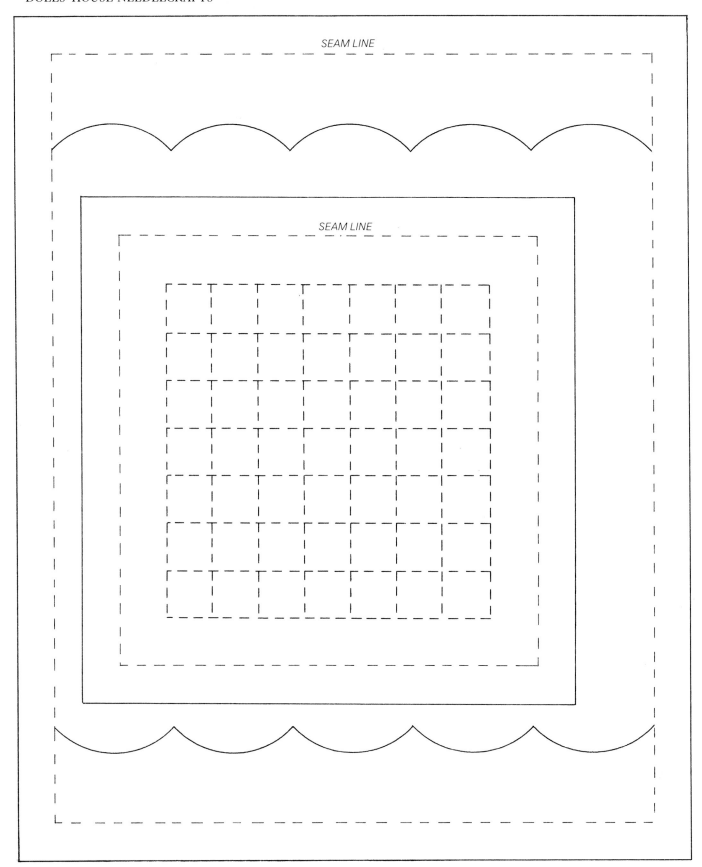

SEAM LINE

SEAM LINE

Square eiderdown and bedspread

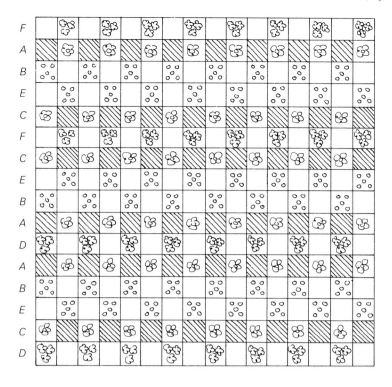

Squares quilt

SQUARES QUILT

(Shown on page 83)

This colourful quilt is made in patchwork squares in co-ordinating print and plain fabrics. Dora has chosen four print and two plain Tana lawns in blue and lilac, lined with plain blue and bound with one of the prints. Choose colours which complement the decorating scheme in your bedroom. This quilt can be made to fit any size bed.

Cut 1 inch wide x 14 inch long strips squarely on the straight grain of the fabric. (To make the pattern shown, print fabrics are identified as A, B, C and D. Plain fabrics are E and F.) Cut three strips each of A, B, C and E. Cut two strips each of D and F. Pin, and stitch the strips together with the smallest possible machine stitch and ¼ inch seams, spacing the print and plain fabrics – (F A B E C F C E B A D A B E C D) – to make a pleasing combination and ensuring that the seams are straight and even. (You may find it easier to cut a ½ inch wide card template to mark straight seam lines on the strips.) As each strip is stitched, press the seam open before stitching the next.

When complete, cut the work into 1 inch strips ACROSS the seams, squarely on the straight grain of the fabric. Reassemble, reversing alternate strips to make a pleasing pattern, and pinning the strips together on the previous seam lines to keep the work square. Stitch the strips together, pressing each seam before stitching the next strip. When the patchwork is complete, press the quilt top carefully on the right side.

Trim the quilt top to the required size, and cut a lining to fit. With wrong sides facing, tack (baste) the two pieces together, then bind the edge all round with 1 inch wide bias strips and ¼ inch seams, overlapping and tucking in the raw ends at each corner. Turn in the raw edge and slip stitch the binding to the lining ensuring that the stitches do not show on the right side.

— CHAPTER FIVE —
Soft Furnishings

The projects in this chapter include curtains (drapes) and bedding and are generally what was once described as 'plain sewing'. The tools and materials used for miniatures are the same as those for plain sewing in lifesize, though we tend to use lighter-weight fabrics and finer needles. The fabrics you choose for soft furnishings are very much a matter of personal taste but as a general rule, finely woven natural fabrics such as cotton lawn (batiste), fine linen, and silk are more effective than man-made fibres, because they crease and hang well and they look more realistic, especially in period dolls' houses. Liberty Tana lawn which is available in plain colours and small prints is particularly good, though most of the fine cottons sold for patchwork will make curtains and sheets in this scale. If you are using patterns, remember that they must be tiny – look at a 6 inch square of the fabric rather than the full width to judge the scale of a print. Fine handkerchief linen, though difficult to find, makes very nice bedding or curtains for period houses and silk can be used for curtains for a grander house. In a period dolls' house you may prefer to use old fabric with faded colours and a well-washed texture rather than new fabrics. Try charity (thrift) shops, jumble (rummage) sales and friends for supplies.

Old handkerchiefs, baby clothes and scarves can all be very useful.

Trimmings too should be delicate; fine braids and narrow cotton lace can be bought from suppliers who specialise in dolls-house trimmings, and tiny braid and fringe can be made by cutting apart a lifesize lampshade trimming and using just one strand of the silky cord or braid from which it is woven. In this type of work it is often neater to stitch seams and hems on a sewing machine rather than by hand, but always use a fine needle and the smallest stitch your machine can make. On some projects, you may find it is easier or neater to glue a hem or trimming in place than to stitch it. Use a white fabric glue such as Aleenes or Hi-Tack or similar for this rather than a general purpose craft glue such as Copydex, as fabric glue will not seep, makes a good bond, and will not turn brown with age. Fabric glues are available from haberdashery (notions) departments in stores, and from the specialist suppliers listed at the back of the book. You will need the bonding materials discussed in the previous chapter for some projects and small, sharp scissors will be essential. Other specific materials or tools are mentioned in the individual projects where they are relevant.

BLINDS AND CURTAINS

ROLLER BLINDS
(Shown on page 99)

This method can be used to make a roller blind (shade) for any size window. You will need a lightweight fabric, Bondaweb (or similar) and a piece of fine wooden dowelling slightly wider than the window. Our blinds are hung from small brass pins which are tapped into each end of the roller and fitted into small eye-hooks screwed into square wooden beads glued to the wall.

Cut the dowelling to the required length to fit the window and tap a pin into each end. Measure the required size of the blind and cut a piece of Bondaweb ½ inch larger all round than this measurement. Cut a piece of fabric twice as long as the Bondaweb, squarely on the straight grain. Fold the fabric in half (wrong sides facing) and iron to crease the fold. Cut a ⅛ inch wide strip of thin card for the lath. Place the Bondaweb on the wrong side

of the fabric against the fold and iron in place. Fold the fabric back over the Bondaweb, inserting the lath in the fold, and iron to bond the two layers of fabric together enclosing the lath and leave to cool.

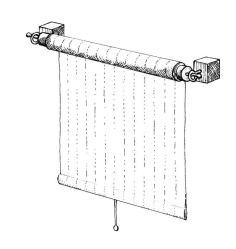

Roller blind

Trace the required size of the blind on to the fabric and cut out. Glue the top edge of the blind to the roller, taking care to line up correctly, allow to dry, then roll the blind tightly around the roller, secured with a little glue if necessary. Define the lath by running your fingernail along the edge to make a sharp crease in the fabric. Make a pull with thread and a tiny bead and glue this to the back of the lath in the centre of the blind.

 ## SHOWER CURTAIN

(Shown on page 99)

Our shower curtain is made in lightweight plastic fabric – I have used a piece cut from a pair of baby pants, though anything similar might be used and plain or printed nylon or fine cotton would be suitable alternatives. The curtain is hung from a brass rail on small brass jump rings from tiny brass eyelets. These eyelets are available from dolls-house and dollmaking suppliers (see Stockists) and are not essential, but they add a professional touch.

Measure around your bath to make a pattern.

AFTER THE BATH
Roller blind, shower curtain, towels, bath mat and pedestal mat (Chapter 5), lady's dressing-gown, shower cap (Chapter 6), straw mat, laundry bin and waste-paper basket (Chapter 8)

The curtain should be just wide enough to look convincing, but not too full to hang well, and long enough to allow for a person standing in the bath. Our curtain is $5\frac{1}{2}$ inches wide x 6 inches long (finished size). Trace the pattern squarely on to the straight grain of the fabric. If you are using a fabric which frays, seal the cutting line with Fraycheck (or similar) – and cut out the curtain. Stitch or glue small hems down both sides, and a slightly larger hem at the bottom. Glue a $\frac{1}{4}$ inch hem at the top. Punch eyelets into the top hem at $\frac{1}{2}$ inch intervals. Stitch a jump ring through each eyelet with thread to match the curtain. Hand pleat the curtain and press lightly over a towel to set the folds. Thread the rail through the jump rings and use pliers to bend the rail to the required shape. Cut the ends of the rail to size with a hacksaw and glue the ends into holes drilled in the wall(s).

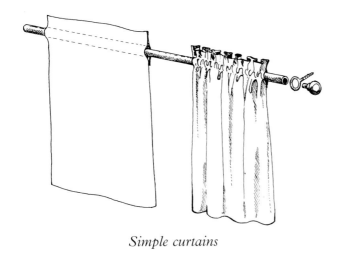

Simple curtains

 ## SIMPLE CURTAINS

(Shown on page 154)

This method can be used to make curtains (drapes) in any light- or medium-weight fabric for windows of any size. I have used a single curtain in muslin (cheesecloth) trimmed with narrow lace for one version, and a pair in velveteen for another. The finished curtains are hung from a pole located through small eye-hooks screwed into the wall and can be opened and closed by drawing along the pole. You will need fine brass tube (from model and hobby shops) for the pole, and a pair of brass doorhandles to fit the tube for finials – or use a commercial brass curtain pole.

Measure the window to make a pattern. The curtains should be 1½-2 times the width of the window depending on the thickness of the fabric, plus hem allowances, and long enough to make the heading described below. If in doubt, cut the curtains over-long and adjust the length as necessary when you make the bottom hems. Trace the pattern squarely on to the straight grain of the fabric and paint the cutting line with Fraycheck (or similar) and allow to dry. Cut out the curtains, taking care to match or line up any pattern. Make small hems on both sides of each curtain, either stitched or glued as you prefer. Fold and stitch a casing at the top of each curtain, ¼-½ inch below the folded edge so that this will form a frill. The casing should be wide enough to insert the pole, but only just, so that the drawn-up curtain will form tight gathers. Make the casing with small machine stitching. Thread the pole through the casing and try in place to check the length of the curtains, adjusting if necessary, then stitch or glue the bottom hems. Thread the curtains on to the pole and draw up to each side. Pin the curtains (on the pole) on to an ironing board with pins in the folds to secure. Hover a steam iron just above the curtains to set the folds and leave to dry. Screw the eye-hooks into the wall and locate the pole through the eyes to check the length. Trim the pole to the required length with a small hacksaw, then relocate it in the eyes and fit the doorhandles into each end of the pole secured with Superglue. If you wish to tie the curtains back, screw small eye-hooks into the wall at either side and thread ribbon or braid through the eyes. See the tie-backs on page 107 and the macramé curtain ties on page 173.

 ## CURTAINS WITH RINGS *(Shown on page 18)*

These simple curtains (drapes) are made in light-weight fabric – I have used printed cotton – and hung from a pole with small brass jump rings. The curtains will open and close.

Measure the window to make a pattern. The curtains should be 1½ times the width of the window, plus hem allowances, and the required length plus allowance for hems at top and bottom. Trace the pattern squarely on to the straight grain of the fabric, paint the cutting line with Fraycheck (or similar), allow to dry and cut out the curtains. Take care to match or line up any pattern. Make small stitched or glued hems on both sides of each curtain and a slightly larger bottom hem. Fold a ½ inch hem at the top edge of each curtain, glue lightly in place and press. With a ruler and pencil, working on the wrong side, mark dots spaced ¼ inch apart across the curtain heading, ¼ inch below the top edge. Mark a second row of dots ⅛ inch below the first row. With matching button thread (or doubled sewing thread), working on the wrong side, make two rows of gathering on the marked dots, taking a very small stitch on the right side of the fabric. Pull up the rows of gathering so that each curtain is the same width and the pair cover the window, and fasten off securely. Ease and stroke the gathering so that it is even. Pin out the curtains on an ironing board, hover a steam iron above the fabric to set the folds, and allow to dry. Stitch jump rings to the top row of gathering on the wrong side, spaced at ¾ inch intervals. Thread the pole through the rings, screw in the eye-hooks, cut the pole and fit the finials as described for the simple curtains. Note that these curtains take up more width when open so you may wish to place the eye-hooks further outside the window frame so that the curtains do not obscure the window.

 ## CURTAINS WITH FRILL *(Shown on page 38)*

These curtains (drapes) with a matching pelmet frill (valance) are designed for lightweight fabrics – I have used printed cotton for our between-the-wars bedroom. They are hung from battens of ¼ inch wide fine woodstrip (available from craft

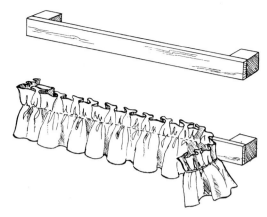

Curtains with frill

made in cotton print with a matching fabric-covered card pelmet supported on a batten of ¼ inch square woodstrip.

Measure the window to make a pattern for the curtains as described above – to hang from a pole suspended from eye-hooks, or from a fine wood-strip batten.

Adjust the pelmet pattern as necessary to fit your window, so that the pelmet is a little wider than the curtains, and trace the patterns on to firm stiff cardboard (posterboard). Score the folding lines as shown. Cover the card with fabric, with the edges folded and glued on to the back of the card, and allow to dry. Fold the covered card to form a 'box' and secure the sides with small oversewing stitches. Glue a batten of ¼ inch square woodstrip to the underside back edge of the pelmet and allow to dry. Glue the curtain batten to the front of the pelmet batten if required. Glue the back of the pelmet batten to the wall above the window.

suppliers), on blocks of ¼ inch square wood or wooden beads. If you prefer the curtains to open and close, make them as described above to hang from a pole and make the frill as described here to fit over the pole.

Measure the window to make a pattern, and cut and make up the curtains as described above except that the gathering is pulled up more tightly to represent curtains which are fully open. Cut a piece of woodstrip (batten) to fit the window and glue the top edge of the curtains to either end of the batten. Pin out the curtains and set the folds as described above. Glue the batten with curtains to the top of the window frame or to the wall just above the window as you prefer.

To make the frill, cut a piece of fabric squarely on the straight grain, twice the width of the curtain batten x 2 inches deep. (Seal the cutting lines with Fraycheck, allow to dry before cutting.) Fold and glue one long edge ½ inch to the wrong side. Fold and glue the other long edge 1½ inches to the wrong side to meet the first edge and press. Cut a woodstrip batten for the frill, ½ inch longer than the curtain batten. Make a row of gathering (machine or hand sewing) on the frill along the line where the folded edges meet, taking care to keep the gathering line straight. Pull up the gathering evenly so that the frill is ½ inch longer than the batten. Glue the batten to the back of the frill, lining up with the row of gathering and leaving ¼ inch of frill at each end. Glue ¼ inch wooden blocks to the wall at either side of the curtain batten and glue the frill batten on to the blocks. Glue the free ends of the frill to the side of the blocks.

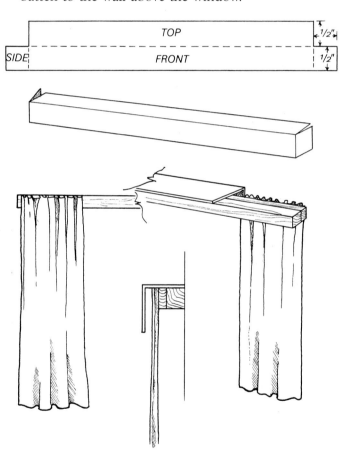

Curtains with box pelmet

CURTAINS WITH BOX PELMET

(Shown on page 138)

This style of simple curtains (drapes) with a box pelmet (valance) was popular from the early part of the twentieth century until the 1960s. In our between-the-wars sitting room, the curtains are

DRAPES WITH SHAPED PELMET

(Shown on page 62)

These elegant drapes, with a shaped box pelmet (valance), are particularly suitable for houses of the eighteenth century when curtains were used more as a decorative feature to 'drape' the window rather

A LADY OF LEISURE

Lacy fringed shawl (Chapter 2), Georgian cushion, parrot picture, button footstool, embroidered fire screen, Florentine medallion carpet (Chapter 3), curtains with swag and tails (Chapter 5), Georgian wing chair and Georgian sofa (Chapter 7), bead and button ornaments, raffia basket, log basket, tapestry frame (Chapter 8)

than to provide warmth or privacy. Joan's drapes and pelmet are made in pale green silk bonded (with Bondaweb or similar) to a lining of cream silk and trimmed with gold cord. You will need stiff card for the pelmet and $\frac{1}{4}$ inch fine woodstrip and $\frac{1}{4}$ inch square woodstrip for the battens.

Using the pattern (on page 107) as a guide, measure the window to make your own pattern. Each drape should be the same width and length (or longer) as the window. Bond the fabric and lining together and allow to cool. Cut a pair of drapes, reversing the pattern for the second. Apply a fine line of glue along both side edges and the bottom edge, press the cord trimming in place and allow to dry. Fold and pin the drapes into pleats, ensuring that the pleats correspond on both drapes. (You might find this easiest to do on a polystyrene ceiling tile, or something similar, pushing pins straight through the fabric into the tile.) Press the pleats with a steam iron to set the folds and secure with a row of small running stitches near the top edge. Glue the drapes to each end of a $\frac{1}{4}$ inch wide, fine woodstrip batten, cut to fit the window.

To make the pelmet, adjust the box pelmet pattern (on page 101) as necessary to fit your window – $\frac{1}{8}$ inch wider than the drape batten – and trace on to stiff card. Score the fold lines, cover with fabric and fold as described for the box pelmet above. Glue a $\frac{1}{4}$ inch square batten to the underside back edge of the pelmet top, and glue the drape batten, with drapes, to the pelmet batten as

described. Using the pattern (on page 107) as a guide, cut in card a decorative pelmet front to fit your own pelmet and cover with fabric as for the pelmet. Apply a fine line of fabric glue to the lower edge, press the trimming in place, and allow to dry. Glue the pelmet front on to the pelmet, so that the top edge rises $\frac{1}{8}$ inch above the pelmet. Glue the pelmet batten on to the wall above the window.

PLEATED BED HANGINGS AND TESTER *(Shown on page 62)*

The elegant hangings on the four-poster bed in our Georgian bedroom are made in pale green silk bonded to a lining of cream silk. The formal pleats are made with a pleater (a ridged, rubber device into which the fabric is pressed and steamed to make the pleats), available from dolls-house and dollmaking suppliers (see Stockists). Joan has dressed a four-poster bed which she painted with gold model paint. The bed hangings and tester can be made quite plain and simple for a modest house, or as grand as you wish by adding swags and decorative panels to the tester, trimmed with cord, tassels, or braid. The curtain tie-backs described below can also be used with these bed hangings.

Paint the bed as required and allow to dry thoroughly. If the bed has finials on top of the posts,

Bed with decorative tester panels, swags,
tie-backs and trimmings

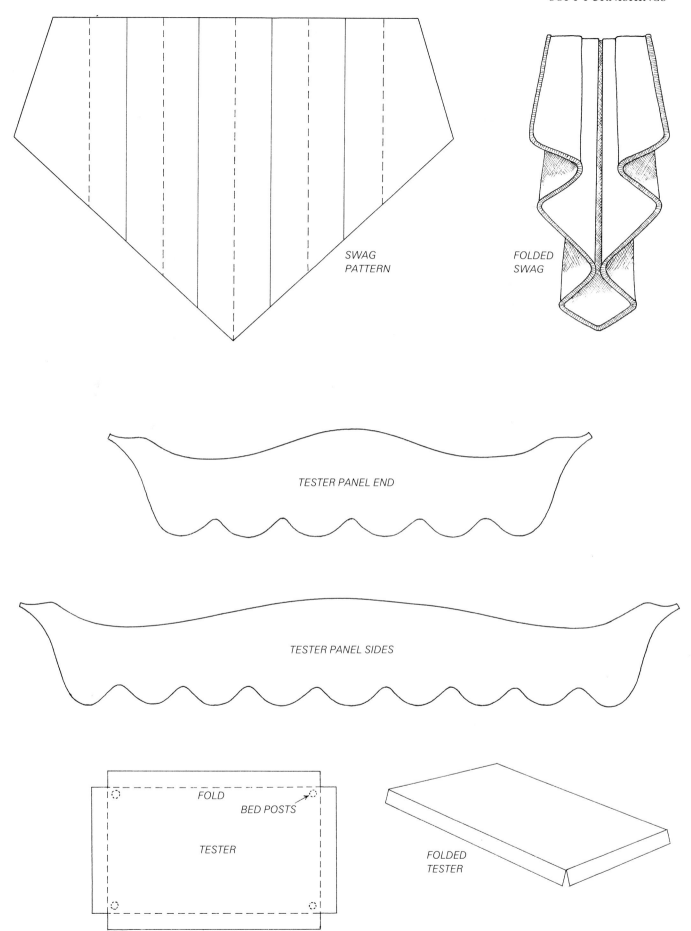

SWAG
PATTERN

FOLDED
SWAG

TESTER PANEL END

TESTER PANEL SIDES

FOLD

BED POSTS

TESTER

FOLDED
TESTER

Pleated bed hangings and tester

remove these while you fit the tester. Make a pattern by measuring the top of your bed and cut a tester in thin stiff cardboard (posterboard) to fit. The top of the tester should fit not too snugly on to the bedposts (to allow for the hangings), with sides approximately $\frac{1}{2}$ inch deep. Score the folding lines and cover the tester with fabric, with the edges folded and glued to the underside. Cut a panel in lining to fit with sealed edges and glue to the underside of the tester to cover the raw edges and allow to dry. Fold the tester to form a box and secure the corners with small oversewing stitches.

The bed can have hangings at the head-end only, or at both head and foot. Cut either two or four hangings in fabric bonded to lining – long enough to reach from the top of the tester to the floor and approximately 5 inches wide. Apply a fine line of glue to the side and bottom edges of each hanging, press the trimming in place and allow to dry. Make pleats over two ridges of the pleater, and secure the head of the pleats with a row of small running stitches. Glue the head of each hanging to the inside of the tester – evenly spaced around the corner of the tester.

Cut a back panel in card to fit from the top of the tester to the bed base, and between the headposts. Pleat a single layer of fabric over one ridge of the pleater to fit, and cover the back panel, with the edges of fabric folded and glued on to the back of the panel. Cut a piece of fabric with sealed edges to fit, and glue on to the back of the panel to cover the raw edges. Glue the top of the panel to the inside of the tester. Fit the tester, with hangings and back panel, on to the bedposts and secure with glue as necessary. (Glue finials on to the top of the tester – or drill holes through the tester to enable you to attach them to the tops of the bedposts.)

Make valances (dust ruffles) for the sides and ends of the bed in fabric, cut with sealed edges, with a small glued hem, and pleated over one ridge of the pleater. Fit the valances to the sides and ends of the bed base and secure them with glue or double-sided tape.

Cut four swags in fabric bonded to lining, apply glue to the side and bottom edges and press trimming in place. Fold the pleats as shown, secure the top edge with small running stitches and press. If you are not adding decorative tester panels, fold and press the top edge of the swags and glue on to the corners of the tester. If you are adding panels, glue the swags in place without folding the top edge. Cut the decorative tester panels in card and cover with fabric, folding and gluing the fabric edges to the back of the card. Apply a fine line of glue and press trimming in place all round the edge of each panel. Glue the panels on to the sides of the tester over the swags, so that the top edge of the panels rise just above the top of the tester. Add tassels, cord bows, etc as required. Make tie-backs as described for the drapes below in fabric bonded to lining with matching trimming if required.

CURTAINS WITH SWAG AND TAILS

(Shown on page 102)

These formal curtains (drapes) with swag, tails and matching tie-backs are most suitable for fairly grand houses. For our Georgian drawing room, Joan has used deep rose-pink silk bonded to a lining of blue silk and trimmed with blue picot braid. Joan used a pleater for the curtain folds – this is a ridged, rubber device into which the fabric is pushed and steamed to make regular pleats. Pleaters are available from dolls-house suppliers, but the curtains can be hand pleated. You will also need stiff card to make the pelmet and $\frac{1}{4}$ inch wide fine woodstrip, and $\frac{1}{4}$ inch square woodstrip for the battens.

Measure the window to make a pattern for the curtains which should be just wide enough to cover the window, and the finished length required. Cut two curtains and two linings. Use $\frac{1}{2}$ inch wide strips of Bondaweb (or similar) applied to each edge to bond the fabric to the lining around the edges of each curtain. Apply a fine line of fabric glue to the side and bottom edges of each curtain, press trimming in place and allow to dry. Pleat the curtains into folds (if using a pleater, work over two ridges for each fold). Set the folds with a steam iron and allow to dry. Cut a pair of tails, from the pattern, in fabric and lining. Bond the edges of the tails together with strips of Bondaweb as for the curtains and glue trimming to the side and bottom edges of each tail. Pleat the tails (ensuring that they are a matching pair), and press to set the pleats. Cut the swag and lining, using the pattern as a guide but adapting the width as necessary to fit your window. Note that the swag is cut on the bias grain of the fabric. Bond the edges of the swag as described, and glue trimming to the lower edge. Fold the swag into pleats and secure the pleats with running stitches at each end. Set the folds by hovering a steam iron above the fabric.

Cut a $\frac{1}{4}$ inch wide fine woodstrip batten to fit the window and glue the FRONT top edge of the curtains to the BACK of the batten at each end. Cut a box pelmet (see page 101) in card to fit your window. Cover the pelmet with fabric and assemble as described. Glue the front of the curtain batten to the inside of the pelmet front. Glue the swag to the outside of the pelmet front. Glue a tail over the swag at each side of the pelmet front. Glue braid around the top edge of the pelmet across the front and continue round the sides to cover the top edges of the swag and tails.

Bond fabric to lining and cut a pair of tie-backs. Apply glue and press trimming along both long edges of each tie-back. Pleat the short edges together, and secure with small stitches. Stitch jewellery jump rings or similar to each end of the tie-back, and loop the rings over small hooks screwed into the wall at either side of the window.

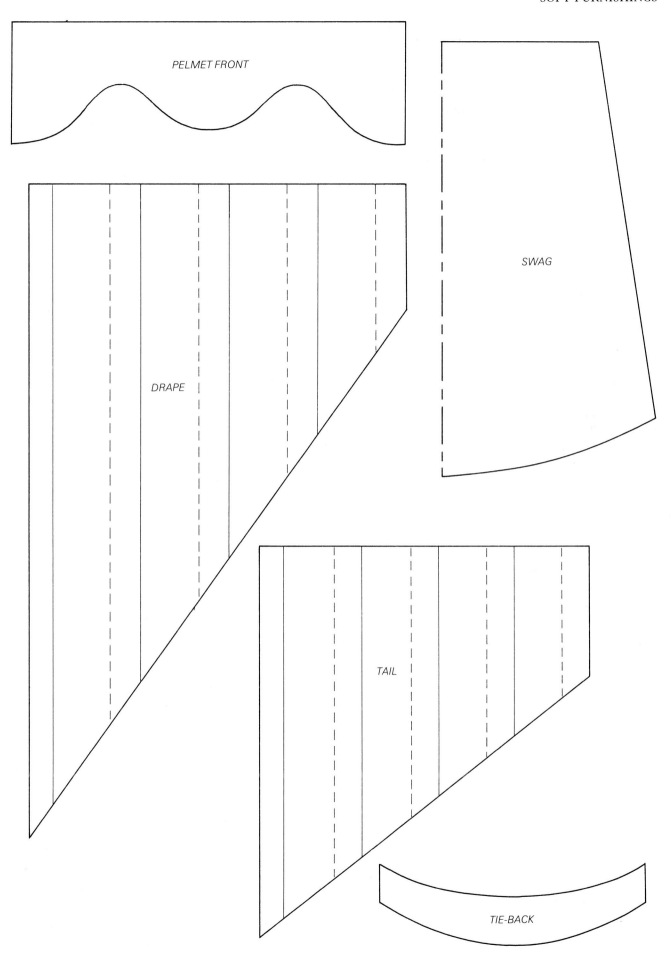

PELMET FRONT

SWAG

DRAPE

TAIL

TIE-BACK

*Drapes with shaped pelmet,
swag and tails*

BEDDING

SHEETS

(Shown on page 83)

Sheets can be made in fine linen or cotton lawn, in white, ivory, or cream for period houses, and in any plain colour or print for modern houses. Standard size for single-bed sheets is approximately 8½ x 6 inches and double size 8½ x 7½ (plus seam allowance), but check these sizes on your own bed and adapt as necessary. The top sheet of the pair might be trimmed with lace or broderie anglais if you wish, or embroidered to match a pillowcase.

Cut the sheet with a ¼ inch allowance at the side and bottom edges and a ½ inch allowance at the top edge and stitch hems by hand or with the smallest machine stitch with mitred or neat square corners. If you prefer, the fabric can be cut to size with sealed edges and simply hemmed at the top. To trim the sheet, either whip (overcast) ¼ inch lace on to the hemmed top edge, or place ½ inch wide lace trimming right sides together, with the scalloped edge of the lace downward, and stitch to the sheet ¼ inch from the edge. Turn the ¼ inch allowance to the wrong side, and hem the straight edge of the lace to cover the raw fabric edge. For embroidery patterns, see Chapter 3.

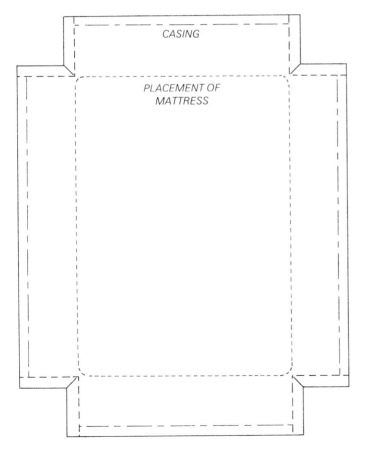

CASING

PLACEMENT OF MATTRESS

Fitted sheet

FITTED SHEET

(Shown on page 111)

The fitted sheet can be useful as an alternative to the bottom sheet of a pair as it reduces bulk when tucking in the bedcovers. It is particularly suitable for modern beds such as the divan in Chapter 7, when used with a duvet.

Use your mattress as a pattern to cut the sheet squarely on the straight grain of the fabric with 1½ inch deep sides as shown. Stitch the edges together at each corner to make a 'box' and trim the seams and corners. Make a narrow casing around the edge of the sheet, leaving a small opening to thread elastic. Thread doubled shirring elastic through the casing, fit the sheet over the mattress, pull up the elastic to fit, and knot the ends. Slip stitch the opening closed and ease the fullness to the corners of the sheet so that the side edges are smooth.

PILLOWS AND PILLOWCASES

(Shown on page 111)

In many dolls' houses, the cover of the pillow serves as a pillowcase, but you might enjoy making Dora's authentic housewife-style pillowcases with flap ends. A single bed will need one or two pillows, a double bed two or four. You will need lightweight cotton fabrics in white or a 'ticking' stripe for the pillows, and white or to match your sheets for the covers, and polyester for the stuffing.

To make a pillow, cut one piece squarely on the straight grain of the fabric and fold in and press both short edges. With right sides facing, fold the fabric across the centre and stitch the side seams. Turn through and stuff lightly so that the pillow will lie flat. Oversew or slip stitch the folded edges together to finish the pillow.

To make a pillowcase, cut one piece on the straight grain of the fabric. (Match the pattern on pairs of cases if using printed fabric.) Make a ⅛ inch hem at both short ends. Fold the pillowcase with right sides facing and stitch the side seams, leaving the flap end clear of the seam. Fold the flap so that the fold is in line with the open end of the pillowcase and slip stitch the sides of the flap to the side seams. Clip the corners, turn through and press with an iron.

FRILLED PILLOWCASE

Cut two pieces on the straight grain of the fabric. Cut a frill in ½ inch wide lace, broderie anglais, or

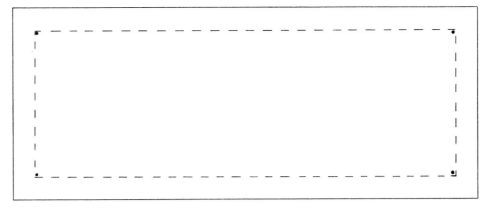

Pillow

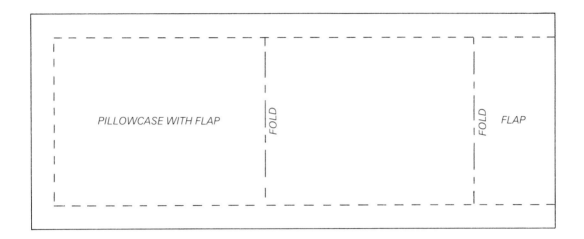

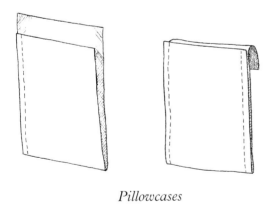

Pillowcases

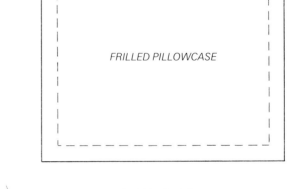

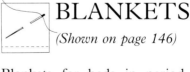

fabric with a sealed edge, approximately 15 inches long. Make two rows of gathering along the raw edge of the frill and pull up to 10 inches. With right sides facing, pin the frill to one piece of fabric, matching the gathered edge of the frill to the outside edge of fabric. Distribute the gathers evenly with a little extra fullness at the corners and stitch. Join the ends of the frill with small blanket stitches. Place the second piece of fabric over the first, with right sides facing, sandwiching the frill. Stitch together around three sides, on the previous stitching line. Trim the corners and turn through. Insert the pillow – or stuff – and slip stitch the fourth side closed, folding in the raw fabric edge and stitching the folded edge to the frill seam.

BLANKETS
(Shown on page 146)

Blankets for beds in period houses should be cream, beige or grey, but modern blankets can be almost any colour you please. Fine wool flannel – either new 'doctors flannel' from fabric shops, or old from Victorian baby clothes – makes excellent blankets, but consider also using material from old baby vests such as 'Chilprufe' or lacy knitted cotton thermal vests. Pink or blue fluffy dusters, Viyella or flannelette and winceyette will also make good blankets. Standard sizes are approximately $8\frac{1}{2}$ x 6 inches for a single bed and $8\frac{1}{2}$ x $7\frac{1}{2}$ inches for a double bed, but check this on your own bed. You will also need Madeira stranded silk (or similar) to match or contrast and $\frac{1}{2}$ inch wide satin or silk ribbon for the edges.

Cut the blanket on the straight grain of the fabric. Cut a strand of Madeira thread 130 inches long (although unwieldy to work with, using one length of thread produces much neater results than joining several shorter lengths). Blanket stitch around two long and one short edges (sides and bottom) of the blanket with small even stitches. Cut ribbon to fit the top edge with a $\frac{1}{4}$ inch allowance at both ends and seal the ends. Fold the ribbon in half along the length and press. Slip stitch one long edge of the ribbon to the top end of the blanket, lining up with the fold. Tuck in the ribbon ends, fold over the edge, and slip stitch the other long edge of ribbon to the other side of the blanket, lining up with the first row of stitches.

LACE BEDSPREAD

(Shown on page 71)

Our pretty bedspread is made from cotton lace edging approximately 2 inches wide with one straight and one scalloped edge and a delicate pattern. You will need approximately $1\frac{1}{4}$ yards of lace to make the bedspread.

Cut four pieces of lace, 8 inches long, matching the pattern on each piece. Carefully matching scalloped edge to scalloped edge, stitch two pieces together with machine or small running stitches

and press the seam open to make the centre panel. Stitch one piece to either side of the centre panel, straight edge to straight edge with whipping or oversewing stitches, and press the seams flat. Cut a piece of lace to fit across one end of the centre panel, matching the pattern, and stitch straight edge over raw edge with machine or small running stitches. Blanket stitch to neaten the raw edges at both of the bottom corners and make a small hem across the top edge, after trimming as necessary to fit the bed.

DUVET AND COVER

(Shown on page 111)

Although duvets have been used in Europe for many years, they are most suitable for British and American houses of the second half of the twentieth century. Our duvet is made in fine white cotton lawn filled with polyester wadding (batting), and the cover is in printed cotton. The duvet is designed to fit a standard-size bed, including the divans in Chapter 7.

To make the duvet, cut a piece of wadding $6\frac{1}{2}$ inches wide x 7 inches long. Cut a piece of white cotton lawn $13\frac{1}{2}$ inches wide x $7\frac{1}{2}$ inches long. Stitch the short edges of fabric together with a $\frac{1}{4}$ inch seam and press the seam open. With the seam to the centre, stitch across the top and bottom edges with a $\frac{1}{4}$ inch seam, leaving a 3 inch opening in the centre of one edge. Turn through and press. Mark lines for stitched channels as shown, in

Lace bedspread

Duvet

MAKING THE BED

Soft ball (Chapter 1), his and hers striped sweaters, baby pram set (Chapter 2), shoulder bag, velvet and needlepoint carpet (Chapter 3), folded-star cushion, rabbit pictures (Chapter 4), lampshade, roller blind, fitted sheet, pillows and pillowcases, duvet and cover (Chapter 5), teddy bear (Chapter 6), divan bed and mattress, cane headboard (Chapter 7)

Fadeaway marker pen on the top side of the case. Fit the wadding inside the fabric case, slip stitch the opening closed and tack (baste) around the outside of the duvet $\frac{1}{2}$ inch from the edge to hold the wadding in place. Stitch the channels as marked with the smallest machine stitch (or make tiny running stitches by hand) and remove the tacking.

To make the duvet cover, cut a piece of fabric $14\frac{1}{2}$ x $8\frac{1}{2}$ inches. Stitch the short edges together with a $\frac{1}{4}$ inch seam, and press the seam open. With the seam centred, stitch across one edge with a $\frac{1}{4}$ inch seam. Make a $\frac{1}{4}$ inch hem around the other edge and turn through and press. Fit the duvet into the cover and close the open edge with French knots worked through both layers of fabric and spaced $\frac{3}{4}$ inch apart to represent press-studs.

LINENS

 ## TOWELS

(Shown on page 131)

There are several materials and methods for making towels, depending on the period of your house. In Tudor or Georgian houses the most realistic towels are linen. In Victorian houses, crêpe bandage can be used to simulate huckaback and in twentieth-century houses, fine towelling or a fluffy cotton fabric such as winceyette is effective. The patterns show standard sizes for towels as a guide.

LINEN TOWELS

Use fine handkerchief linen or a slightly rough-textured cotton such as unbleached calico (muslin) in off-white, cream or ivory rather than bleached white. Trace the pattern squarely on to the straight grain of the fabric. To make an unfringed towel, paint Fraycheck (or similar) around all four edges on the cutting line, allow to dry, and cut out the towel. Turn the smallest possible hem around each side and stitch with the smallest machine stitch, or hem. To make a fringed towel, cut out the towel and pull threads from both ends to make fringes, then paint Fraycheck along both sides, allow to dry and hem. Note that on closely woven fabrics, hemming may be unnecessary as the Fraycheck should prevent the fabric from fraying – a line of machine stitching as close to the edge as possible could be used instead to make a firm edge. Simple but effective 'linen' towels can be made from lengths of cotton tape with fringed or hemmed ends. If you wish, linen (or tape) towels can be decorated with embroidery or cross stitch or a line of machine stitching in colour. The 'cheats' method is to use fine-point fibre-tipped pens and a very light touch to draw 'embroidered' motifs. Note that cotton tape can also be used to make roller towels, with a stripe in red or blue, machine-stitched or drawn along both edges.

HUCKABACK TOWELS

Huckaback was a coarsely-woven linen with raised weft threads which was used for towels from the eighteenth to the twentieth century. Our towels are made from crêpe bandage, available in several widths from chemist shops (drug stores or pharmacies). The cream colour and texture are very realistic, and the towels are fringed with strips of

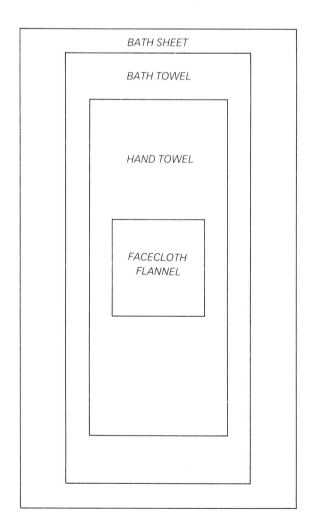

Towels

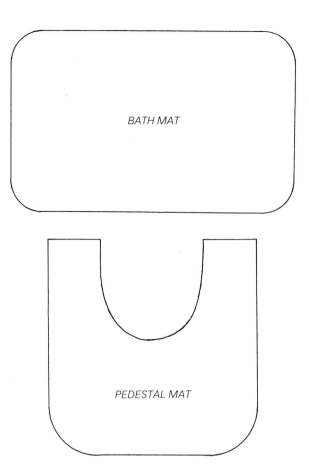

Bath mat and pedestal mat

unbleached calico (muslin) torn against the selvedge. Cut lengths of crêpe bandage as squarely as possible. Tear a $\frac{1}{4}$ inch wide strip of calico along the selvedge and pull threads to make a fringe. Cut pieces to fit the ends of the towel, seal the short ends with Fraycheck and allow to dry. Apply fabric glue to the back of the fringe strip along the selvedge, allow the glue to become tacky, then press the fringe strip on to the end of the crêpe towel. Press with a steam iron. If required, make a line of machine stitching on the selvedge in matching, or contrasting red or blue, thread. You will find that narrow crêpe bandage also makes excellent old-fashioned roller towels.

TERRY TOWELS

Single-sided terry towelling can be bought by the yard in some department stores, but if you have trouble finding it, use a pair of towelling baby pants, a Babygro, baby's face flannel or similar. This fabric has a slight stretch, but is much finer and thinner than ordinary towelling. Trace the pattern on to the fabric as squarely as possible and seal the cutting line with Fraycheck on the wrong (flat) side. Allow to dry, then make a line of the smallest machine stitching around the cutting line. If you have an overlocking stitch on your machine, stitch around the cutting line with this or oversew by hand. Cut out the towel as close as possible to the stitched line. As a substitute for terry towelling, fluffy fabrics such as winceyette will make effective towels.

Winceyette is available in plain colours and patterns including fine stripes which are suitable for modern towels. Make a winceyette towel as described for linen towels.

BATH MAT AND PEDESTAL MAT

(Shown on page 131)

This very simple set of towelling mats is suitable for a twentieth-century bathroom. You will need single-sided terry towelling in the colour of your choice (I used a pair of baby pants), plain cotton fabric to match or in white for backing, and medium-weight Bondaweb, Heat 'n Bond or a similar iron-on bonding material.

Check the cut-out on the pedestal mat against your own loo and adjust the pattern to fit if necessary. Bond terry towelling to cotton fabric backing and allow to cool. Trace the patterns on to the backing and cut out the mats.

TABLECLOTHS

(Shown on page 18)

The tablecloths, shown in pictures throughout the book, are either rectangular or round and though fabrics and trimmings vary, the method is basically the same for all. Making a tablecloth is simple but the trick is to get the cloth to hang realistically and the method described can be used for any light- to medium-weight fabric. Our tablecloths are made in printed cotton or lightweight velveteen, hemmed and/or trimmed with lace, narrow picot braid, or fringe pulled from lifesize lampshade-trimming braid. The round lace cloth is made from a commercial table-mat, with the lace border removed and re-stitched after the mat was cut down to the required size. (See also the embroidery motifs used for projects in Chapter 3 if you wish to make an embroidered tablecloth.) You will need the fabric and trimming of your choice, thin stiff card (postcard thickness is ideal), craft glue and narrow double-sided tape.

RECTANGULAR CLOTH

Trace around the outline of the table top on to thin card. Decide the length of overhang required and draw a line ¼ inch less than this, outside the line of the table top. Cut out the card, cut square notches at each corner, and score the table-top line to fold. Fold the card to form a 'box' and secure the corners with adhesive tape. Run a line of narrow, double-sided tape around the lower edge. Put the card on to the table.

Trace the outline of the tablecloth to fit your table

on to the wrong side of the fabric. Seal the cutting line with Fraycheck (or similar), allow to dry, and cut out the cloth. Make a hem, or glue trimming to the edge with fabric glue and press. Place the cloth over the card cover, secured at the centre with a little double-sided tape. Smooth the overhang down the sides of the card so that the lower edge sticks to the tape, and arrange the corners into neat folds.

ROUND CLOTH

Trace around the outline of the table top on to thin card and cut out this circle. Decide the length of the overhang required and cut a strip of card this width and long enough to go round the outside of the card circle. Mark, score and fold a line ¼ inch from one long edge of the card strip. Snip along this edge at ¼ inch intervals to make a 'fringe'. Wrap the card strip around the table, so that the fringed edge lies flat on the table top and secure the short ends together with adhesive tape. Glue the card circle on to the fringed edge of the side strip. Run a piece of narrow double-sided tape around the lower edge of the side strip.

Trace the outline of the tablecloth to fit your table on to the wrong side of the fabric. Seal the cutting line with Fraycheck (or similar), allow to dry, and cut out the cloth. Make a hem or glue trimming to the cloth with fabric glue. Centre the cloth on the card cover, secure with a little double-sided tape. Smooth the overhang down the sides of the cover at four equidistant points, then at four equidistant points between the first, so that the cloth hangs in

Tablecloths – card-table covers

eight even folds with the back of each fold stuck to the tape.

If you wish to use a smaller overcloth with a round tablecloth, cut and make up the overcloth in fabric or lace, trimmed as required, and spray the back with a light coat of mounting spray (available from art and craft suppliers), so that the overcloth will 'cling' to the folds of the tablecloth.

TEA TOWELS AND CLEANING CLOTHS

(Shown on page 186)

No kitchen is complete without tea towels (dish towels) and cleaning cloths, but you should choose materials for a period house carefully. White or cream cotton tape with fringed ends makes good old-fashioned tea towels which might have a red or blue stripe machine-stitched or drawn with fibre-tipped pen down each side. Small rectangles of fine cotton fabric, marked squarely on the grain and

THE END OF THE TRAIL

Simple blanket (Chapter 1), combinations (Chapter 2), hexagon bedspread (Chapter 4), sheets, pillows and pillowcases, towels, rag rug (Chapter 5)

sealed with Fraycheck before cutting, are also effective if you choose the appropriate pattern or colour. Small blue, red, or green and white checks or gingham look good, and fine stripes or prints will fit well in a twentieth century house. Most tea towels are approximately 1½ x 2½ inches.

Small pieces of lifesize cloths will make good miniature cleaning cloths, from orange dusters edged with red overlocking stitch, and tiny chamois leathers, to miniature 'J' cloths and tiny rectangles of sponge-cloth or Brillo pad for a modern house. Measure the lifesize item to judge the size of the miniature. (See also the knitted cloth on page 16.) If yours is a modern house, don't forget such things as bin liners, paper towels and aluminium foil or cling film all of which can also be made from the lifesize product.

RUGS AND LAMPSHADES

 ## BRAIDED-WOOL RUGS *(Shown on page 38)*

This is a traditional 'cottage craft' method for making rugs which was particularly popular in the nineteenth century. Our rugs are made in tapestry wool (yarn), available in a wide range of colours and you will need three skeins of wool for each rug. These can be plaited (braided) together in separate or mixed colours as you prefer to make a mottled or striped effect. For the round rug, I used brown, rust, and cream plaited together for the centre and a stripe of each colour plaited separately for the borders. The oval rug is made in ecru, coffee, and pink stripes plaited separately. There are endless possible permutations, and some beautiful subtle effects can be achieved by using three shades of the same colour. The rug is backed with iron-on non-woven interfacing of the type normally used in dressmaking.

Cut three strands of yarn approximately 6 feet long. Knot the strands together at one end and fasten this knotted end to the arm of a sofa (couch) or armchair with a safety pin. Plait the strands together as tightly as possible and knot the other end. The traditional method of shaping the rug is to stitch the rounds of plaited yarn together with matching yarn or thread, taking care not to pull the thread too tightly so that the rug does not become distorted. The following method, though unconventional, is very effective and much quicker. Spray a piece of thin cardboard (posterboard) with mounting spray (available from art and photography suppliers). Working on this tacky surface, press the plaited yarn on to the card (note that as you work, the uppermost surface of yarn will be the underside of the finished rug). Begin at the centre and work outward, wrapping one round of plaited yarn around the previous one so that there are no gaps. To shape an oval rug, work the first two or three rounds straight up and down, then work outward, shaping the oval. To shape a circular rug, work the first round around the knotted end in the centre and work outward. Press each round of plaited yarn firmly on to the tacky card and add in more lengths, or different colours as required, bringing all knots to the upper surface of the work. When the rug is the required size, taper the end gradually into the previous round and secure with a little fabric glue. Cut a backing in iron-on interfacing, very slightly smaller than the rug, and working on the card, iron the backing on to the plaited yarn and allow to cool. Peel the rug off the card and oversew the outer edge of the backing to the last round of plaited yarn. Press the rug carefully on the right side, under a damp cloth.

 ## RAG RUG *(Shown on page 114)*

Rag rugs were traditionally made from odd scraps of fabric on a backing of hessian or canvas. Our rag rug is made authentically and, though the method is not difficult, it needs patience! I have used a card of Liberty Tana lawn bias binding in a small print for the rags, on a backing of tapestry canvas. You will also need 1 yard of strong cotton crochet yarn and two safety pins.

Cut the bias binding down the centre of the length, and then through each fold down the length to make four $\frac{1}{8}$ inch strips. Cut a piece of stiff card approximately $1\frac{1}{2}$ inches wide. Wind the strips of fabric around the card and cut through each end so that the whole length of bias binding is now cut into pieces $\frac{1}{8}$ x $1\frac{1}{2}$ inches – these are the 'rags'. Cut a strand of crochet yarn approximately 28 inches long, knot each end to form a loop and pin the looped ends to something firm so that the yarn is taut. (I work with the yarn pinned across the arms of my armchair.) One at a time, tie the rags around the crochet yarn in a half knot, pulled tight. Slide each knotted rag along the yarn, butted against the previous one so that there are no gaps. When all the rags are knotted on to the yarn, ease them out to cover a 24 inch length evenly, and with small sharp scissors, trim the ends of each rag to approximately $\frac{1}{4}$ inch. Cut a piece of canvas $3\frac{1}{2}$ x $2\frac{1}{2}$ inches for the backing. With a sewing needle and matching thread, working from the underside, stitch the thread of rags to the backing, making the first row close to the edge, and working from side to side across the backing as shown. Make eight rows, turning at each end as shown, with the rows spaced $\frac{1}{2}$ inch apart. Trim and secure both ends firmly. Trim the corners of the backing slightly rounded, and trim the 'pile' of the rags if required. Press the rug carefully on the wrong side.

 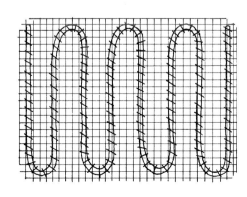

Rag rug

115

FUR RUGS

(Shown on page 22)

Our fur rugs are made from fur fabric of the type used for making soft toys, with a short pile and knitted backing. The fur fabric is bonded to a backing of iron-on interfacing. The rug in the nursery is a rectangle in white fur and the 'leopard skin' in the Victorian drawing-room is cut from an area of fullsize leopard print with a small pattern.

Iron interfacing to the back of some fur fabric and allow to cool. Draw an outline on to the back of the fabric, using a rectangle of the required size with slightly rounded corners, or the shape of the tiger-skin pattern on page 81. Cut out the rug, snipping only through the knitted backing of the fur fabric, and not cutting the pile. Ease the pile apart. Brush the rug with an old toothbrush (or similar) so that the pile overhangs the edge of the rug.

LAMPSHADES

(Shown on page 171)

These simple lampshades can be used on commercial lights, or on bases made from commercial vases in the same way as the lamps made from large beads in Chapter 8. The lampshades are made in fine cotton or silk fabrics, bonded to a white cotton lawn lining and trimmed with fine braid, lace, or fringe. Patterns are given for three sizes, the method is the same for all.

Using lightweight Bondaweb, Heat 'n' Bond or a similar material, bond white cotton lawn to the back of the fabric, placing straight grain to straight grain, and allow to cool. Trace the lampshade pattern on to the lining, so that the curve is on the bias grain of the fabric, and cut out the lampshade. Apply a fine line of fabric glue with a toothpick (or a similar instrument) to the top and bottom edges of the lampshade and allow to dry slightly so that it is tacky. Press the trimming in place and allow to dry completely. (Take care to align the trimming accurately and evenly with the edge of the lampshade, or the finished shape will appear distorted.) With the scalloped-edge pattern, use a pin to ease the trimming into place. Apply fabric glue to the lining side of one short edge of the shade, allow to become tacky, then curve the shade and press the glued edge over the other short edge as shown to form the seam. Hold the seam in place with your fingers as the glue dries. (See page 169 for instructions on fitting the finished lampshade onto a lamp base.)

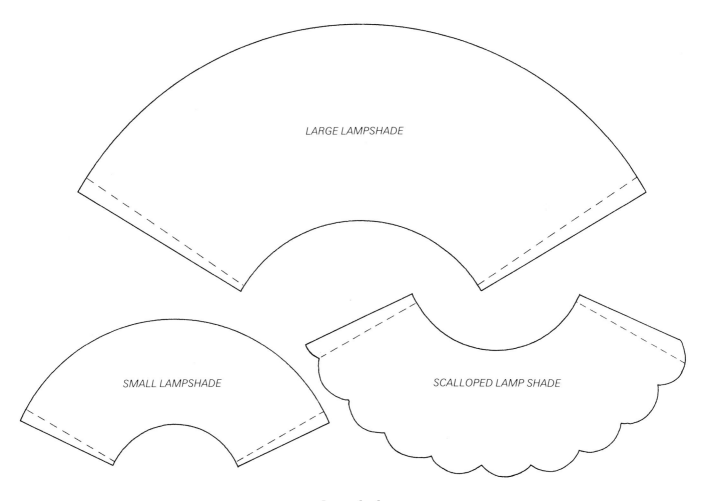

Lampshades

— CHAPTER SIX —
Dressmaking

The patterns in this chapter are simple, mostly one-piece patterns for clothes and costume accessories which will fit standard-size man, lady, child and baby dolls-house dolls. If you do not wish to use the clothes to dress your dolls, they can be displayed in the dolls' house – perhaps a dressing-gown hung on the back of the bathroom or bedroom door, or a nightgown laid out on the bed. The patterns are suitable for clothing of the eighteenth to twentieth centuries depending on the fabrics and trimmings you choose. All fabrics should be finely woven and lightweight; and natural fabrics such as silk or cotton – especially Liberty Tana lawn – produce better results than man-made fibres. Trimmings such as lace and ribbons should be very delicate and any patterns should be tiny in scale. The clothes can be stitched by hand or machine as you prefer, but use a fine needle and the smallest stitches. Small-scale fabrics, lace, braid and ribbons, tiny buttons or beads, and the tiny brass eyelets which are used for parasols, etc, are all available from dolls-house suppliers including those listed at the back of the book. These suppliers also sell tools for making tiny bows and ribbon roses which produce finer results than can be achieved by hand. You will also need Fraycheck or a similar product for sealing the cut edge of fabrics, light-weight iron-on interfacing, small sharp-pointed scissors and fabric glue as discussed in previous chapters. Other specific materials required for individual projects are mentioned where relevant.

Dressmaking in this scale is fiddly, but the patterns and methods have been designed to make it as simple as possible. It is essential to eliminate bulk and to handle the clothes as little as possible so the following method can be applied to all the clothes patterns in this chapter. If the garment is intended to be worn by a doll, cut the pattern in kitchen paper and try it on the doll to check the fit, especially hem and sleeve lengths, and make any necessary adjustments. Trace the pattern on to the fabric with a Fadeaway marker pen or well-sharpened dressmakers' pencil. Paint a fine line of Fraycheck (or similar) all round the cutting line, and allow it to dry. Cut out the pieces (a small seam allowance is included on all patterns), with small sharp scissors. Make any pintucks and apply the trimmings to the garment wherever possible before the seams are stitched. Trimmings can be stitched in place by machine or hand as you prefer, or glued with a light application of fabric glue allowed to become tacky before the trimming is pressed in place. Stitch the seams by hand or machine, using the smallest possible stitches. Clip corners and curves where necessary, and turn the garment through to the right side. Where possible, press seams open with an iron or, on tiny parts, by running your thumbnail down the seam. Hems can be stitched or glued as you prefer and pressed. Ribbon straps or bows are best glued in place. Tiny buttons or beads are stitched to the finished garment in the 'buttoned-up' position – working through both layers of fabric if the garment is not to be worn, or through the top layer only before the garment is put on to the doll and the opening is closed with slip stitches. If a garment intended to be worn has gathered cuffs or waist, work the gathering before the garment is put on to the doll, and pull up to allow for the width of the doll's hand – or pull up and fasten off when the garment is actually on the doll.

If you wish to hang a garment on a hook, or drape it over a bed or chair, pin it out on an ironing board in the folds required, and hover a steam iron above the fabric to set the folds. Allow to dry on the ironing board.

UNDERWEAR

CHEMISE AND DRAWERS *(Shown on page 119)*

This set of underwear is particularly suitable for Victorian and Edwardian ladies. I have used white Tana lawn trimmed with white cotton lace and pink embroidery-thread (floss) 'ribbon' with matching silk ribbon bows.

Trace the patterns on to the fabric, seal the cutting lines and cut one chemise on the bias grain of the fabric and two drawers pieces on the straight grain of the fabric. Stitch or glue lace to the top and bottom edges of the chemise and to the leg ends of the drawers so that the lace overhangs each edge. Make small running stitches through the lace with three strands of embroidery thread to imitate insertion ribbon. Make a line of gathering at the

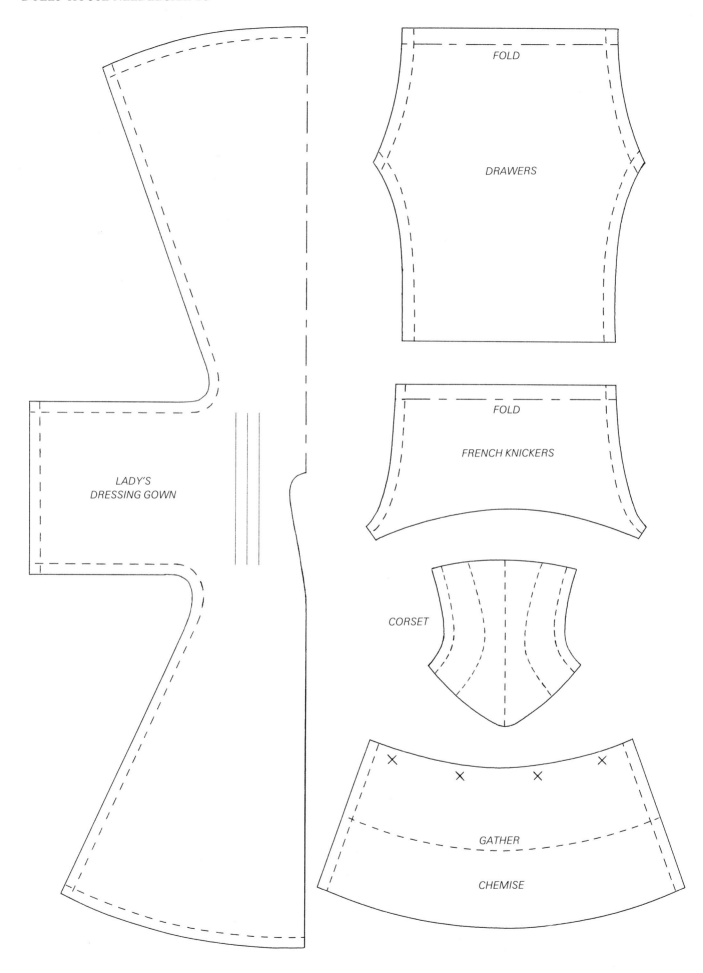

Lady's underwear and dressing-gown

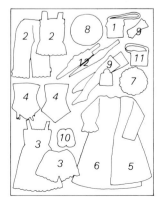

THE LADY'S COLLECTION *(see key)*

1 Shoulder bag (Chapter 3), 2 chemise and drawers,
3 French knickers and petticoat, 4 corsets,
5 dressing-gown, 6 nightgown, 7 mobcap, 8 straw
hat, 9 stockings and gloves, 10 slippers, 11 handbag,
12 parasol (Chapter 6)

waist of the chemise, as shown, with shirring elastic or sewing thread. Pull up slightly and fasten off. Stitch the centre back seam of the chemise and turn through. Stitch the leg seams of the drawers, then stitch the two legs together from front to back through the crotch and turn through. Fold a single turning at the waist edge of the drawers and run a line of tiny gathering stitches in matching doubled thread or single shirring elastic. Pull up and fasten off. Cut two 1¼ inch straps of lace and glue to the inside of the chemise at back and front as shown. Make three tiny ribbon bows and glue to the chemise front and the legs of the drawers.

FRENCH KNICKERS AND PETTICOAT

(Shown on page 119)

This set of underwear is most suitable for twentieth-century ladies, as coloured underwear was considered extremely 'fast' until the turn of the century. Pastel colours were very fashionable in the 1920s and 1930s so I have used pink Tana lawn trimmed with white lace and pink silk ribbon bows. The petticoat pattern can also be used (lengthened as required) to make a twentieth-century nightdress in lawn or silk.

Trace the patterns on to the fabric, seal the cutting lines, and cut one petticoat on the bias grain of the fabric and two knicker pieces on the straight grain of the fabric. Stitch or glue lace to the top and bottom edges of the petticoat and to the knicker legs so that the lace overhangs each edge. Make a line of gathering around the waist of the petticoat, as shown, in matching shirring elastic or doubled thread, pull up slightly and fasten off. Stitch the back seam of the petticoat and turn through. Stitch the leg seams of each knicker piece then stitch the legs together from back to front through the crotch and turn through. Turn in the top of the knickers and gather the edge with small running stitches in matching doubled thread or single shirring elastic, pull up and fasten off. Cut two 1¼ inch straps in ribbon and glue the ends inside the petticoat at back and front as shown. Make four tiny ribbon bows and glue one each to the petticoat top and hem, and to the legs of the knickers.

CORSETS

(Shown on page 119)

The four corsets shown in different pictures in the book are all made from the same pattern, using different coloured silk or satin fabrics and trimmings. One version is made in scarlet satin trimmed with black lace, picot braid, and scarlet ribbon; the second is emerald green satin trimmed with emer-

Corset with chemise and drawers

ald braid, white lace, and black ribbon. These bright colours are most suitable for the later nineteenth century or for 'fast' ladies! More modest versions of the corset are made in pastel colours; the first in pink satin trimmed with ivory lace, and the second in cream silk trimmed with cream lace and pink ribbon. The corset can have suspenders and shoulder straps made from matching ribbon if you wish, and is laced down the back with matching thread. (If a doll is to wear it, lace the corset when it is on the doll.)

Bond iron-on interfacing to the back of the fabric and allow to cool. Trace the pattern, seal the cutting line, and cut two pieces on the straight grain of the fabric. Stitch the 'bone' lines shown on the pattern in matching or contrasting thread with the smallest machine stitch (or back stitch), on one piece (front). On the second piece, stitch the bone lines as shown but make two rows of stitching close together down the centre. Seal with Fraycheck, then cut this piece down the centre line between the rows of stitching (back). Stitch the side seams, clip the curves, and press open. Stitch or glue lace and braid trimming to the top and bottom edges of the corset and make running stitches in embroidery thread to represent ribbon insertion as required. Work cross stitch up the centre back in matching thread to represent lacing, working over the rows of stitching. Glue ribbon 'suspenders' to the lower edge of the corset and ribbon straps to the top edge and add a tiny ribbon bow or rose to the front as required.

NIGHTWEAR

GENTLEMAN'S DRESSING-GOWN

(Shown on page 123)

Our gentleman's dressing-gown (robe) is made in fine silk with a checked pattern in maroon and beige and lined with beige silk. If you prefer to make an unlined version in a slightly heavier fabric, see the instructions for the lady's dressing-gown.

Trace the pattern on to fabric and lining, seal the cutting lines and cut both pieces on the straight grain of the fabric. Stitch the side seams from the wrist to the hem, clip the curves, turn through and press (on both fabric and lining). With right sides facing, slip one piece inside the other, and stitch fabric to lining all round the outside edge – from centre back hem, up one front, around the neckline, down the other front, and around the hem – leaving a 2 inch opening at the centre back hem to turn through. Clip the curves and corners and turn through. Press to make crisp edges and slip stitch the opening closed. With the dressing gown inside out, pull the sleeve lining over the sleeves, turn up the sleeve ends and slip stitch to the lining. Turn through and press. Work belt loops at either side of the dressing-gown on the side seams, in buttonhole stitch (or oversewing) and thread a narrow braid belt through the loops. Add a pocket, and work a hanging-loop at the back neck, if required.

LADY'S DRESSING-GOWN

(Shown on page 119)

Two versions of this lady's dressing-gown (robe) are shown to demonstrate that a different choice of fabric and trimming can be used to create quite different effects. The first version is made in plain scarlet Viyella with topstitched hems and a pocket, and the second (shown on page 99) is in pale blue lawn trimmed with pintucks, lace, and picot braid. With the right choice of fabric and trimming the pattern could be used to make a dressing-gown for any period lady. For example, in a tiny floral-print linen it might be a 'bedgown' of the eighteenth century, or in fine towelling it could be a late twentieth-century bathrobe.

Trace the pattern on to the straight grain of the fabric, seal the cutting line, and cut one piece. If you wish to make pintucks on the shoulders, fold the fabric on the lines shown on the pattern and whip stitch (overcast) over the folded edges in matching thread. Make six pintucks and press.

For the plain dressing-gown, fold and tack

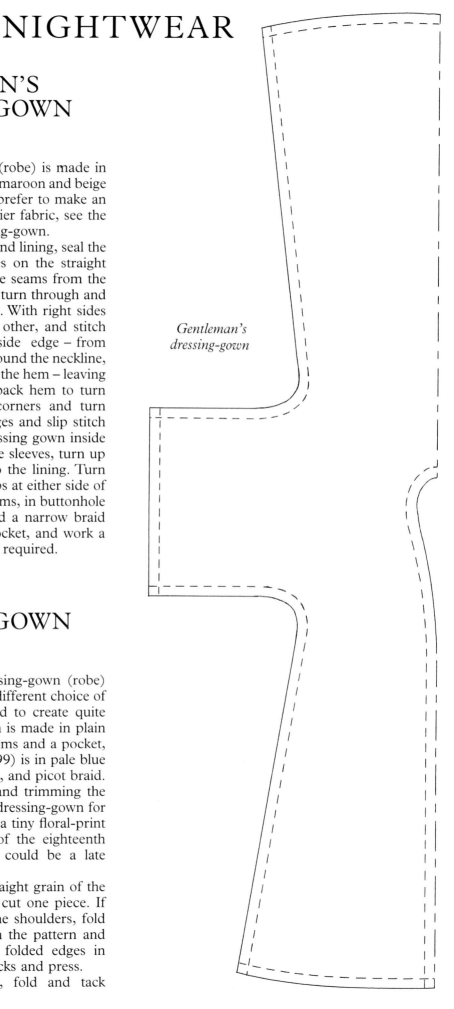

Gentleman's dressing-gown

(baste), or glue a small hem at the front edges and around the neckline, snipping as necessary. Press, then topstitch this hem. Fold and topstitch hems at the sleeve ends. Stitch the side seams, clip the curves, turn through and press. Turn and stitch, or glue, a hem at the lower edge.

For the trimmed version, stitch or glue lace trimming to the sleeve ends. Stitch the side seams, clip the curves, turn through and press. Whip fine picot braid or lace around the edge, from the centre back hem, up one front, around the neckline, down the other front and round the hem.

Work belt loops on the side seams and thread a ribbon or braid belt. If required, cut a pocket in matching fabric, turn in and tack a small allowance around the edge, slip stitch or glue the pocket in place, press and remove the tacking. Work a hanging-loop at the back neck if required.

CHILD'S DRESSING-GOWN

The child's dressing-gown pattern can be made up in any of the versions described for the gentleman's or lady's dressing-gown or, as an alternative, the edges could be bound with ¼ inch wide bias strip cut from fine silk or lawn (bias binding). Suggested fabrics for this method include Viyella, winceyette, and single-sided towelling.

LADY'S NIGHTGOWN

(Shown on page 119)

This pretty little nightgown is suitable for any lady from the eighteenth century to the present day. It can be made in fine cotton lawn or silk, though white, cream, or ivory are usually the most appropriate colours. The lace trimming should be very delicate and approximately ¼ inch wide. I have used tiny pearl beads as buttons. The pattern can be adapted to make a nightgown for a little girl by using the stitching line as the cutting line, shortening the sleeves to the gathering line, and trimming the length as required.

Trace the pattern on to the straight grain of the fabric, seal the cutting line and cut one piece. Seal the cutting line before slashing the front opening. To make pintucks on the shoulders, fold the fabric on the lines shown and whip stitch (overcast) the folded edges in matching thread. Make six pintucks and press. Bind the edges of the front opening and the neckline with lace, scalloped edge to the right side and straight edge to the wrong side. Ease the lace around the curve of the neckline and line up neatly at the bottom of the front opening. Stitch tiny beads or buttons to one side of the front, and work thread loops around the buttons down the other side, to represent a loop and button fastening.

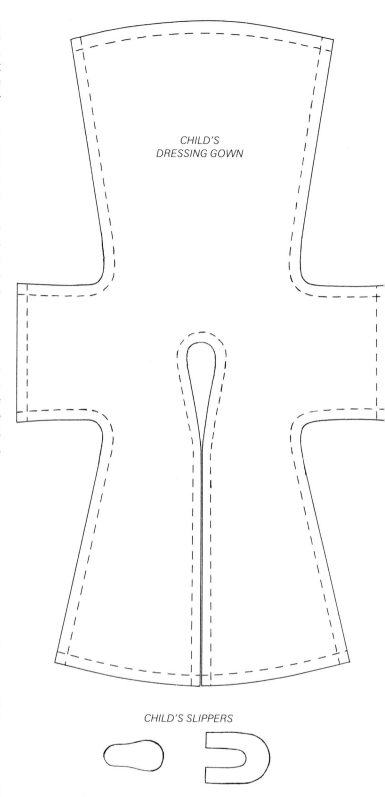

CHILD'S
DRESSING GOWN

CHILD'S SLIPPERS

Child's dressing-gown and slippers

Stitch the side seams and clip the curves. Fold the sleeve ends and stitch or glue in place. Place lace over the sleeve hem and work gathering stitches through lace and fabric to make wrist frills. Pull up (over a pencil or similar) and fasten off. Join the cut ends of lace with small blanket stitches or glue. Turn through and press. Turn and stitch, or glue, a small hem at the lower edge. Add tiny ribbon bows to front neckline and sleeve frills if required.

THE GENTLEMAN'S COLLECTION
*1 Knitted dressing-gown, 2 striped sweater,
3 combinations (Chapter 2), 4 dressing-gown,
5 nightshirt and nightcap, 6 straw hat, 7 socks and
gloves, 8 slippers, 9 belt, scarf and tie, 10 umbrella
(Chapter 6)*

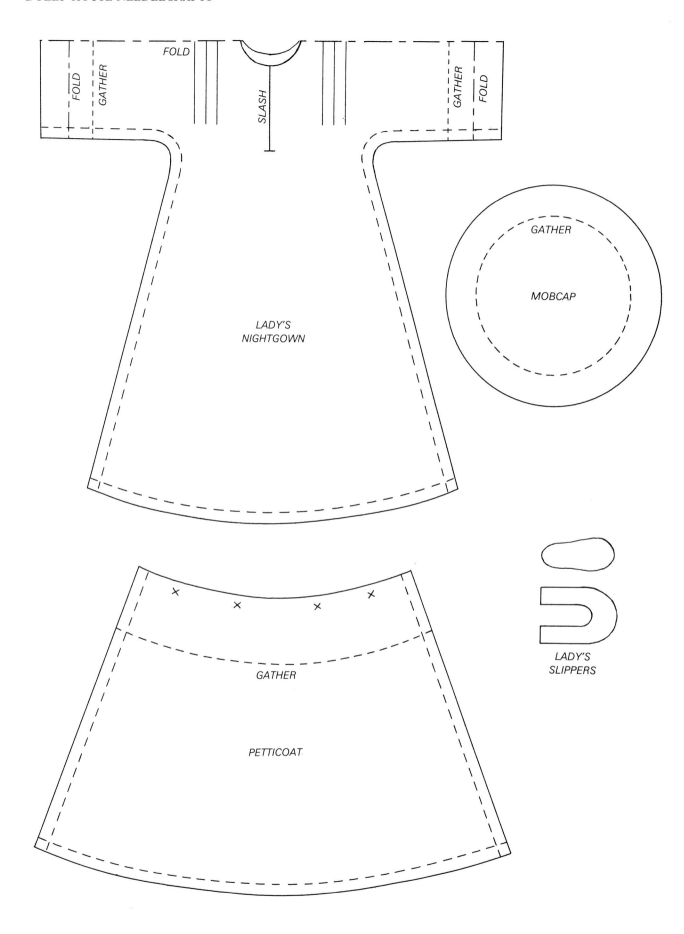

Lady's nightgown, petticoat, slippers
and mobcap

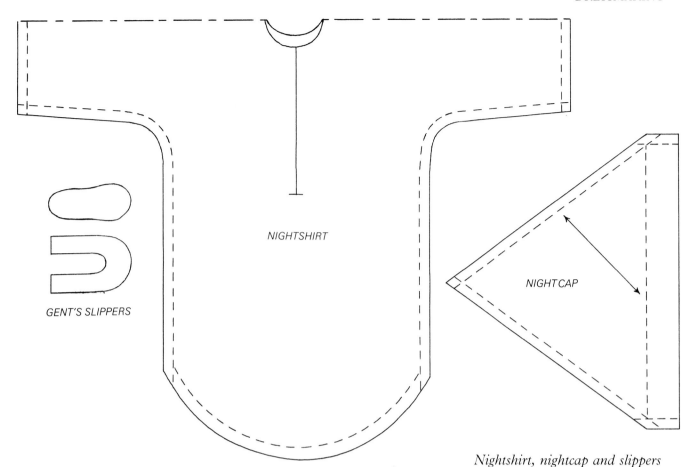

Nightshirt, nightcap and slippers

NIGHTSHIRT

GENT'S SLIPPERS

NIGHTCAP

NIGHTSHIRT AND NIGHTCAP *(Shown on page 123)*

This old-fashioned nightshirt and cap are particularly suitable for Victorian gentlemen. I have used an old well-washed cotton lawn with a fine beige and white stripe – old fabrics are especially good for nightwear of this type as they lend the simple pattern a little character. The pattern can also be used to make a shirt by using the stitching line as the cutting line, and making the garment shorter.

Trace the pattern on to the straight grain of the fabric, seal the cutting line, and cut out one piece. Seal the cutting line before slashing the front opening. Bind the edges of the front opening and the neckline with a ¼ inch wide bias-cut strip of fine

cotton (bias binding) and press. Make a small pleat at the lower end of the opening, so that one bound edge overlaps the other, and secure with small stitches. Stitch tiny buttons or beads to the overlapping side and slip stitch the overlap in place. Stitch the side seams and clip the curves. Turn up the sleeve ends and hem or glue in place. Turn through and press. Make a small pleat at each sleeve end and stitch a tiny button or bead to represent a cuff. Turn and stitch, or glue, a hem at the lower edge.

To make the nightcap, trace the pattern on to the bias grain of the fabric, seal the cutting line and cut one piece. Stitch the back seam and turn through. Turn and stitch, or glue, a hem around the lower edge. Make a small tassel in sewing thread and stitch the tassel to the point of the nightcap.

OUTERWEAR

APRON AND PINAFORE *(Shown on page 127)*

The apron and old-fashioned wrapover pinny are both made in tiny-print fine cotton fabrics and have edges bound with ³⁄₁₆ inch (4mm) silk ribbon. The ribbon is a little fiddly to ease around the curves, but it does make a much finer bound edge than cotton binding.

Trace the pattern on to the fabric, seal the cutting line, and cut out the apron or pinafore on the straight grain of the fabric.

APRON

Cut a piece of ribbon for each straight side and fold and press in half down the length. Apply a fine line of glue to the right side edge of the fabric, allow to dry slightly until it becomes tacky, then press one

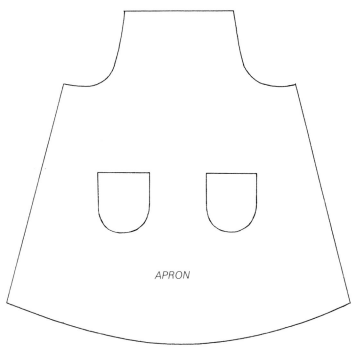

APRON

Apron and pinafore

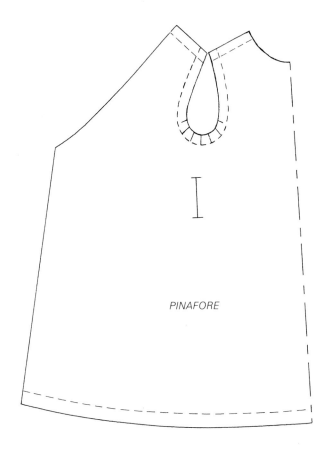

PINAFORE

edge of the ribbon in place, lining up the fold with the edge of the fabric, and allow to dry. Glue the back of the fabric and fold and press the other edge of the ribbon in place on the wrong side. Cut, fold, and glue ribbon to the hem in the same way, then to the top of the bib. Cut one piece of ribbon 12 inches long, fold and press along the length and mark the centre point. Apply glue to the curved side edges of the bib, then, working from the waistline at

COPING MANFULLY
*Crocheted cushion, tie-on seat cushion, pet blanket,
dishcloth, pot holder (Chapter 1), combinations
(Chapter 2), parrot picture, Turkoman rug (Chapter
3), tablecloth, cleaning cloths, lampshade (Chapter
5), apron and pinafore, shopping bag, umbrella
(Chapter 6), plant-pot hanger, laundry bin, pet
basket, picnic hamper, kitchen accessories (Chapter 8)*

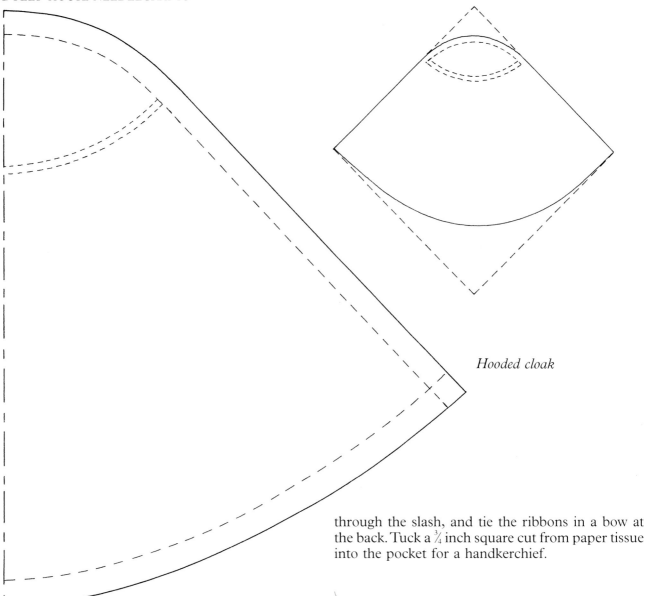

Hooded cloak

through the slash, and tie the ribbons in a bow at the back. Tuck a $\frac{3}{4}$ inch square cut from paper tissue into the pocket for a handkerchief.

HOODED CLOAK
(Shown on page 27)

This style of hooded cloak was very fashionable in the eighteenth century and was still worn by country women at the end of the nineteenth century. Traditionally, it was made in scarlet wool – I have used Viyella, but you could use any colour. If you do not have a doll to wear the cloak, it can be hung on the back of the kitchen door.

Trace the pattern on to a 7 inch square of fabric as shown, including the gathering line at the neckline. Seal the cutting line and cut out the cloak. Turn and stitch, or glue, a hem all the way round the outside edge and press. With matching button thread or doubled sewing thread, make a row of tiny gathering stitches around the hood, $\frac{1}{4}$ inch from the edge. Pull up slightly to form a frill and fasten off. Make two rows of gathering around the neckline on the marked line, pull up and fasten off. Secure the gathering around the hood and neckline by working oversewing stitches through each gathering stitch on the inside. Stitch or glue narrow ribbon ties to either side at the front neckline.

one side, leave an end of ribbon for the tie, and press ribbon on to the bib side. Leave a loop at the top, centred on the mark, press ribbon to the other bib side and leave the other end for a tie. Trace the pockets, seal the cutting line, cut pockets, and bind the top edges with ribbon. Apply glue to the outside edge of the pockets and press in place.

WRAPOVER PINNY

Cut ribbon, press in half along the length, and glue to the straight skirt front edges and the curved bodice front edges, mitring at the corners. Glue ribbon to the back neckline, easing around the curve. Stitch the shoulder seams and press open. Turn in and glue hems around the armholes, snipping as necessary. Turn and glue a hem at the lower edge. Cut the pocket, glue ribbon around the edge, easing around the curve, and glue the bound edge of the pocket to the pinny. Apply Fraycheck (or similar), and cut a small slash at one side of the bodice as shown. Glue ribbon ties to each corner of the wrapover front, thread the underwrap tie

SHAWLS *(Shown on page 18)*

Simple but effective shawls are made by cutting a 4½ inch square of fabric precisely on the straight grain, and pulling threads from each edge to make a fringe. The green silk shawl shown draping a table in our Victorian parlour has a border of two rows of machine stitching worked in gold thread. The scarlet shawl in the Victorian kitchen is made from Viyella which is an excellent substitute for wool in this scale. White or cream Viyella will make a good baby shawl, and strong or pastel colours in plain or print silk, cotton, or Viyella can be used for ladies shawls. Look out for tiny Paisley prints for Victorian ladies, and consider also embroidering a plain shawl with one of the motifs in Chapter 3.

BABY GOWN

(Shown on page 43)

This pattern can be used to make everyday gowns for Victorian babies, or a christening gown for a twentieth-century baby. Use a very fine cotton or silk and the most delicate narrow lace in white or ivory for the best results.

Trace the pattern on to the straight grain of the fabric, seal the cutting line and cut one piece. If the gown is not to be worn, do not slash the back opening; if it is to be worn, seal the cutting line before slashing. Stitch or glue bands of lace trimming to the front of the gown, as shown by the dotted lines on the pattern, to make the front panel. Place the horizontal bands first, then the vertical bands at either side. Bind the neckline with lace, or whip stitch (overcast) slightly-gathered lace around it. Stitch or glue lace to sleeve ends. Stitch the side seams, clip the curves, turn through and press. Gather the sleeve ends above the lace to make frills, pull up slightly, and fasten off. Stitch or glue lace around the lower edge. To make the sash, thread silk

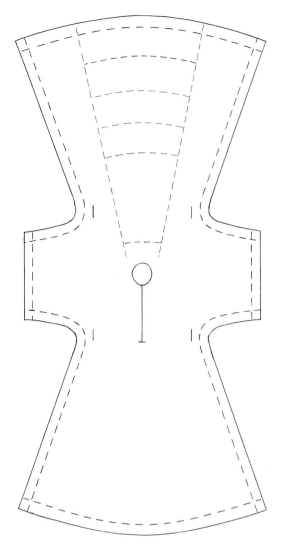

Baby gown

ribbon in a needle and stitch through each side of the gown at the waistline as shown, bringing the ribbon ends to the front. (Put the gown on to the doll and slip stitch the back opening closed.) Tie the ribbon ends in a bow and trim.

HATS AND ACCESSORIES

MOBCAP AND SHOWER CAP

(Shown on pages 119 and 131)

This pattern can be used to make a plain mobcap in white cotton lawn for a cook or housemaid, or for a lady to wear with the Victorian bathing costume in Chapter 2. Trimmed with lace, the mobcap is appropriate for an eighteenth- or early nineteenth-century lady both as day wear and as a nightcap. The same pattern, made in thin plastic material (I used a piece cut from a lifesize shower cap), will

make a shower cap to be worn in the twentieth-century bathroom.

Trace the pattern (on page 124) on to the fabric (seal the cutting line on cotton fabrics), and cut one piece. To make a plain mobcap, simply gather around the cap as shown with single shirring elastic or doubled sewing thread, pull up and fasten off. For a lace-trimmed cap, stitch ⅜ inch wide lace trimming with the gathering so that the lace overhangs the edge of the cap slightly. Add some tiny ribbon bows to decorate as required.

For the shower cap, turn in and glue outside edge ⅛ inch, and gather 1/16 inch from folded edge.

STRAW HATS
(Shown on page 119)

Our hats are made in ³⁄₁₆ inch (4mm) wide hat straw which is available in a range of colours from dolls-house and dollmaking suppliers (see Stockists). If you prefer, the hats can be made in tightly-plaited (braided) raffia – but iron the plaited raffia before you begin, to make it as flat as possible. The

Straw hats

method is the same for all hats, but the colours and trimmings you choose will make it suitable for any period. Our hats are trimmed with narrow ribbon, silk ribbon roses, picot braid, and tiny feathers, which are all available from the same suppliers as the hat straw. You can shape the hat in your hands as you work if you wish, but it is usually easier to make a simple block by gluing half of a 1 inch diameter wooden bead (for a round crown), or a slice of 1 inch dowelling (for a flat crown, found on a boater), to a small piece of scrap wood.

Dampen the hat straw (or raffia) slightly to make it more pliable. Pull the cotton thread woven into one edge of the hat straw to curl the straw. The tension of this thread controls the amount of curl – pull tighter at the beginning for a tight curl, and less as the work proceeds for a looser curl. Begin at the centre of the crown, coiling the first round of straw as tightly as possible and work outward, oversewing each round to the previous one with the smallest stitches in matching thread. Shape the crown of the hat as you work by adjusting the tension on the pull-thread, then outward for the brim, lessening the tension with each round. When the hat is the required size, taper the end of the straw into the brim gradually, cut the end at an angle and secure it to the underside with a little glue. Steam or dampen the hat and press it over your block to refine the shaping. Smooth the crown with the point of an iron, make a flat brim for a boater by ironing firmly, and leave the hat on the block to dry.

Glue the trimmings to the hat with fabric glue, working on the block. Our boater on page 123 is trimmed with a band of blue and white striped ribbon and a small bow. The blue hat on page 62 has picot braid glued around the edge of the brim, and a wreath of pink silk ribbon roses with green ribbon leaves around the crown. The pink hat on page 78 is trimmed with brown picot braid around the brim, and loops of braid around the crown with cream ribbon roses and a brown feather.

STOCKINGS AND GLOVES *(Shown on page 119)*

These simple little accessories, though not wearable, can be used to give the dolls-house bedroom a 'lived-in' feel, or used to fill the glove box on page 172. Ladies stockings can be made in any black or white sheer fabric such as chiffon, organdie, voile or tulle (or ballet net) for an eighteenth- or nineteenth-century house, or from a lifesize nylon stocking for a twentieth-century house. Socks are made by the same method from any fine knitted fabric, such as T-shirt cotton or 40-60 denier nylon. The gloves are made from scraps of the thinnest glove leather in any colour you please. (See also the yellow household gloves on page 186, which are made by this method from a piece of lifesize lightweight household glove.)

To make the stockings (or socks), cut a strip of fabric approximately 2 inches wide and long enough to cut the pattern twice. Cut a strip of

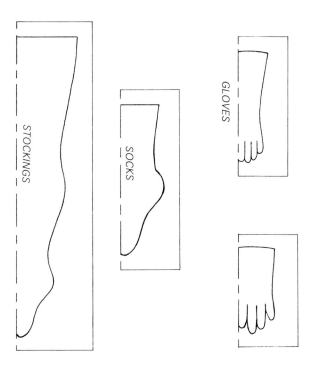

Stockings and gloves

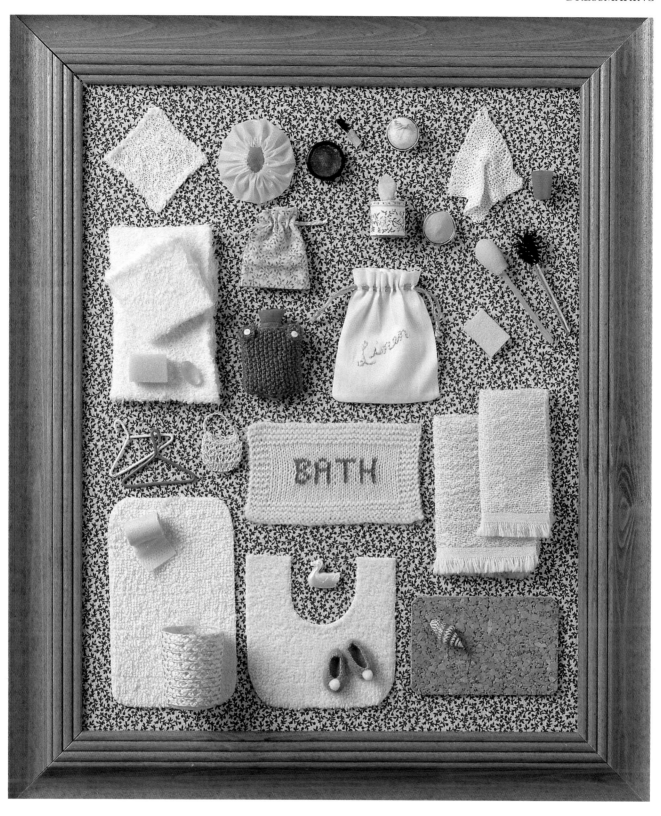

THE BATHROOM COLLECTION
1 knitted flannel, 2 small string bag,
3 hot-water bottle cover, 4 bath mat (Chapter 1),
5 towels, 6 bath mat and pedestal mat (Chapter 5),
7 shower cap, 8 slippers, 9 linen bag and sponge
bag (Chapter 6), 10 bead and button accessories,
11 straw waste-paper basket, 12 cork bath mat,
13 loofah and loo brush (Chapter 8)

Bondaweb (or similar), 1 inch wide. Iron the fabric strip along the length to make a sharp crease. Iron the Bondaweb to the inside of the fabric, lined up on the fold, and iron the other side of the fabric to enclose the Bondaweb. Trace the pattern on to the fabric. If you want seams, machine stitch along the cutting line with the smallest stitch, down the back of each stocking. Paint Fraycheck (or similar), along the cutting line of any fabric which frays, and along the stitching line if you have made seams, and allow to dry. Cut out the stockings, cutting as close as possible to the seam line. Glue a narrow lace trimming around the top of the stockings as decoration if required.

To make gloves, cut 1 inch wide strips of leather, fold down the length, and glue the two inner faces of the leather together with fabric glue, allow to dry. Trace the pattern on to the leather and cut out the gloves.

SLIPPERS
(Shown on page 119)

Patterns are given for these simple slippers in lady's, gentleman's and child's sizes, (see pages 124, 125 and 122), the method is the same for each. You can adapt the pattern as necessary to fit a specific doll, or make a pair of slippers to put under the bed. I have used felt which was pressed with a steam iron to shrink and tighten the texture as much as possible before cutting, though you can use any similar non-fray or minimum-fray fabric. I trimmed the slippers with tiny pom-poms (from a craft shop), though tiny ribbon bows or roses would make a good alternative.

Trace the pattern on to the fabric (seal the cutting line on any fabric which frays), and cut a pair of uppers and a pair of soles. Work tiny blanket stitches around the top edge of each upper in matching or contrasting thread. Join the back seam with blanket stitch on the wrong side and stitch the upper to the sole with tiny blanket stitches, working on the right side, in matching thread. Use a round-ended tool such as a small paintbrush handle to ease the slippers to shape. Glue pom-poms or ribbon bows to the fronts as required.

BAG, BELT SCARF AND TIE
(Shown on page 123)

These are simple little costume accessories which can be worn or used to add character to the dolls' house. Handbags and belts are made from scraps of fine glove leather and scarves and ties from scraps of fabric.

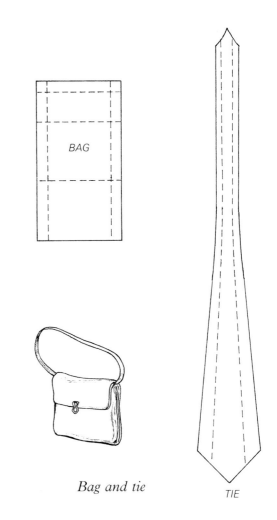

Bag and tie   TIE

HANDBAG *(Shown on page 119)*

Cut the pattern in leather, and fold and glue both long and one short edges. Fold the bag as shown and glue the side edges together. Glue the ends of a thin strip of leather under the flap for the strap, and glue an oddment of jewellery finding to the front of the flap for a catch.

BELT

Cut a strip of leather 3½ inches x ¼ inch wide. Fold and glue both long edges to the centre, and trim one end to a point. Glue a tiny buckle (from dolls-house suppliers) to the other end.

SCARF

Cut a piece of fabric (I have used Viyella), 6 inches long x 1 inch wide squarely on the straight grain of the fabric. Pull threads to make a fringe on both short ends, then paint Fraycheck (or similar) along both long edges, and allow to dry. Trim the long edges to make the scarf ⅞ inch wide, cutting through the sealed fabric.

TIE

Trace the pattern on to lightweight fabric (I have used silk), on the bias grain, and seal the cutting line. Cut the inner outline shown on the pattern in Bondaweb (or similar) and iron it on to the centre of the tie, and allow to cool. Cut out the tie and fold and press the long edges to meet at the centre, enclosing the Bondaweb.

Consider also making handkerchiefs from squares of fine cotton lawn with edges sealed with Fraycheck (or similar) before cutting – 1 inch square for gents' hankies or $\frac{3}{4}$ inch square with glued-on trimming for ladies. Gentlemen might also have a ribbon rose for the buttonhole.

SHOPPING BAGS *(Shown on page 127)*

Our two shopping bags can be used as costume accessories or displayed in the dolls-house kitchen. The larger bag (shown on page 179) is made from ribbon $1\frac{1}{2}$-2 inches wide with handles of narrow ribbon – Isobel has used a woven tapestry ribbon in red, green, and black with black handles. The smaller bag is made in lightweight fabric – I have used printed cotton.

LARGE BAG

Cut a piece of ribbon approximately $3\frac{1}{2}$ inches long and stitch or glue a small hem at each end. Place the narrow ribbon, as shown, on the right side of the bag, and stitch or glue it in place. Fold the bag in half, with wrong sides facing, and oversew the side seams with tiny stitches in matching thread.

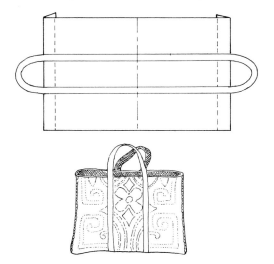

Large shopping bag

SMALL BAG

Trace the pattern on to the straight grain of the fabric, paint the cutting line with Fraycheck (or similar) and allow to dry. Cut the bag, fold in half with right sides facing, and stitch the side and bottom edges together. Clip the corners and turn

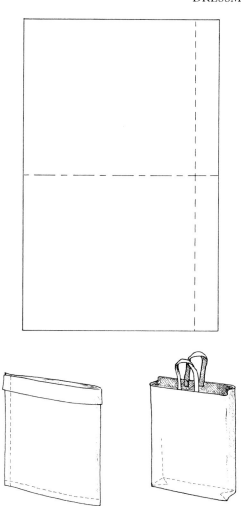

Small shopping bag

through. Fold and glue a small hem around the top edge. Using a toothpick or similar pointed tool, poke the corners at the bottom of the bag inward, apply a little fabric glue, and press the folded edges together to shape a rectangular base for the bag. Cut a rectangle of thin card to fit, and glue it flat inside the base. Crease the sides of the bag in line with the ends of the base and press. Fold and glue a narrow strip of fabric or ribbon and cut two handles. Glue the ends of the handles to the inside of the bag.

LINEN BAG AND SPONGE BAG
(Shown on page 131)

These drawstring bags are made in lightweight cotton fabrics. The laundry bag for dirty clothes goes well in the bathroom or bedroom, and any 'failed' dressmaking projects will make excellent laundry to fill it! The pattern for the sponge bag can also be used to make a reticule for a nineteenth-century lady.

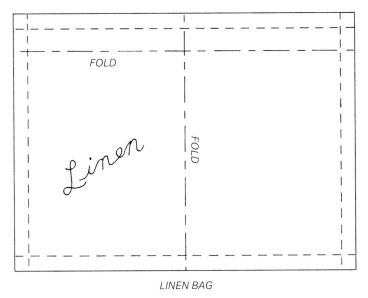

LINEN BAG

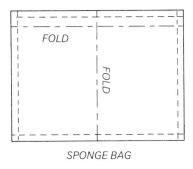

SPONGE BAG

Linen bag and sponge bag

LINEN BAG

Cut a piece of plain coloured cotton fabric 4 x 3 inches. Trace the pattern on to the fabric and embroider 'Linen' with one strand of thread in a contrasting colour in back stitch. Fold and stitch a hem at the top edge as shown. With right sides facing, fold the bag in half, stitch the side and bottom seams, and turn through. Cut two 6 inch lengths of embroidery cotton (floss) – six strands – for drawstrings. Work small running stitches around the top of the bag just below the hem with the first length, beginning and ending at the side seam. Knot the thread ends together. Work a second row of small running stitches just below the first with the second length, beginning and ending opposite the side seam, and knot the ends together. Pull up the drawstrings to close the bag.

SPONGE BAG (OR RETICULE)

Trace the pattern on to the fabric, seal the cutting line, and cut the bag. Turn and glue a ⅛ inch hem at the top edge. Seam the side and bottom edges as above and turn through. Work the drawstrings as above with doubled sewing thread or two strands of embroidery thread.

PARASOLS AND WALKING-STICKS

(Shown on pages 78 and 62)

These simple parasols, umbrellas, and walking-sticks are made from wooden toothpicks. The handles are either beads or small pieces of brown plastic-covered wire cut from ordinary three-core electric cable. I have trimmed the sticks with tiny brass eyelets as ferrules, which though not essential, add a realistic touch. The fabric covers should be lightweight silk or cotton in plain colours or prints and trimmed with fine braid or lace.

To make a walking-stick, paint, stain, or polish, the toothpick if required and glue a brass eyelet on to the lower end with Superglue. Glue another eyelet and a bead to the top end for a knob handle. Note that it may be necessary to sand the toothpick slightly with very fine-grade abrasive paper in order to push the eyelets far enough up (or down) the shaft of the stick.

To make a curved handle, cut 1 inch of plastic-covered wire, scrape the plastic covering away from one end, and use pliers and a twisting motion to pull the stranded wires ⅛ inch out of the end, leaving ⅛ inch of hollow plastic tube at the other end. Glue a brass eyelet on to the stick, then push the end of the stick into the hollow plastic tube, secured with Superglue. Bend the plastic-covered wire to a curve and trim the end to the required length. Heat the end of the handle carefully with a match to melt the plastic slightly, and roll the softened plastic between your fingers to cover the wire ends.

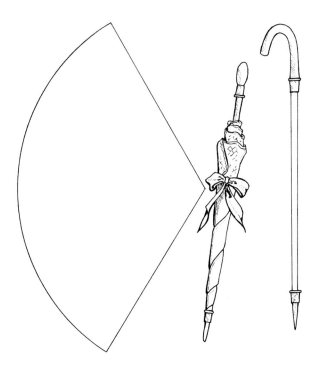

Parasol and walking-stick

IN THE BOUDOIR
Flower-trellis rug (Chapter 3), chemise and drawers, corset, straw hat, stockings and gloves, handbag, parasol (Chapter 6), dressing-table stool, fabric-covered screen, Louis armchair (Chapter 7)

To make a parasol or umbrella, trace the cover pattern on to fabric, seal the cutting line and cut out. Stitch or glue trimming to the curved edge as required, seam the straight edges together to make a cone and turn through. Push the point of the stick through the point of the cover and secure with a touch of glue. Glue an eyelet on to the end of the stick, to butt against the point of the cover, and secure with Superglue. Wrap the cover around the stick in neat folds and secure with stitches or glue. Make a bead knob or plastic-wire handle as described above. Add a ribbon band, bow, or ribbon roses as required.

 TEDDY BEAR AND DOLL *(Shown on page 43)*

These little toys can be held as accessories by most child-size dolls, but also look attractive displayed in the nursery. The teddy bear can be made from any fine non-fray or minimum-fray fabric. The doll is made from a $\frac{1}{4}$ inch bead and a pipecleaner, and dressed in $\frac{1}{4}$, $\frac{1}{2}$ and 1 inch matching nylon ribbon.

TEDDY BEAR

Trace the pattern twice (reversing for the second piece) on to fabric with a very sharp pencil. If the fabric frays at all, paint the cutting line with Fraycheck (or similar), allow to dry, and cut two pieces. Stitch the back and front together wrong sides facing, around the edge with tiny blanket stitches in matching thread, leaving a small opening under one arm for stuffing. Stuff the bear with wisps of polyester, pushed in with a toothpick, and blanket stitch the opening closed. Tie a narrow silk ribbon bow around the neck and mark the face with a black fine-point fibre-tipped pen.

DOLL

Fold a pipecleaner and push and glue it into the bead. Trim to length as shown, and bend the feet forward. Cut the arm length in pipecleaner and glue it to the body. Bind the body with a piece of surgical tape (available from chemists or pharmacies). To thicken the doll's legs, dip them in Gesso – a liquid plaster available from art shops – and leave to dry. Paint the head, arms, and legs flesh colour, and paint boots or shoes as required. Glue a scrap of lace around the body, caught between the legs with a few stitches, for knickers. Glue pieces of $\frac{1}{4}$ inch ribbon around the arms for dress sleeves. Cut 1 inch of $\frac{1}{2}$ inch ribbon for the bodice, snip a neck hole, and slash open at the back, and glue the bodice on to the doll, over the sleeves. Cut a 3 inch length of 1 inch ribbon for the skirt. Fold along the length to make two tiers, and press. Blanket stitch the back seam, and gather along the folded edge with tiny stitches. Put the skirt on the doll over the bodice, pull up the gathering to fit, and fasten off. Slip stitch the skirt to the bodice around the waist. Make the hair with a dozen strands of embroidery thread (floss), with a small stitched parting in the centre, and glue the hair on to the doll's head. Make tiny silk ribbon bows and glue to the dress waist and hair. Mark the doll's eyes with a black fine-point fibre-tipped pen.

The method can be used to make larger or smaller dolls as you wish. See also the knitted doll and teddy bear in Chapter 1.

Teddy bears and doll

— CHAPTER SEVEN —

Furniture and Upholstery

The patterns in this chapter range from very simple stools made from cotton reels to authentic upholstered sofas and chairs. Most of the projects require only the minimum of woodworking skill, but the right tools and materials will make the job easier. The furniture is made in basswood – a smooth white hardwood with a small grain – or in balsawood, both of which are available from craft shops. To cut the wood you will need a small razor-toothed saw for straight lines and a fret saw for curves. You will need a small mitre block to cut mitred joints and an engineers' set square to measure accurate right-angles. The wood should be sanded smooth with a fine-grade abrasive paper and stained with a spirit-based woodstain to represent mahogany or walnut. The wooden pieces are glued together with a white woodwork glue such as Evostick Resin W, and the furniture can be finished with several coats of wax polish or with an acrylic varnish. You will also need a craft glue such as UHU and a fabric glue.

Padding for upholstered furniture is foam, in $\frac{1}{8}$, $\frac{1}{4}$ and $\frac{1}{2}$ inch thicknesses, as specified in the patterns, and this can be taken from packaging or bought from craft shops. Upholstery fabrics are a matter of personal taste, but lightweight cotton fabrics are the best choice for the beginner as they are the easiest to use. Experienced miniaturists might try lifesize upholstery fabrics with carefully chosen patterns for the more challenging projects at the end of the chapter. The fine braids used for trimming are available from dolls-house and dollmaking suppliers, including those listed at the back of the book, or made by cutting apart a lifesize lampshade-trimming braid. Other specific requirements have been discussed in previous chapters or are mentioned where relevant.

STOOLS

COTTON-REEL STOOLS *(Shown on page 167)*

This very simple method will make a useful little footstool for the parlour of any dolls' house from the late eighteenth century to the present day, depending on the fabric you choose for the cover. I have used a printed velveteen for our footstool, and made another version in glove leather with a small chess piece as a pedestal to make a piano stool. If you have an old-fashioned wooden cotton reel (thread spool), this is a good way to use it, but any ordinary plastic reel is suitable. Consider also using one of the motifs in Chapter 3 to embroider a cover for your stool.

Saw the cotton reel in half through the centre, and cut a circle in stiff card to fit the cut end of one half. Cut a circle of $\frac{1}{4}$ inch foam to fit, and glue it on to the card. Cut a circle of fabric (or leather) $\frac{1}{2}$ inch larger all round than the padded card and make a line of gathering in strong thread around the outside of the fabric. Centre the padded card on the wrong side of the fabric and pull up the gathering tightly and fasten off. Glue the covered card on to the cut end of the cotton reel. Cut a strip of fabric on the straight grain to fit around the cotton reel with allowances to turn in both long edges to meet, and make a butt join at the short edges. Seal the short edges with Fraycheck (or similar), turn in the long edges to meet, and press. Glue the folded fabric strip around the side of the cotton reel so that the top edge of the strip meets the outside edge of the padded top. Glue narrow braid trimming around the edge(s) as required. For the piano stool, glue a $1\frac{1}{2}$ inch tall chess piece, or similar turned wood, into the hole on the underside of the reel.

Cotton-reel stools

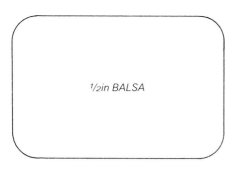

1/2in BALSA

1/2in BALSA

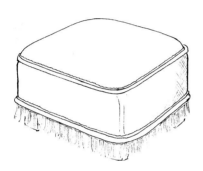

Square stools

straight grain $\frac{1}{2}$ inch larger all round and make a line of gathering around the edge. Centre fabric over the padded card, pull up gathering and fasten off. Glue the covered card on to the top of the balsa. Cut a piece of tapestry canvas to fit and glue it on to the underside of the balsa (optional). Cut a strip of fabric on the straight grain, $1\frac{1}{8}$ inch wide to fit around the sides of the stool with a butt join. Seal the short ends with Fraycheck (or similar), fold the long edges to meet at the centre, and press. Glue the fabric strip around the sides of the stool so that the top edge of the strip meets the outside edge of the padded top. Glue braid and fringe trimming to the top and bottom edges of the side as required. Glue beads, or push and glue painted push-pins, into the underside at each corner with Superglue.

DRESSING-TABLE STOOL *(Shown on page 62)*

This elegant stool can be made in the long version shown on the pattern, which is designed to fit at the foot of a bed, or shortened to 2 inches to make a dressing-table stool. Our stool is made from commercial picture-frame moulding and four 1 inch cabriole legs available from most dolls-house shops. The seat is $\frac{1}{8}$ inch wood, and the seat pad can be

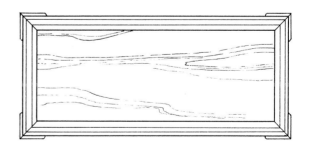

VIEW THROUGH A-A

SQUARE STOOLS

(Shown on page 90)

There are several versions of this stool shown throughout the book – in pale green or brown velvet trimmed with braid and fringe, in green leather, and the longer version in printed cotton. The method is simple but the choice of materials will make a variety of different effects. The stool is made in $\frac{1}{2}$ inch thick balsawood, padded with foam, and covered with fabric or leather. The feet can be small square or round beads in black or brown wood or plastic, or plastic push-pins (from stationers) painted black or brown. I have used a braid and fringe cut from lampshade trimming. Consider also embroidering a cover for your stool in Florentine stitch, or adapting one of the patterns in Chapter 3.

Trace the pattern (either size) on to the balsawood and cut out with a razor-toothed saw. Sand the edges and sides smooth. Cut the pattern in stiff thin card, and in $\frac{1}{4}$ inch foam, and glue the foam on to the card. Cut a piece of fabric (or leather) on the

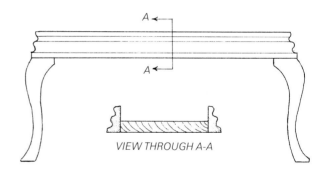

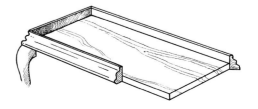

Dressing-table stool

TEA AT GRANDMA'S HOUSE
Simple knitted cushion, pet blanket, knitted teddy (Chapter 1), hat, scarf and mittens, sweater and shorts (Chapter 2), ribbon-patch tea-cosy (Chapter 4), curtains with box pelmet, tablecloth, lampshade (Chapter 5), cotton-reel stool, square stool (Chapter 7), bead and button ornaments, cushions and antimacassars, pet basket (Chapter 8)

covered in any fabric you choose. The cross stitch seat cover pattern in Chapter 3 (see page 57) will fit the longer version.

Cut the seat in ⅛ inch wood. Cut the seat frame in moulding with mitred corners, and glue the seat frame around the seat as shown. Stain the seat and frame to the required colour. Sand the cabriole legs carefully and thoroughly to refine the shaping and stain to match the seat. Glue the legs to the underside of the seat as shown, allow to dry. Apply several coats of wax polish, well buffed between coats, or varnish. Cut a piece of stiff, thick cardboard (posterboard) to fit loosely into the well in the seat, and cut ¼ inch foam to fit. Glue the foam on to the card. Cut a fabric cover on the straight grain, ½ inch larger all round than the card. Centre the padded card on the fabric and fold and glue the fabric to the underside. Trim the fabric to make neat mitred corners at each end. Glue the covered seat pad into the well in the seat.

SIMPLE FURNITURE

OTTOMAN

(Shown on page 38)

The ottoman is a fabric-covered seat or storage box which became fashionable in the early nineteenth century, and in its twentieth-century incarnation is usually used as a blanket box. Our ottoman is made in ³⁄₁₆ inch wood covered with printed cotton and has a ribbon-hinged padded lid edged with narrow braid. The pattern is designed to make a box to fit at the foot of the bed, but can easily be adapted to make any size ottoman you choose.

Cut a base, back, front, two sides and a lid from the pattern in ³⁄₁₆ inch wood, and sand the pieces.

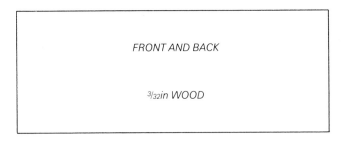

FRONT AND BACK

³⁄₃₂in WOOD

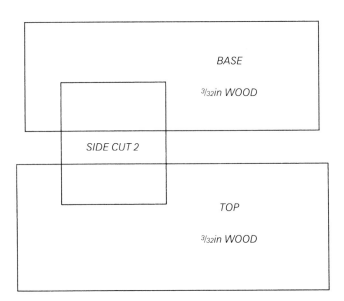

BASE

³⁄₃₂in WOOD

SIDE CUT 2

TOP

³⁄₃₂in WOOD

Ottoman pattern

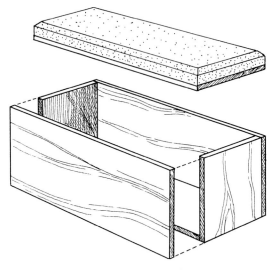

Ottoman assembly

Assemble the box with woodwork glue as shown, and allow to dry. Cut a piece of ¼ inch foam to fit, glue it on to the lid and trim the top edges rounded, as shown.

Cut a piece of fabric on the straight grain, ½ inch larger all round than the lid. Centre the fabric over the padding, apply glue to the edges of the lid, smooth the fabric on to the glued edges so that the padding is covered, and allow to dry. Trim the edge of the fabric flush with the underside of the lid. Note that it is easier to do this if you glue fabric to one long edge first, then the second long edge, then the short edges, allowing each edge to dry before gluing the next. Cut a piece of fabric on the straight grain ¹⁄₁₆ inch larger all round than the underside of the lid. Apply fabric glue, smoothed all over the underside of the lid with your fingers, and allow to become tacky. Smooth the fabric on to the wood, folding and gluing the edges of fabric to the edges of the lid, snipping as necessary to neaten each of the corners (the raw edge of the fabric will be covered by the narrow braid).

Cut a 3 inch wide strip of fabric (with the cutting line sealed), long enough to fit around all four sides of the box and overlap by ¼ inch. Turn in ⅛ inch at both short ends and glue. Working on one side of the box at a time, coat the wood with fabric glue and allow it to become tacky, then smooth the fabric on to the wood. Begin at one (back) corner and centre the fabric so that $1\frac{1}{2}$ inches overhangs the top edge of the box and $\frac{1}{4}$ inch overhangs the base of the box. Wrap the fabric around the four sides so that the folded short ends meet at the first corner, and allow to dry. Snip and mitre the corners and glue the $\frac{1}{4}$ inch fabric allowance to the underside (base) of the box. Cut a piece of fabric 1 x 3 inches with sealed edges, and glue this centred to the underside of the base. Snip the corners and fold and glue the $1\frac{1}{2}$ inch fabric allowance over the top edge and to the insides of the box. Cut a piece of fabric to fit with sealed edges and glue it on to the inside base of the box. Both box and lid are now covered and lined.

To hinge the lid, fit the lid on to the box and hold it in place with an elastic band. Glue a piece of matching narrow silk ribbon (or a strip of fabric with sealed edges) to the back edge of the lid and the back of the box, and allow to dry. Glue narrow braid around the edge of the lid (covering the ribbon), with the ends meeting at the centre back. Glue some braid around the top of the box for decoration if required.

FABRIC-COVERED SCREEN *(Shown on page 142)*

The folding screen is a very useful piece of furniture. It can be placed in the drawing room or bedroom to block draughts or to afford privacy, or by a window to offer shade from the sun. Most Victorian houses had one or two screens and they are still popular today – though used more now as a decorative feature than for practical reasons.

Our screen is made in $\frac{1}{8}$ inch wood, covered with printed cotton, edged with narrow braid, and hinged with $\frac{3}{16}$ inch (4mm) wide silk ribbon. Choose a colour or pattern which complements the décor of the room. You may prefer to face both sides of the screen with the same fabric, or use different fabrics on each side to make a reversible screen. The embroidered silk panels shown in Chapter 3 can also be used to cover a screen made from this pattern. Stitch the embroidery first, and back it with lightweight iron-on Vilene (or similar) before cutting the panels.

Cut three panels in $\frac{1}{8}$ inch wood ensuring that they are exactly the same size and shape, and sand the edges smooth. Using one panel as a template, draw six panels on the wrong side of the fabric with a sharp pencil – ensuring that they are squarely on the straight grain and taking care to match any pattern. Cut out the fabric panels about $\frac{1}{2}$ inch outside the drawn lines.

Spread fabric glue thinly and evenly over one side of each wooden panel with your fingers so that it is completely coated and leave for a moment to

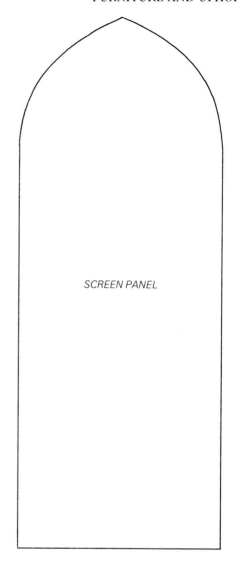

SCREEN PANEL

Fabric-covered screen

become tacky. Place the glued panels on the wrong side of three of the fabric panels, lining up with the drawn lines. Smooth the fabric on to the wood, easing out any wrinkles, and leave to dry.

When the glue is dry, trim the fabric around each panel with small sharp scissors to leave $\frac{1}{16}$ inch outside the wood. Apply fabric glue thinly and evenly around the edge of the wooden panel with your finger and leave to dry slightly. Fold the fabric edges over the wooden edges, clipping and trimming at the corners, and press the fabric smoothly on to the glued edge. When the glue is dry, cover the other side of each panel in the same way.

To hinge the panels, place one on top of the other, lined up precisely, and hold all three together with clothes pegs (pins) at top and bottom. Cut two pieces of silk ribbon $4\frac{1}{2}$ inches long. Apply glue with your finger to the back edges of one outside panel and the centre panel and place one piece of ribbon evenly down the length of both as shown. When the glue is dry, turn the three panels over and glue the second piece of ribbon to the other outside panel and the centre panel in the same way.

THE LULLABY
Lacy fringed shawl (Chapter 2), layette dress and bootees (Chapter 2), simple curtain (Chapter 5), fabric-covered screen, draped cradle (Chapter 7)

To edge the panels, working on one at a time, apply glue with a toothpick all around the edge. Beginning at the bottom, press narrow braid in place around the glued edge, covering the ribbon hinge and the raw edge of fabric and trimming the end to fit. Repeat for the other panels, taking care to keep the braid straight and even all the way round each section of the screen.

SCRAP SCREEN

This pattern and method can also be used to make a traditional scrap screen. As it is virtually impossible to find and cut pictures tiny enough to be realistic in this scale, compose each panel on a sheet of A4 paper, using the smallest 'scraps' you can find from magazine and catalogue illustrations. It is reasonably easy to work in this larger size and to compose authentically complex panels. Glue the scraps on to the paper to make three panels (or six if you prefer to have scraps on both sides of the screen). Take your panels to the local printer and have them reduced and colour photocopied to fit the screen panels. Make up the screen as described above, using your photocopied panels and dolls-house wallpaper instead of fabric.

DIVAN BED AND MATTRESS *(Shown on page 146)*

Our divans are standard-size single and double beds which are suitable for modern houses. With the addition of a headboard (see below), and the appropriate bedding, they might also be used in a period house. The bed base is made from $\frac{3}{4}$ inch

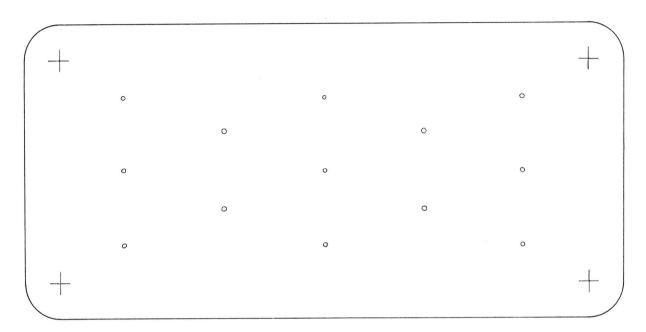

Divan beds and buttoning guide

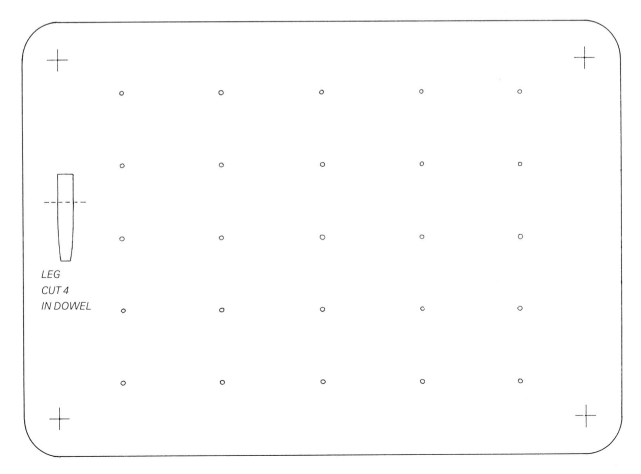

LEG
CUT 4
IN DOWEL

balsawood, covered with white felt (from needle-work and craft suppliers) and fabric, and the mattress is $\frac{1}{2}$ inch foam covered with white felt and fabric. You will also need Bondaweb, Heat 'n Bond or a similar lightweight bonding material. The bed legs can be made from $\frac{1}{4}$ inch wooden dowelling whittled to shape, or from plastic push-pins painted black or brown. Choose a lightweight cotton fabric for the covers in an appropriate print or 'ticking' stripe. The patterns for bedding in Chapter 5 will fit these beds. The method is the same for both single and double beds.

To make the base, cut the pattern in $\frac{3}{4}$ inch balsawood, in white felt and (optional) in tapestry canvas. Sand the edges and sides of the balsa smooth and glue the felt on to the top of the balsa. (Glue the tapestry canvas on to the underside of the balsa.) Cut a piece of fabric $\frac{1}{4}$ inch larger all round than the base, and place it over the felt. Glue the edges of the fabric to the sides of the base, smoothing the fabric taut and trimming, easing out and snipping any puckers at the corners. Cut a strip of fabric $1\frac{1}{2}$ inches wide on the straight grain, and long enough to fit around all sides of the base with a $\frac{1}{4}$ inch overlap. Cut a strip of Bondaweb (or similar) $\frac{3}{4}$ inch wide and the same length. Iron the Bondaweb to the centre of the fabric, then turn in both long edges to meet and iron the fabric to enclose the Bondaweb. Turn in $\frac{1}{8}$ inch at both short ends, glue, and press flat. Beginning at the centre of one end (top) of the base, glue the fabric strip around the sides of the base so that the ends meet with a butt join at the top end of the bed. Whittle dowelling legs to shape and drill holes in the underside of the base to receive them, or paint push-pin legs. Attach the legs with Superglue.

To make the mattress, cut the base pattern in $\frac{1}{2}$ inch foam, twice in white felt and, adding $\frac{1}{4}$ inch seam allowance, twice in fabric. Cut a strip of fabric $1\frac{1}{2}$ inches wide and long enough to fit around the base with $\frac{1}{2}$ inch overlap. Fold the fabric strip in half lengthwise and press. Fold in $\frac{1}{8}$ inch at both short ends and press. Beginning at the centre of one end (top), with right sides facing, stitch the double thickness (raw edges) of fabric strip to one mattress piece with a $\frac{1}{4}$ inch seam and the smallest machine stitches. Stitch the other (folded) edge of the doubled strip to the second mattress piece, leaving a 3 inch opening at the top end to allow for stuffing, and turn through. Glue one piece of white felt to each side of the foam and allow to dry. Slip the felt-covered foam inside the mattress case and slip stitch the opening and the short edges of the strip closed. Mark the positions of the buttons (shown on the base pattern), on both sides of the mattress with a Fadeaway marker pen (or similar) and work the buttons in French knots, using button thread and working from the centre of the mattress outward, making a French knot on both sides of the mattress. Pull the thread tightly enough to indent, but not enough to distort the shape of the mattress.

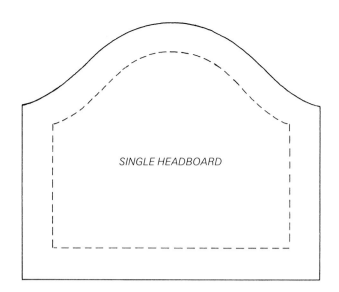

Padded or cane headboards

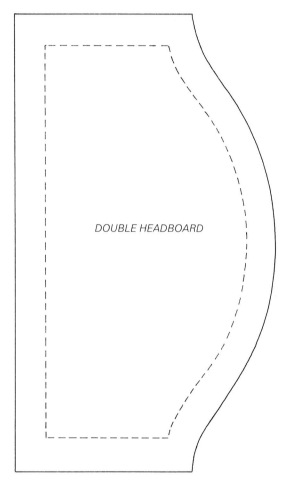

PADDED HEADBOARD

(Shown on page 146)

This headboard can be made to fit either the single or double divan bed, and can be plain, as shown, or quilted. You will need $\frac{1}{8}$ inch wood, thin stiff card, $\frac{1}{8}$ inch foam, and the fabric of your choice. Our headboard is covered in pale blue Liberty Tana lawn, but a small print – perhaps to match the bedspread – would be equally attractive. The headboard is fixed to the divan base with battens of fine woodstrip and small brass pins.

Cut the pattern in wood, in foam, and in thin card. Adding a ¼ inch seam allowance all round, cut a back cover and, adding a ½ inch seam allowance, cut a front cover in fabric, squarely on the straight grain. Spread fabric glue on the card, allow to become tacky, then centre the card on the back cover. Snip the curves and corners as necessary and fold the fabric edges and glue to the back of the card. Glue the foam on to the wood, allow to dry, and trim the foam edges rounded. Centre the padded wood on the front cover, and fold and glue the fabric edges to the back of the wood, making the cover as smooth and taut as possible, snipping curves and corners as necessary. Glue the back of the covered card to the back of the covered wood, running your thumbnail around the edges to make a smooth, tight join.

To fix the bedhead to the divan base, cut two battens 1½ inches long in fine woodstrip. Glue the top ¾ inch of each batten to the back of the headboard about ½ inch from each side and allow to dry. Fit the headboard on to the bed base and tap small pins through the lower part of the battens and into the bed base.

QUILTED HEADBOARD

To make the quilted version of the padded headboard, cut the wood, card, foam, and fabric as above, and cut a second front cover (backing) in fine lawn. Mark the dotted line shown on the pattern on the front cover in Fadeaway marker pen (or similar). Place the foam, centred on the backing fabric, and front cover over the foam and tack (baste) round the edge of the foam to hold in place. Quilt through the three layers, on the marked line with tiny machine stitches or back stitch. Trim the backing in line with the foam. Apply glue to the wood, allow to become tacky, then centre the quilted fabric on the wood. Fold and glue the fabric edges to the back of the wood, cover the card, and glue the two pieces together as above. Cut battens and fix the headboard to the divan as above.

CANE HEADBOARD

(Shown on page 111)

This rather elegant headboard can also be used for both the single and double divan beds. The frame is cut in ⅛ inch wood and the panel is tapestry canvas. The design is a simple traditional shape which is suitable for beds from the turn of the century to the present day and our version is in walnut-stained wood with a natural canvas panel. For a modern bedroom, consider white-painted wood with a white canvas panel.

Cut the pattern in wood and cut out the centre on

the dotted line with a fret saw. Sand the wood thoroughly and round off the edge of the cut-out and the outside edge on the front of the frame. Stain or paint the wood as required and apply several coats of wax polish to the front and edges, well buffed between each coat, or varnish. Cut the panel in tapestry canvas, ⅛ inch outside the dotted line on the pattern. Centre the canvas and glue in place on the back of the frame with craft glue. Pull one thread from scrap canvas and glue it around the outside edge of the panel to make a neat edge. Cut battens and glue and pin the bedhead to the divan base as described for the padded headboard.

DRAPED CRADLE

(Shown on page 142)

This pretty cradle (crib) is very simple to make, but if you choose a good lace with a very delicate pattern for the drapes it will complement even the grandest nursery. The cradle is made from ½ inch balsa and stiff cardboard (posterboard) which should be strong but pliable so that it will curve well. The canopy support is fine brass rod (from craft and model shops) and I have used white-painted push-pins for the legs. Our cradle is covered with 1½ inch wide satin ribbon in pale pink

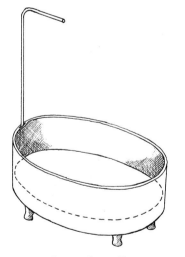

Draped cradle

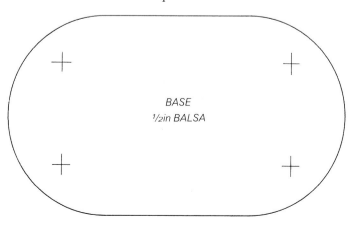

BASE
½in BALSA

and 1¼ inch wide ivory cotton lace – but you can of course choose other colours if you prefer. You will need 24 inches of ribbon and approximately 2 yards of lace. The bedding is made from scraps of fine white lawn, pink silk, and white lace with a small mattress made with ¼ inch foam.

To make the cradle, cut the base pattern in ½ inch balsa and sand the edges smooth. Cut a piece of card 1½ inches wide and long enough to fit around the base and meet edge-to-edge. Cut two pieces of 1½ inch ribbon to fit the card with a ½ inch seam allowance. Glue the card around the balsa base, with lower edges flush and tape the ends of the card securely together. Stitch the short ends of each piece of ribbon together (with a maximum ¼ inch seam) to make loops, and press the seam open. With wrong sides facing, and the seams at opposite ends, whip the two pieces of ribbon together along one edge with the smallest oversewing stitches. Ease the ribbon cover over the card, with one seam at the head of the cradle (outside) and the other at the foot of the cradle (inside). Pull the outside cover down so that the bottom edge is level with the bottom edge of the card, securing with a fine line of glue if necessary. Glue the bottom edge of the inside cover on to the base, snipping as necessary so that it lies flat. Paint the heads of the push-pins white and push and glue them into the underside of the base.

To make the lace cover, cut two pieces of lace to fit around the cradle plus ½ inch seam allowance. Cut one piece of lace 1½ times the length of the first pieces. Whip (overcast) the two shorter pieces

THE GUEST ROOM BED

Hot-water bottle cover, knitted teddy (Chapter 1), random-stripe rug (Chapter 3), hexagon bedspread (Chapter 4), sheets, pillows and pillowcases, blankets, towels (Chapter 5), divan bed and mattress, padded headboard (Chapter 7), laundry bin (Chapter 8)

together, straight edge to straight edge along the length. Make two rows of gathering along the straight edge of the longer piece and pull up the gathering to fit one scalloped edge of the shorter piece. Distribute the gathering evenly and stitch the two pieces of lace together with tiny running stitches so that the scalloped edge of the shorter piece overlaps the gathered edge, fasten off securely. Seam the cut edges of lace together to make a loop, trim, and neaten the seam with blanket stitching. Ease the lace cover over the cradle so that the bottom edge of the frill hangs fractionally below the bottom of the cradle. Make a row of gathering near the top (scalloped) edge of the cover and pull up gently, so that the lace folds smoothly over the top edge of the cradle, down the inside and the top edge is gathered over the base. Fasten off the gathering securely. Note that made by this method, the cover lace can be removed for washing.

To make the canopy support, cut a piece of fine brass rod 5 inches long and bend a right-angle 1 inch from one end. Using a large needle, toothpick or something similar, gently make a small hole down through the head end of the cradle between the card and the lining of ribbon. Ease the brass rod into this hole. If necessary, secure the rod with a little glue and/or a few small stitches.

To make the canopy, cut three pieces of lace 10½ inches long, carefully matching the pattern. Stitch the three pieces together with tiny running stitches, with the scalloped edge of one piece overlapping the straight edge of the next, and press. Fold the piece in half, and whip the straight edges together to form a 'hood'. Make a hem on the raw edge which will be the bottom edge of the canopy. Make two rows of gathering, close together, from the point of the 'hood' to the scalloped (front) edge of the canopy. Pull up the gathering evenly to 1¼ inches and fasten off. Wrap a little double-sided tape around the canopy support to secure it, and drape the canopy over the support, pressing the gathering on to the tape. Make silk ribbon bows and glue or stitch the bows to the canopy at each side and/or the top, and to the foot of the cradle to decorate as required.

To make the bedding, cut a mattress from the base pattern in ¼ inch foam. Cut two covers in white lawn with a ¼ inch seam allowance all round. Stitch the covers together, leaving an opening at one side for stuffing. Clip the curves and turn through. Slip the foam inside the cover and slip stitch the opening closed. Cut a top sheet in white lawn with sealed edges to fit the cradle and hem the top edge and whip or glue on narrow lace trimming. Make a tiny pillow in pink silk, stuffed very lightly, and whip narrow lace trimming around the edges. Using the base pattern as a guide, cut a piece of wadding (batting) for the quilt, ⅔ the length of the base. Cut two covers in silk with a ¼ inch seam allowance. Stitch the covers together, leaving a small opening on the straight edge. Clip the curves and turn through. Slip the wadding inside the cover and slip stitch the opening closed. Trim the quilt with a row or two of machine or hand stitching through all three layers around the edge, and add an embroidered motif.

UPHOLSTERED FURNITURE

Buttoned wing chair

These patterns for authentic upholstered chairs and sofas (couches) are based on lifesize pieces of antique furniture and are designed to be made by more experienced miniaturists. If you have an electric vibro saw and hand drill, you will find them useful, but the furniture can be made with the basic hand tools discussed at the beginning of this chapter. You will also need wire snips, a craft knife with a selection of sharp new blades and small wood files or needle files.

The choice of upholstery fabric is important. It should be appropriate for the period in colour and pattern and the pattern should be as small in scale as possible. Joan has used lifesize upholstery fabrics which make very realistic furniture, but because of their thickness and tendency to fray, these fabrics are difficult to work with. You may find it easier to use a lighter-weight, woven cotton fabric – or fine leather – for your first venture. It is important to match the pattern on fabric for the various parts of the chair, especially if you use a fabric with a larger pattern such as the one shown on our Georgian wing chair and sofa. The simplest way to do this is to cut pattern templates for the back, seat, arms, and sides in tracing paper which can be placed over the fabric – showing the pattern clearly. The method for assembling the furniture is similar for all pieces — the various parts are cut and padded, and covered individually before the chair or sofa is assembled.

BUTTONED WING CHAIR *(Shown on page 150)*

This splendid leather-upholstered chair with its buttoned back and cabriole legs would look most impressive in any dolls-house study. If you have never made upholstered furniture before, you will find leather easier to work with than fabric because it stretches slightly and does not fray. Joan has chosen dark green, but glove leather is available in a wide range of colours (see Stockists) – though the chair looks most authentic in rich dark colours.

To make the chair you will need $\frac{1}{8}$ inch balsa-wood for the back and sides, $\frac{3}{16}$ inch balsa for the base and $\frac{3}{8}$ inch balsa dowel for the arms. The back legs are cut from $\frac{3}{16}$ inch thick basswood and the front cabriole legs from $\frac{5}{8}$ inch square basswood – or you could use a pair of 1 inch long commercial cabriole legs. The stretchers are cut from $\frac{1}{8}$ inch dowel. For padding you will need $\frac{1}{8}$, $\frac{1}{4}$ and $\frac{1}{2}$ inch thick foam. The leather for the covers should be good quality glove leather and our chair is finished with tiny brass nails (see Stockists).

Cut two sides and a back on the straight grain in $\frac{1}{8}$ inch balsawood. Cut a base in $\frac{3}{16}$ inch balsa. Sand all edges smooth.

Make a card template and use it to mark the cabriole legs on two adjacent sides of the length of

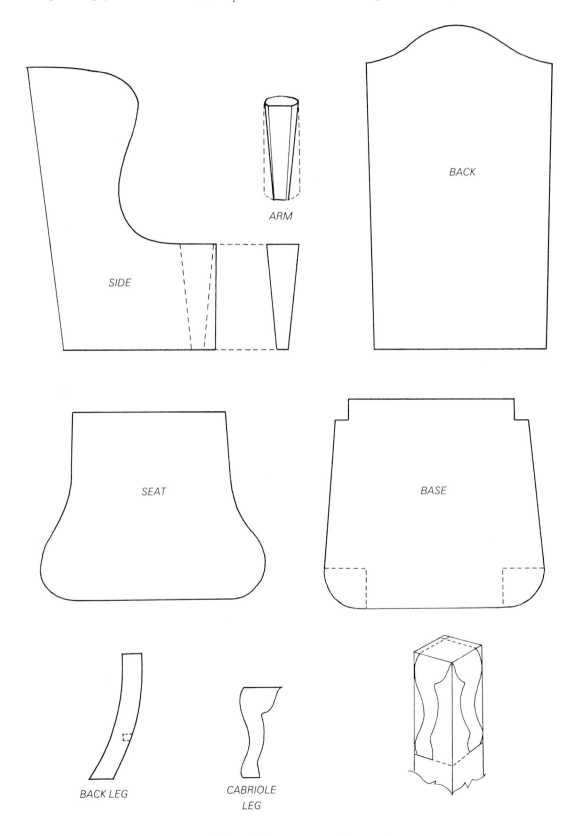

Wing chair – patterns for wood

$\frac{5}{8}$ inch square wood as shown. Use a fret saw (or jewellers' saw) to cut along all four marked lines, then cut across the bottom to shorten the leg to the correct length. Use needle files and abrasive paper to refine the shaping of the leg and foot.

Cut two back legs in $\frac{3}{16}$ inch wood and sand thoroughly. Drill $\frac{1}{16}$ inch holes into the back legs as shown to accommodate the stretchers.

Cut two arms from $\frac{3}{8}$ inch balsa dowel and use a craft knife and sandpaper to shape the arms into cones as shown. Sand one side of each arm to make a flat surface. Glue the arms to the outer sides as shown on the pattern. Trim away the excess wood on the sides with a craft knife and use abrasive paper to shape a smooth curve around the front edge of the arm and side.

To assemble the base and legs, glue the back legs into the notches in the base so that the top edges are flush, and allow to dry. Glue the cabriole legs to the underside of the base as shown. To give added support to the cabriole legs, drill carefully through the base and $\frac{1}{8}$ inch into the legs with a $\frac{1}{16}$ inch bit and glue small pegs, which can be whittled from toothpicks, into the holes.

Cut two 2 inch long stretchers in $\frac{1}{8}$ inch dowel. Use a craft knife to shape one end of each stretcher as shown, to fit into the holes in the back legs. Try the stretchers into the back legs and mark the position on the front legs where the stretcher will fit. Drill holes in the cabriole legs to receive the stretchers. Mark correct length on the stretchers, allowing $\frac{1}{32}$ inch to fit into the cabriole legs. Trim and shape the other end of the stretchers. Drill a hole $\frac{1}{2}$ inch from the front of each stretcher to receive the cross-stretcher. Apply a little glue to the holes in the legs and ease the side stretchers in place – ensuring that the holes for the cross-stretcher are aligned. Cut, shape and glue the cross-stretcher between the side-stretchers. Stain and polish the leg assembly as required, and leave until it is thoroughly dry.

Cut $\frac{1}{2}$ inch foam padding for the back and $\frac{1}{4}$ inch padding for the sides. Glue the foam to the inner faces of the back and sides. Note that on the sides, the foam is positioned $\frac{1}{8}$ inch from the back edge to allow room for the back when the chair is assembled. Roll and glue the foam around the curve of the arms and trim where the arm meets the outer side. Trim the foam to round off the edges around each piece.

Use the guide to mark the positions of the 'buttons' on the OUTSIDE of the back in pencil.

Cut the inner back cover in leather and place over the padding. Apply glue to the side and top edges of the wood and press the leather firmly and smoothly in place, trimming the corners and easing out puckers. Trim away any excess leather flush with the back edge of the wood. Allow the glue to dry thoroughly.

To button the back, follow your pencilled guide and, working one row at a time from the top, push

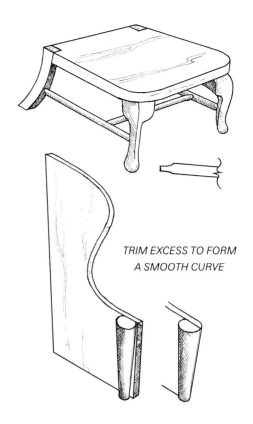

TRIM EXCESS TO FORM
A SMOOTH CURVE

Wing chair – assembly

glass-headed pins through the leather, foam, and wood from the front, to guide the buttoning. Use a fine leather-needle and one strand of matching strong thread. Knot the thread and insert the needle, from the back, through the pinhole to the front. Remove the pin, make a small stitch through the leather, and return the needle through the pinhole to the back. Pull the thread tight to indent the leather. Make each button in the row in the same way, then pin and stitch the next row, down to the bottom.

Cut a pair of covers for the inner sides in leather and place over the padding. Glue the straight back edge of each side on to the exposed $\frac{1}{8}$ inch of wood. Apply glue to the edges of the wood and press the leather firmly and smoothly in place, easing out any puckers. Roll and glue the leather around the curve of the arms and trim neatly where the arm meets the outer side. Trim away any excess leather flush with the outside edge of the wood.

To assemble the back and sides, apply glue to the unpadded back edge of each side and to the side edges of the back. Position the back between the sides so that the top and bottom edges of each piece line up. Hold the pieces temporarily with strips of masking tape around the outside. Apply glue to the lower edges and position the arms and back on the wooden base ensuring that the outside edges are flush. Hold with masking tape and support as necessary until the glue dries. To strengthen the assembly, push dressmakers' pins (or fine wire)

THE NEEDLEWOMAN'S CORNER
Round table centre (Chapter 1), Georgian cushion (Chapter 3), lampshade (Chapter 5), square stool, buttoned wing chair (Chapter 7), bead rosebowl, lined sewing basket (Chapter 8)

through the base and $\frac{3}{8}$ inch into the sides and back – two pins in each piece. Glue the pins in place with Superglue and snip off the protruding ends.

Cut a cover for the front edge of the base in leather, centre the cover and glue it in place to fit between the outside arms. Snip, fold, and glue the excess leather on to the top and underside of the wooden base.

Cut padding for the outside of the chair (inner line) in $\frac{1}{8}$ inch foam and glue it in place to leave $\frac{1}{8}$ inch of wood around the edges.

Cut a cover for the outside of the chair (outer line) in leather. Apply glue to the unpadded $\frac{1}{8}$ inch around the chair and position the leather over the padding. Press the leather firmly and smoothly in place, trimming as necessary so that the outside cover edge meets the inner cover edge neatly. Fold and glue the lower edges on to the underside of the base, trimming the back corners around the legs.

Cut a pair of arm rests (inner line) in thin card and (outer line) in leather. Glue the card to the inside of the leather and snip, fold, and glue the edges of the leather to the back of the card. Glue the arm rests on to the arms.

Cut a seat in firm card and in $\frac{1}{2}$ inch foam. Glue the foam on to the card and snip to round off the foam edges. Cut a seat cover in leather and place over the foam. Snip, fold, and glue the edges of the cover to the underside of the card. Glue the seat on to the base.

To insert the tiny brass 'nails', make holes with a fine darning needle held in a pin-vice, $\frac{1}{8}$ inch apart all around the edges of the back, sides, base, and arm rests and push the brass pins in place.

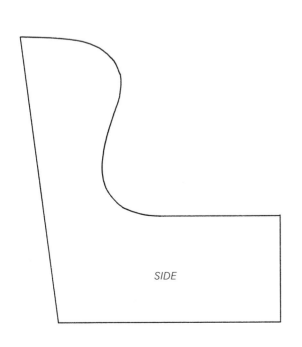

SIDE

BACK

BUTTONING GUIDE

Wing chair – patterns for padding

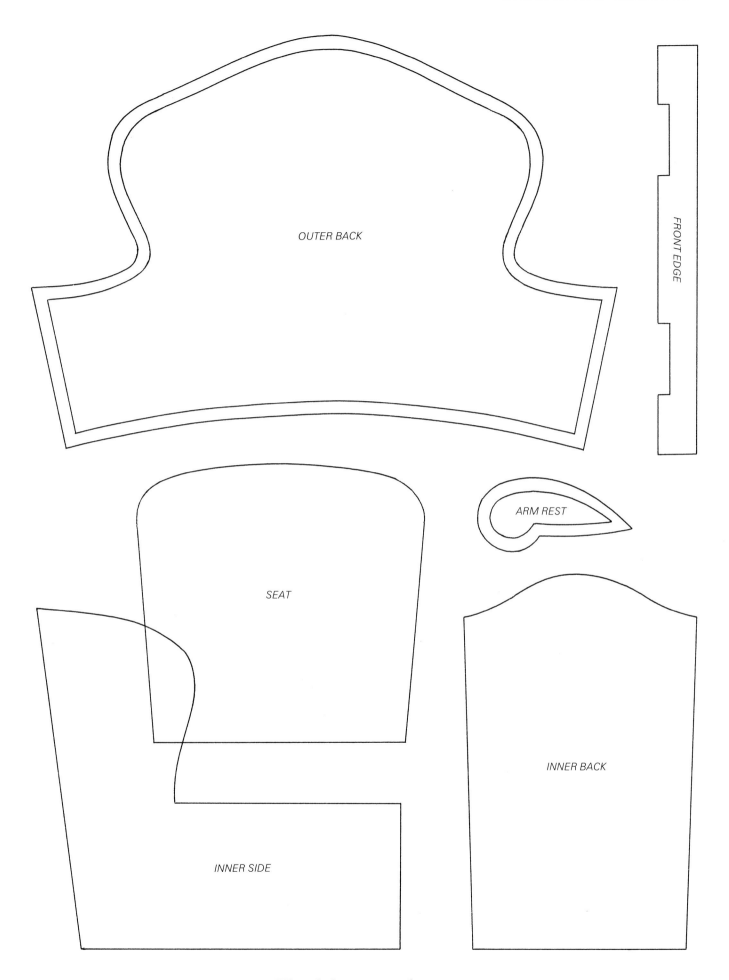

Wing chair – patterns for covers

151

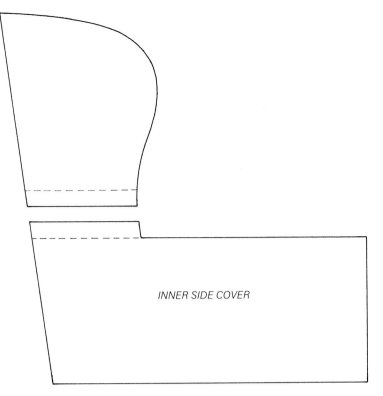

INNER SIDE COVER

Georgian wing chair – inner side cover

 GEORGIAN WING CHAIR *(Shown on page 102)*

The Georgian wing chair is essentially the same in construction as the leather-covered chair (above), but is covered with fabric. Joan has used an upholstery fabric with a pattern of stripes and flowers in shades of cream, green, and pink and trimmed the chair with a silky cord taken from lampshade-trimming braid. This chair is made in basswood rather than balsa, and you will need $\frac{1}{8}$ inch wood for the back and sides and $\frac{3}{16}$ inch wood for the base. The back legs and stretchers are made from $\frac{3}{16}$ inch square wood and $\frac{1}{8}$ inch dowel and the front legs from $\frac{5}{8}$ inch square wood – or use a pair of 1 inch long commercial cabriole legs. The padding is $\frac{1}{8}$ and $\frac{1}{4}$ inch foam. Rather than repeating the pattern, the reader is referred to the figures and instructions given for the leather-covered chair where relevant.

Cut two sides and a back in $\frac{1}{8}$ inch wood and a base in $\frac{3}{16}$ inch wood. Make cabriole front legs and cut back legs. Cut two arms in $\frac{3}{8}$ inch balsa dowel, and assemble the arms. Assemble, stain, and polish the leg assembly as for the leather-covered chair.

Cut padding for the back and sides in $\frac{1}{4}$ inch foam and glue padding on to wood.

Cut covers for the inner back, outer back, and the inner sides in fabric. Note that the inner side covers are cut in two pieces as the fabric will not stretch sufficiently to round the curve of the arm in one piece. Glue the fabric over the padding for the inner back. Then glue fabric over padding to the

inner sides, stroking the lower edge of the upper piece over the top edge of the lower piece to smooth the join neatly. Ensure that the fabric is firmly and smoothly glued to the edges of the wood and trim any excess fabric so that it is flush with the back edge of the wood.

Assemble the back and sides, and position the arms and back on to the wooden base as for the leather-covered chair. Cover the front edge of the chair with fabric, cut to fit between the outside arms, and snip, fold, and glue the excess fabric to the top and underside of the base. Cut padding in $\frac{1}{8}$ inch foam, and cover in fabric for the outside of the chair. Glue in place, ensuring that the outside cover edge meets the inner cover edge neatly, and trim excess fabric. Fold and glue the lower edges on to the underside of the base, trimming and gluing the back corners around the legs. Cut the arm rests in card, and a pair of covers in fabric. Assemble the arm rests and glue in place. Cut a seat in firm card and in $\frac{1}{2}$ inch foam, glue the foam on to the card and trim to round off foam edges. Cut seat cover in fabric and cover the seat. Glue seat on to base.

Apply a fine line of glue to the meeting edges of the covers around the back, sides and arm rests of the chair and press cord trimming in place to cover the raw edge. Apply cord trimming to the lower edge of the base, all round the chair. Neaten the underside of the chair with a piece of black iron-on interfacing (or similar), cut to fit and glued in place to cover the raw edges of fabric.

 GEORGIAN SOFA

(Shown on page 102)

This elegant little sofa (couch) might be covered and trimmed to match a wing chair for the drawing room as Joan has done, or covered to complement a bedroom. The sofa is made in $\frac{1}{8}$ inch basswood with back legs of $\frac{3}{16}$ inch wood. The front cabriole

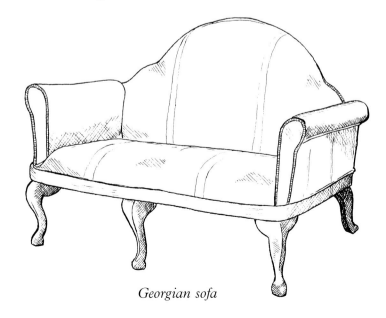

Georgian sofa

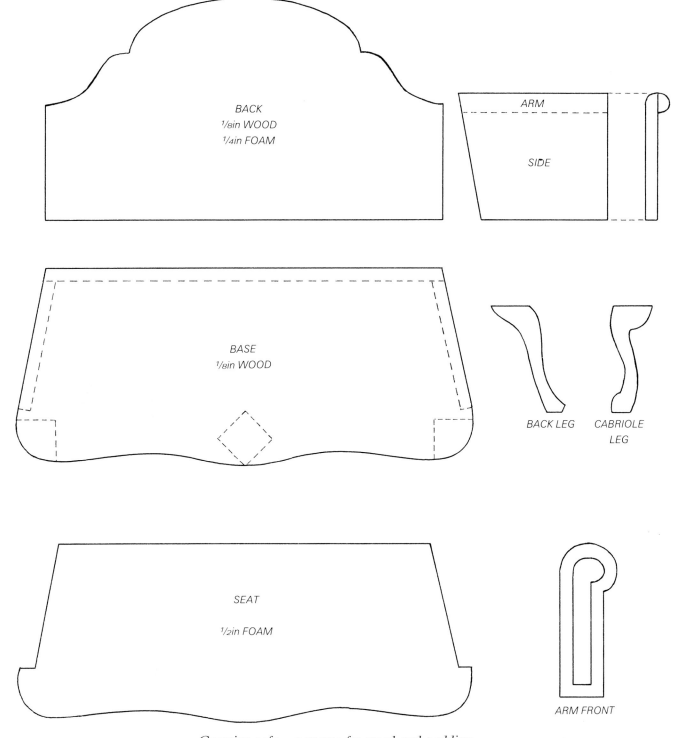

BACK
1/8in WOOD
1/4in FOAM

ARM

SIDE

BASE
1/8in WOOD

BACK LEG

CABRIOLE
LEG

SEAT

1/2in FOAM

ARM FRONT

Georgian sofa – patterns for wood and padding

legs are made in ⅝ inch wood, or you could use three commercial 1 inch cabriole legs. The seat of the sofa is faced with a ⅜ inch wide strip of mahogany wood veneer and the arms are ³⁄₁₆ inch balsa dowel. The padding is ¼ and ½ inch foam. The method of assembly is essentially the same as for the buttoned wing chair on page 147, so the reader is referred to this pattern where relevant.

Cut the base, back and sides in ⅛ inch wood. Cut three back legs in ³⁄₁₆ inch wood and make three cabriole legs as for the wing chair. Glue and pin the legs to the underside of the base as shown. Cut a strip of mahogany wood veneer to fit, and glue on

to the front and sides of the base with the lower edges flush. Hold the veneer in place with masking tape to fit tightly around the curves until the glue is dry. Cut and glue veneer to the back of the base in the same way. Sand thoroughly, and stain and polish the base assembly as required.

Cut a pair of arms in ³⁄₁₆ inch dowel, sand one side of each arm to make a flat surface, and glue the arms to the outer sides as shown. Cut padding in ¼ inch foam for the inner back, and the sides and arms, and glue the padding on to the wood, rolling the foam around the arms and trimming to taper (chamfer) where the arm meets the outer side. Cut

THE VICTORIAN PARLOUR

Small rug or throw, round table centre, square antimacassar
(Chapter 1), Victorian flower cushions, needlepoint fire
screen (Chapter 3), simple curtains, tablecloths, fur rug
(Chapter 5), cotton-reel stool, square stool, fabric-covered screen,
Victorian armchair and sofa (Chapter 7), bead and button
ornaments, ribbon workbox (Chapter 8)

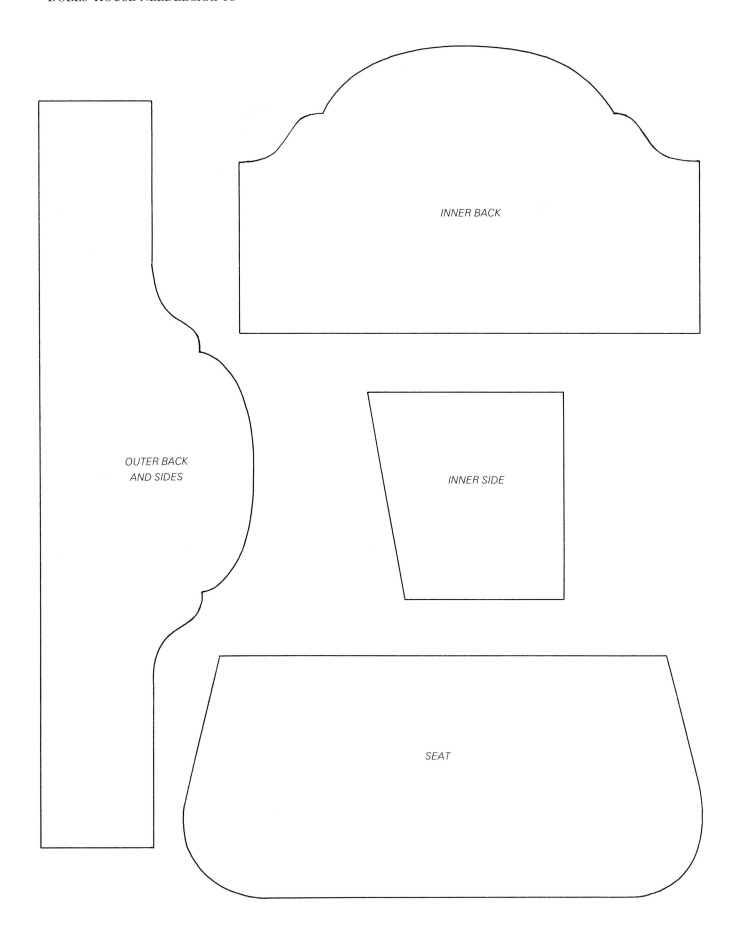

INNER BACK

OUTER BACK
AND SIDES

INNER SIDE

SEAT

Georgian sofa – patterns for covers

a cover in fabric for the inner back and glue the cover over the padding, ensuring that the fabric is smoothly and firmly glued to the edge of the wood. Trim any excess fabric flush with the back edge of the wood. Cut a pair of inner side covers in fabric, and glue the covers over the padding, rolling the fabric around the arm and trimming and gluing to fit neatly where the arm meets the outer side. Fold and glue excess fabric at the front and back edges around the edge, as smoothly as possible, and trim.

Assemble the back and sides as for the wing chair and glue the back and sides on to the base to fit inside the veneered edge. Cut arm fronts (inner line) in card, and a pair of covers (outer line) in fabric. Cover the arm fronts and glue them on to the front edge of each arm.

Cut a seat in firm card and check to ensure that it fits on to the base behind the veneer edging. Pad the seat with $\frac{1}{2}$ inch foam and cover with fabric as for the wing chair. Glue the seat on to the base. Apply a fine line of glue to the meeting edges of fabric around the sofa back, arms, arm fronts, and lower edge and press cord trimming in place to cover the raw edges.

CHAISE-LONGUE

(Shown on page 78)

The Regency style of this elegant chaise-longue, or day-bed, makes it appropriate for any house of the early nineteenth century to the present. Joan has covered our chaise-longue in gold silk trimmed with picot braid to complement the Victorian bedroom, but you could use any fabric you prefer, though plain colours or stripes in rich or pastel colours are most typical of the style. The chaise-longue is made in $\frac{1}{8}$ inch basswood on a frame of $\frac{1}{4}$ inch square wood, with arms of $\frac{3}{8}$ inch dowel. The 'carving' is made with small pieces of commercial moulding (such as Shortwood Carvings No AG 10). The padding is $\frac{1}{4}$ and $\frac{1}{2}$ inch foam. The chaise-longue can be made left- or right-handed as you prefer, by simply reversing the patterns.

Cut a base in $\frac{1}{8}$ inch wood. Cut two frame sides and two frame ends in $\frac{1}{4}$ inch square wood and assemble the base and the frame as shown, with all the top edges flush.

Cut two left arm supports and two right arm

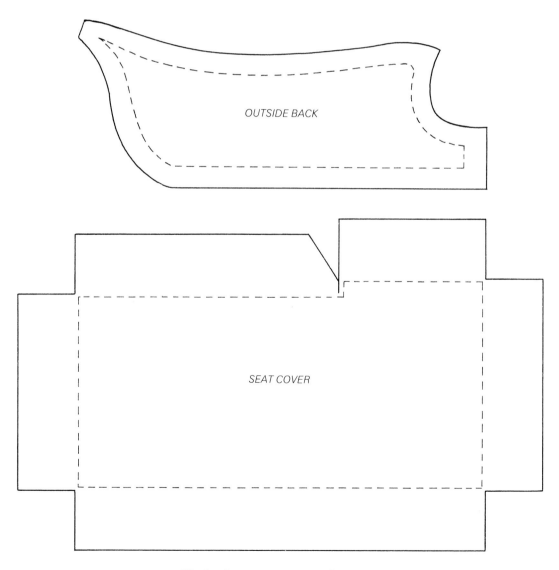

Chaise-longue – patterns for covers

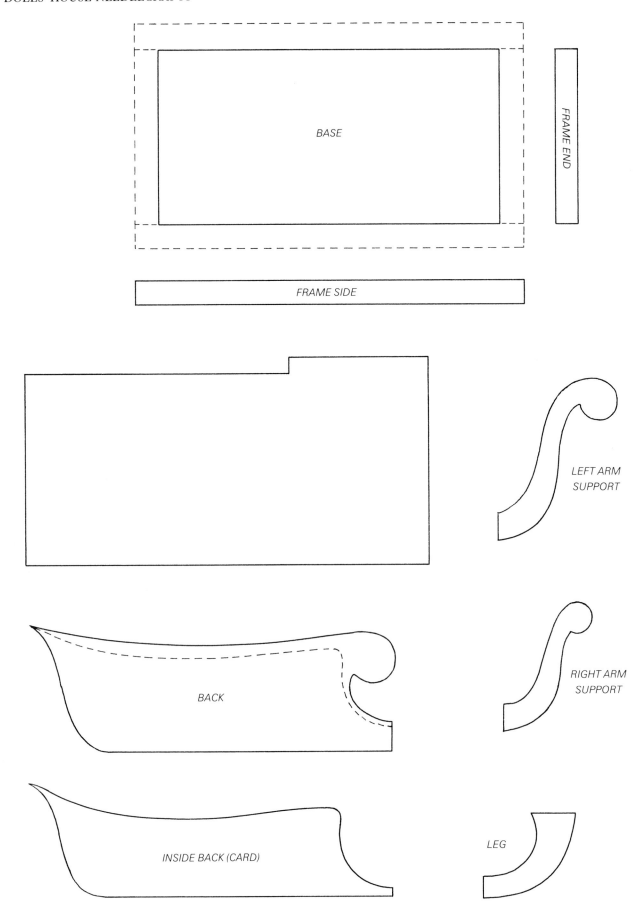

BASE

FRAME END

FRAME SIDE

LEFT ARM SUPPORT

RIGHT ARM SUPPORT

BACK

INSIDE BACK (CARD)

LEG

Chaise-longue – patterns for wood and padding

supports in ⅛ inch wood. Pin and glue the arm supports to the base frame as shown. Cut one piece of ⅜ inch dowelling to fit for each arm, and glue the dowelling between the left and right arm supports as shown. Cut strips of light thin card (postcard) to fit between the arm supports, from the top of the base, around the dowel arm to the underside. Glue one edge of the card strip to the underside of the arm, roll the card over the arm and glue the other edge to the top of the base as shown, on both left and right arms.

Cut a back in ⅛ inch wood, drill and pin the back on to the base frame with back edges flush but do not glue the back in place at this stage. Cut four legs in ⅛ inch wood, drill and pin the legs to the base frame with back and front edges flush but do not glue the legs in place at this stage.

Sand the wooden parts of the chaise-longue thoroughly then apply woodstain as required. If you are using applied mouldings, sand the back of each piece to make the mouldings as thin as possible, trim to the required size and shape and glue the mouldings on to the wood with Superglue, used sparingly so that it does not seep. Apply sanding sealer and sand again. Paint the mouldings with gouache or acrylic paint to match the wood-stain. When the paint is dry, apply polish or varnish as required.

Cut strips of ¼ inch foam to fit the arms, and glue one edge of the foam to the top of the base. Glue the foam to the inner side of the card, rolled over the arm, and down the outside of the card as shown. Cut strips of fabric to fit and cover the padded card arms. Glue one end of fabric to the top of the base, apply glue lightly to the side edges of the foam and allow to dry a little and become tacky. Smooth the fabric on to the foam, around the dowelling to shape the arm, and glue the other end of fabric to the outside edge of the base frame.

Cut an inside back in thin card, and with a ¼ inch allowance all round, in fabric. Wrap the card with fabric, snipping as necessary, and glue the edges to the back of the card. Cut an outside back in card

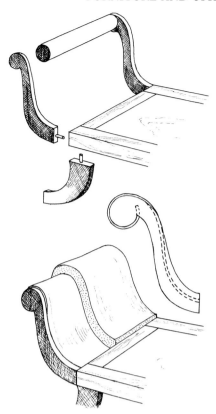

Chaise-longue – arm assembly

(inner line) and fabric (outer line) and make up in the same way. Glue the inside back and outside back to the centre of the back of the chaise-longue to leave a surround of wood. Glue the back on to the base frame. Glue the legs to the base frame.

Cut a seat in card and in ½ inch foam, and glue foam on to card. Cut a seat cover in fabric. Wrap the cover around the padded card with mitred corners and the edges glued to the back of the card. Glue the seat on to the base.

Apply a fine line of glue to the top edges of the inside back and arms, all edges of the outside back and the lower edges of the seat, and press picot braid trimming in place. If you wish to make a bolster cushion for your chaise-longue, see the method and adapt the pattern on page 65.

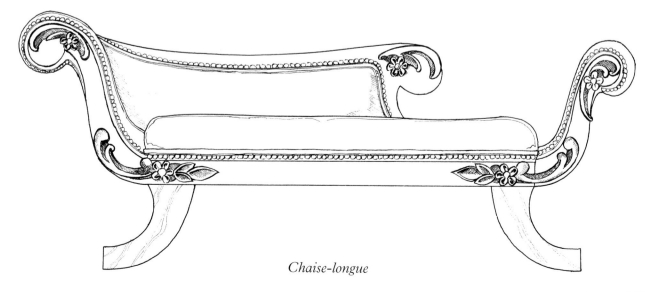

Chaise-longue

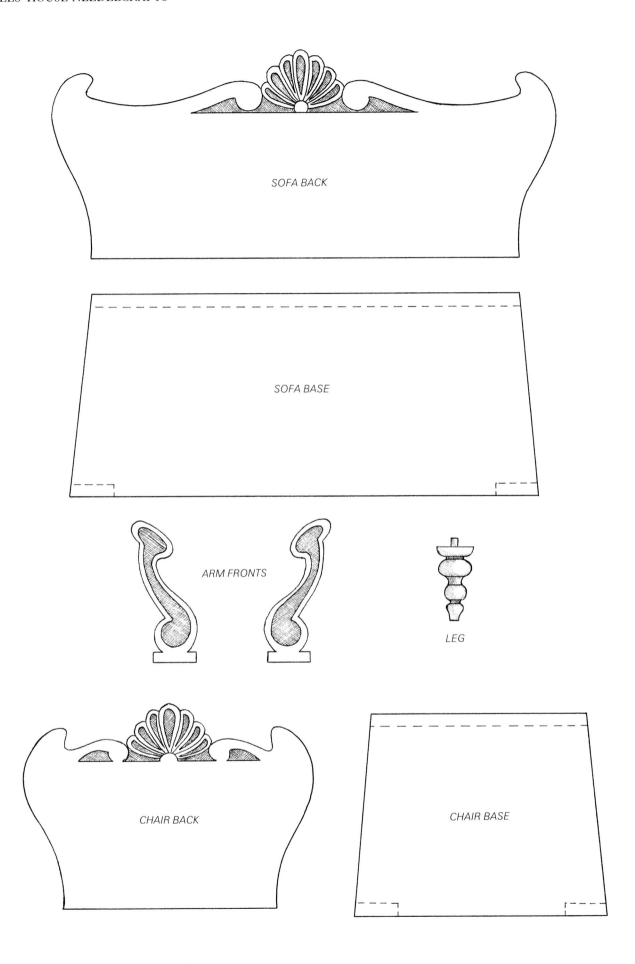

Victorian armchair and sofa – patterns for wood

VICTORIAN ARMCHAIR AND SOFA *(Shown on page 154)*

Victorian armchair

The style of this matching chair and sofa (couch) with their carved and turned legs is typically Victorian. Joan has used a dull-gold upholstery fabric for the covers and a narrow picot braid for trimming, but a sombre-coloured velveteen would be equally appropriate. You will need $\frac{1}{8}$ inch basswood to make the furniture with $\frac{3}{8}$ inch dowel for the arms and a piece of $\frac{1}{4}$ inch wide moulded woodstrip to trim the front edges. The carving can

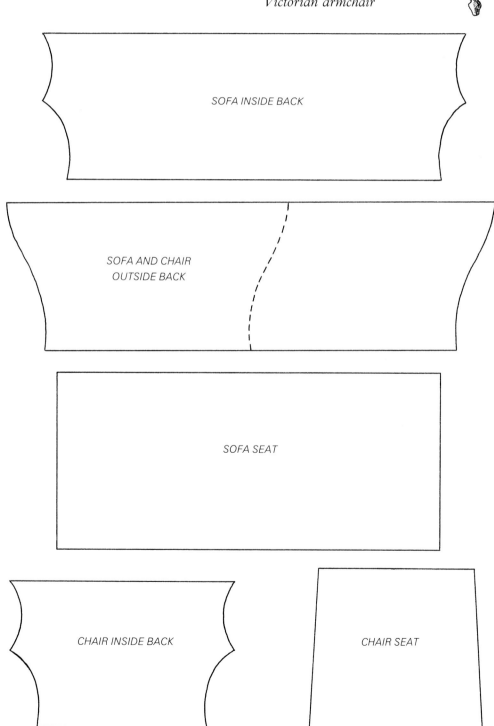

Victorian armchair and sofa – patterns for padding

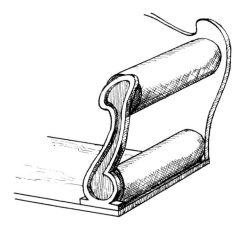

Victorian armchair and sofa – arm assembly

be done with an electric drill, or by hand with a craft knife with a 10A blade and a small pointed file. The chair and sofa legs are turned from $\frac{1}{2}$ inch dowel, but you could use commercial $\frac{3}{4}$ inch turned legs if you prefer. The method is the same for both chair and sofa.

Trace the patterns for the back and a pair of arm fronts on to the wood, squarely along the grain, and work the carving before cutting the pieces. Pare away the shaded areas shown on the pattern with a small burr in the electric drill, or a craft knife, and refine the shaping with a fine pointed file. When the carving is complete, cut the back and arm fronts and cut the base. Glue and pin (dressmakers' pins or fine wire) the back on to the base, lining up the back edges. Glue the arm fronts on to the base, lining up the front corners. Cut four pieces of $\frac{3}{8}$ inch dowel to fit, and glue in place between the top and bottom of each arm front and the back as shown. Cut a piece of moulded woodstrip to fit, and glue it to the front edge of the base. Turn four legs in $\frac{1}{2}$ inch dowel as shown. Glue and pin the legs to the base. (If you have turned the legs as shown, drill holes to accommodate the pegs.) Sand thoroughly and stain and polish the chair/sofa until the required effect is achieved.

Cut two pieces of $\frac{1}{4}$ inch foam to fit between the arm front and the back. Glue one edge of the foam along the underside of the top dowel on each arm, roll the foam over the dowel to the outside of the arm, and glue the other edge to the bottom dowel, to fill the sides of the chair. Trim the foam and chamfer the edges neatly. Cut the arm covers in fabric, as a strip wide enough to fit between the arm fronts and the back, and long enough to fit from the inside bottom edge of the arm, over the arm, to the outside bottom edge. Apply fabric glue sparingly to the foam padding on each arm and allow it to dry a little and become tacky. Wrap the fabric strip over the foam and smooth it on to the foam around the top dowel to define the shape of the arm. Glue both bottom edges of fabric securely in place.

Cut an inside back in thin firm card and in $\frac{1}{4}$ inch foam and glue the foam on to the card. Cut an inside back cover in fabric with a $\frac{1}{2}$ inch allowance all round, and wrap the padded card with fabric, trimmed as necessary and with the edges glued to the back of the card. Glue the covered inside back to the back of the chair/sofa. Cut an outside back in card, and an outside back cover in fabric with a $\frac{1}{4}$ inch allowance all round. Cover the card with fabric, and glue the covered outside back to the back of the chair/sofa.

Cut a seat in card and in $\frac{1}{2}$ inch foam and glue the foam on to the card. Cut a seat cover to fit in fabric and wrap the fabric around the padded card, mitring the corners and trimming as necessary, and glue the edges to the back of the card. Glue the seat on to the base of the chair/sofa.

Apply a fine line of glue around all edges of the outer back and the arms, the top edge of the inner back, and front edges of the seat and press picot braid trimming in place.

LOUIS ARMCHAIR
(Shown on page 135)

This classic Louis armchair is a very versatile style which looks charming in an eighteenth-century drawing room, will fit happily into a nineteenth-century room and would add an elegant touch to a modern house. Joan has made hand-embroidered covers in shades of pink and green trimmed with a toning picot braid, but you could use a lightweight fabric if you prefer. The chair is made in $\frac{1}{8}$ inch basswood, and the legs from $\frac{5}{8}$ inch square wood – or you could use four commercial 1 inch cabriole legs. The shaped aprons which trim the underside of the chair are cut in $\frac{1}{2}$ inch square and $\frac{3}{32}$ inch wood and the sides are rounded with $\frac{1}{4}$ inch dowel. The embroidered covers are worked in DMC or

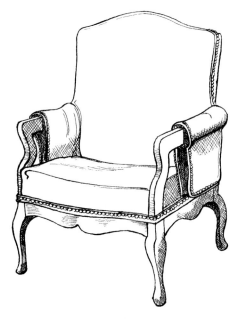

Louis armchair

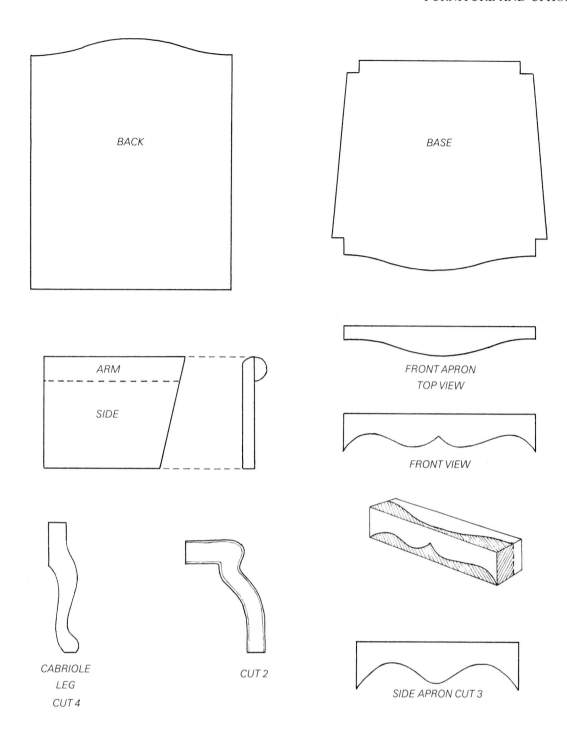

Louis armchair – patterns for wood and padding

similar cotton thread (floss) in four shades of each colour on silk gauze with 38 holes to the inch and the padding is $\frac{1}{8}$, $\frac{1}{4}$ and $\frac{1}{2}$ inch foam.

Trace the patterns for the covers on to 38-hole silk gauze with a well-sharpened pencil, allowing plenty of space around each piece for cutting out. Work the embroidery with one strand of thread in four shades of each colour – from dark to light – in Florentine stitch, taking care to line up the pattern on the back and seat covers, and both side covers. The back and outer sides of the chair can be covered with a toning plain fabric if you prefer.

Cut a base, a back, two sides, and two arms in $\frac{1}{8}$

inch wood. Cut four cabriole legs as for the wing chair (page 147) in $\frac{5}{8}$ inch square wood. Cut a front apron in $\frac{1}{2}$ inch square wood, and side and back aprons in $\frac{3}{32}$ inch wood. Cut $\frac{1}{4}$ inch dowel arms to fit, with one side sanded flat, and glue to the wooden sides as shown.

Glue the legs into the notches in the base with top edges flush. Glue the side and back aprons to the edges of the base, to fit between the legs, with outside edges flush. Glue the front apron to the underside of the base to fit between the front legs as shown. Use a small file to refine the shaping so that there is a smooth curve from leg into apron. Sand

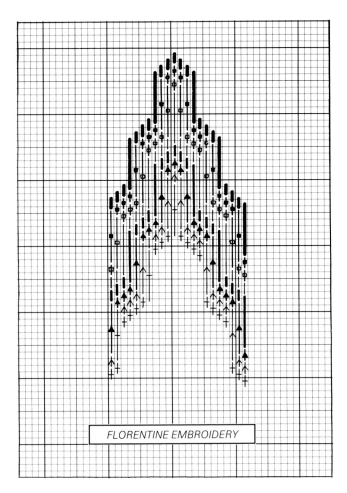

FLORENTINE EMBROIDERY

the edges. Cut the back cover in (embroidered) fabric, with $\frac{1}{2}$ inch allowance all round, and cover the padded back, smoothing the cover taut over the padding and trimming and glueing the fabric edges on to the back of the wood. Cut the side covers in (embroidered) fabric with a $\frac{1}{4}$ inch allowance all round, mitre the corners and fold in the allowance all round. Cover the padded sides by gluing one edge of the fabric to the lower edge of the dowel and wrapping the fabric around the dowel and down the inner side.

Assemble the back and sides (as for the wing chair on page 147) and glue and pin the back and sides on to the base. Cut padding for the outer back and sides in $\frac{1}{8}$ inch foam and glue on to the wood. Cut a cover for the outer back and sides in fabric and place over the padding, gluing the edges all round to meet the inner back and side covers. Trim as necessary. Cut a strip of fabric $\frac{1}{4}$ inch wide to fit around the front edge of the chair from side to side. Fold in both long edges to meet, and press. Glue the folded strip around the front edge of the base with the ends meeting the outer side cover. Glue and pin the arms to the front edges of the sides and on to the base as shown.

Cut a seat to fit in stiff card and in $\frac{1}{2}$ inch foam and glue the foam on to the card. Cut the seat cover in (embroidered) fabric with $\frac{1}{2}$ inch allowance all round, and wrap the cover around the padded card with mitred corners and edges glued to the back of the card. Apply a fine line of glue all round the meeting edges of the outer back and side covers, and press picot braid trimming in place to cover the raw edge. Apply glue and press the trimming around the front edges of each side. Glue the seat on to the base. Apply glue, and press trimming to the top edge of the front base cover with the ends meeting the trimming around the front edge of the sides.

thoroughly, and stain and polish, or varnish, the assembly as required. Sand the arms to round off the top and front edges and stain and polish the arms to match the leg assembly.

Cut back padding in $\frac{1}{4}$ inch foam and glue on to the back. Cut $\frac{1}{4}$ inch foam to fit and glue to each side from the lower edge of the dowel, rolled over the dowel, to the inside. Trim the foam to chamfer

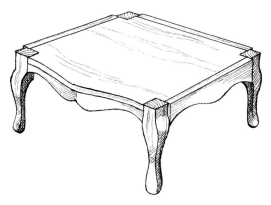

Louis armchair – base and leg assembly

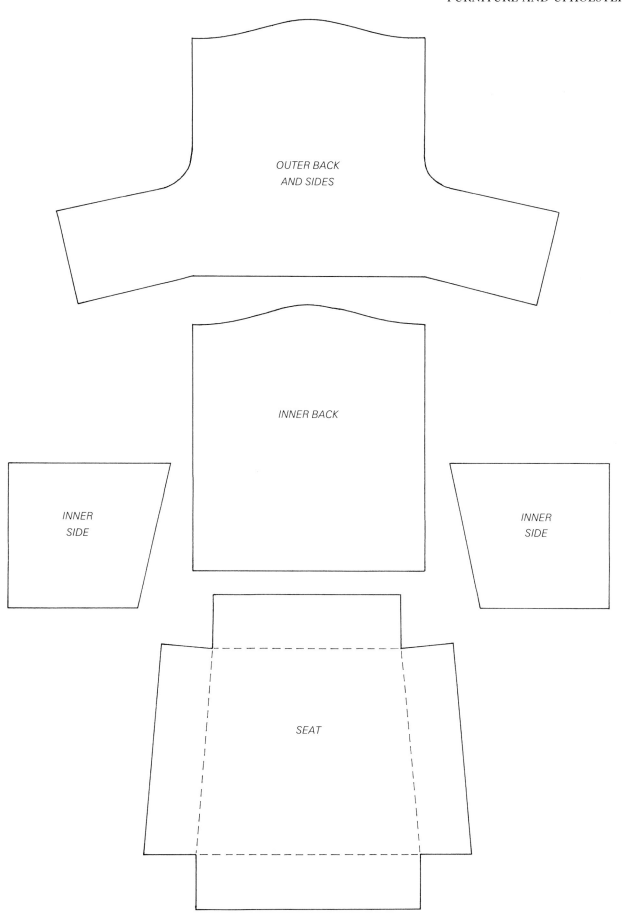

Louis armchair – patterns for covers

CHAPTER EIGHT

Crafts and Accessories

The projects in this chapter cover a range of crafts including macramé and basketwork, and simple accessories made from scraps of ribbon or beads and buttons. As hoarding is an instinct with miniaturists, readers will probably have the necessary materials already 'in stock' to make most of these projects.

There is such a vast range of beads in glass, ceramic, wood, clay, and plastic available from specialist shops and suppliers that we are almost spoiled for choice. If you buy a catalogue in which the beads are illustrated full size, it is virtually a book of ideas for dolls-house ornaments (see Stockists). Old beads from broken jewellery can be found in junk shops or jumble (rummage) sales and can usually be bought very cheaply. There are lots of bead projects here to start you off, but this is one area where the raw material is often the inspiration – so don't be afraid to 'do your own thing'. Buttons too, when viewed with a miniaturist's eye, offer endless possibilities. Most haberdashery (notions)

departments have a good selection, but raid friends' button boxes and try charity (thrift) shops and jumble sales as well. Ribbon also suggests a host of ideas – try your local department store or craft and needlework supplier for new ribbons, but look out for old ribbon too as this is often finer, softer and in more subtle colours than modern ribbon.

The other materials used in this chapter, including fabrics, lace, and wood, embroidery threads and canvas, and crochet cotton, have been discussed in previous chapters. Any other specific materials or tools are mentioned in this chapter with the relevant project.

Imagination rather than skill is often the key to good miniature accessories. Most of the projects in this chapter are simple and many of them take only minutes to make but if you choose your materials well, the finished result can be a pretty, or witty, accessory which will add charm and a touch of life to any room in your dolls' house.

BEADS AND BUTTONS

To make most of the ornaments described below you will need Superglue – and will probably find the non-drip gel variety easiest to use. Rather than using it straight from the tube, squeeze a drop of glue on to a piece of scrap card and apply it to the bead with the point of a wooden toothpick. To stand properly, beads with rounded bases should be sanded flat. The easiest way to do this is to tape a piece of abrasive paper on to the work surface, hold the bead upright and rub the bottom firmly across the abrasive paper – from side to side, then with a circular motion. You will need a medium-grade paper for wood, plastic, or clay beads, a rough-grade for glass, ceramic, or metal beads, and a fine-grade for smoothing. Ceramic and glass beads need some effort to sand flat, but be careful with clay which sands very easily. *Take care not to inhale the dust created by sanding beads.*

If you are gluing a number of beads together to make a jar or bottle, work upward from the base and, where possible, support the beads with a pin or toothpick through the centre holes to help align them. Sand the base flat first, or glue the bead on to

a flat button base and secure the bead or button to the work surface with a little double-sided tape. Glue the next bead or jewellery finding or fitting on to the first, and allow it to dry before adding more. Sight at eye level to ensure that you glue each piece upright, and allow the glue to dry at each stage before adding the next.

ORNAMENTS AND ACCESSORIES

(Shown on page 171)

Our collection of vases, perfume bottles, and ornaments are made from a range of beads, buttons, and jewellery findings such as jump and split rings, and bell caps. You will also need dressmakers' pins, glass-headed pins, and wire snips to make these items.

Our 'African pottery' is simply clay beads with the bases sanded flat. The 'Greek' vases are small round beads in red and white, or red, white, and

black painted clay with the base sanded flat and a matching small tubular bead glued to the top as the neck of the vase. The matching lidded jar is a similar round bead with the base sanded and a painted line on the bead used to indicate the 'lid' of the jar – the knob is a black glass-headed pin, cut to ¼ inch and glued into the hole in the bead.

Our 'silver' rosebowl, tobacco box, spirit flask, and 'chased-silver' jar are all silvered plastic beads. The rosebowl is a ribbed ring, filled with Fimo, or similar modelling clay, to give it weight, with a posy of ribbon roses or tiny dried flowers pushed into the clay. The jars are urn-shaped beads with the bottoms sanded flat and small flat spacers glued

Bead and button ornaments

THE SMOKING ROOM
Spray of berries cushion, wall hanging, embroidered screen panels, tiger-skin rug (Chapter 3), gentleman's dressing-gown (Chapter 6), cotton-reel stool (Chapter 7), bead vase, hookah pipe, art-nouveau lamp (Chapter 8)

and pinned with dressmakers' pins as lids. The tobacco box is a large patterned spacer with a similar pinned lid. The 'silver' candlesticks are a pair of hexagonal tubes filled with clay for weight and dolls-house candles pushed into the top end.

The 'Chinese' vases are blue and white ceramic beads glued on to bases of small black or white flat buttons. The lids are gilt disc-shaped beads on gilt split rings with white glass-headed pins as knobs.

The perfume bottles are made from small glass beads with the bottoms sanded flat or glued on to split ring or jump ring bases. Lids are tiny glass beads, spacers, or discs, and tiny gilt or silver bell caps secured with dressmakers' pins.

Other simple accessories include glass buttons used as ashtrays with a smidgin of cigarette ash for realism, and a clock made from a plastic clock-face button sanded as thin as possible and glued to a flat

167

wooden button. The large 'copper' plant-pot is a coppered plastic bead with a large hole. The base was sanded flat, the bead filled with clay, and a plant, made from painted paper leaves on wire stems, was pushed into the clay.

The 'decorator' tree is a compressed cotton or polystyrene ball glued on to a wooden toothpick. To make the coating, squeeze a model landscape tree or bush over a saucer to loosen some of the green fibre coating. Mix a little fabric glue with green paint and coat the bead all over. Roll the glued bead in the fibre and leave to dry. Our trees are set in clay in commercial dolls-house flowerpots but you might use a toothpaste-tube cap painted matt terracotta as an alternative. Our Christmas tree baubles are gilt beads wired and glued together and hung from fuse-wire loops.

A large wooden or glass button will make a good fruit bowl filled with fruit modelled in Fimo or a similar medium. Flat buttons with small rims will make frames for pictures cut from magazine or catalogue illustrations. Small dish-shaped buttons with flat bases will make a soap dish with a small piece of real soap or bath sponge; or a powder bowl with a tiny cotton ball trimmed with a ribbon bow as a powder puff. A small bowl-shaped button can be filled with white soap as a shaving bowl with a shaving brush cut and trimmed from the end of a nail varnish or typing correction-fluid brush. (Clean the brush with nail varnish remover or correction fluid thinner.)

Try making a box of tissues from a $\frac{1}{2}$ inch diameter tubular wooden bead (or a cube-shaped bead), covered with a scrap of dolls-house wall-paper. Cut a $\frac{3}{4}$ inch square of paper tissue and push it on to the hole in the top of the bead with a toothpick. A baby's rattle can be made from a tiny, pretty bead with a handle of twisted wire or a piece of toothpick glued into the hole. A small round bead with the holes filled will make a child's ball, and small square beads with the holes filled will make building blocks.

HOOKAH PIPE

(Shown on page 167)

This amusing accessory for the Victorian gentleman's study was suggested by the shape and size of the brass-coated plastic bead. Hookah pipes were made in a variety of different forms and are often shown in contemporary illustrations, so choose a large bead, approximately 1–1½ inches tall, which resembles the type of pipe you wish to make. You will also need a dolls-house eggcup, goblet, or dish to make the bowl of the pipe and a length of cord – I have used a soft tubular cord striped in gold and black with fine parcel string pulled through it.

Sand the base of the bead flat so that it will stand perfectly upright. Drill a hole into the body of the

bead, approximately halfway up, at a downward angle using a drill bit fractionally larger than the diameter of your cord. Cut a 6 inch length of cord, and soak approximately 1 inch at each end with fabric or craft glue to stiffen it and allow to dry thoroughly. Glue one stiffened end of the cord firmly into the hole in the bead so that it protrudes at an upright angle. If necessary, bind the first inch of cord with fine fuse wire to further stiffen the angle. Roll and squeeze the other end of the cord in your fingers to narrow it – if you have used string covered with tubular cord, scrape away a little cord to expose the string – to represent a mouthpiece. Glue the bowl on to the top of the bead with Superglue.

ART-NOUVEAU LAMP *(Shown on page 167)*

This type of lamp was very fashionable in the early twentieth century when electricity was a new invention and lamps were often more decorative than functional. You will need a white metal figure (available from dolls-house shops), and a flat button for the base. The lampshades are three flower-shaped pink glass beads with small, round, plain glass beads as light bulbs. You will also need three 3 inch silver head pins and bronze-coloured model paint (Humbrol enamel or similar).

Clean any flashing on the white metal figure with a craft knife, and glue the figure on to the button base with Superglue. Paint the assembly with bronze paint, and allow to dry. Thread one round bead and one flower bead on to each head pin and secure them with Superglue. Twist the head pins together from 1½ inches below the shades to the bottom. Gently bend the top ½ inch of each head pin to splay the shades outward. Paint the head pin stems bronze and allow to dry. Trim the stem ends so that the shades are 2 inches above the base, and glue the twisted wire to the back of the figure and to the base with Superglue. Support as necessary as the glue dries. Apply a second coat of bronze paint to the figure, base, and head pin stems, and allow to

Hookah pipe, art-nouveau lamp and bead ornaments

dry thoroughly. Apply a little black-lead polish to the painted parts of the lamp with a cotton-wool bud and buff until it gleams – taking care not to get polish on the shades.

BEAD-BASE LAMP

(Shown on page 171)

This simple lamp base is designed to support a shade made from the patterns on page 116. A variety of different bases is shown in pictures in the book, and you can use almost any bead you wish, though it should be in proportion to the size of the shade. You will need a scrap of thin stiff card, a toothpick, and a compass.

Bead-base lamp

Sand the base of the bead if necessary so that it stands perfectly upright. If the bead has a very large hole or is particularly lightweight, fill the hole with Plasticine, Blu-tack, or clay, and push the toothpick into this – otherwise, glue the toothpick into the hole. Try the shade in place and cut the top end of the toothpick so that it is $\frac{1}{2}$ inch shorter than the shade. Use a compass to draw a circle and mark the centre on thin card. The diameter of the circle should fit inside the shade to support it $\frac{1}{4}$–$\frac{1}{2}$ inch above the bottom of the shade. Cut the card disc and pierce a hole in the centre just large enough to fit on to the toothpick. Try the shade in place to judge the correct height for the disc, and glue the disc in place – ensuring that it is horizontal – and allow to dry. Apply a thin smear of glue around the edge of the disc and position the lampshade.

JUG COVER

(Shown on page 186)

This little cover, used to keep flies from the contents of a jug or bowl, can be made from a circular motif cut from lace, or in net, tulle, or muslin (cheesecloth), edged with blanket stitch or

very narrow lace trimming. The tiny glass beads (seed beads) around the edge which weight the cover can all be the same colour or, alternatively, in different colours.

Cut a circular motif in fine lace approximately 1 inch in diameter. Or trace a circle approximately $\frac{3}{4}$ inch in diameter on to net or tulle, seal the cutting line with Fraycheck (or similar), and allow to dry. Cut out the circle and stitch narrow lace trimming around the outside edge with whipping or running stitches, and press flat. Or trace a 1 inch diameter circle on to fine muslin or lawn, seal the cutting line with Fraycheck (or similar), cut out and blanket stitch around the outside edge.

Stitch tiny glass beads, evenly spaced, around the outside edge. Soak the cover in water and mould over the jug or bowl – secured with a small elastic band until dry.

BEADWORK CUSHION *(Shown on page 59)*

Beadwork was very fashionable among the leisured ladies of the nineteenth century and most Victorian homes displayed at least one example of the craft. Our beadwork cushion is worked on Aida fabric with 14 holes to the inch, with seed beads in four colours. Dora has used two shades of pink and gold on an emerald green background, but you can, of course, choose any colours you prefer. The cushion is backed with silk in a colour to match the background beads. For the best results, we recommend dyeing the Aida with drawing ink (available from art shops) to match the background beads and the backing fabric.

Paint a piece of Aida, approximately 3 inches square, with drawing ink and allow to dry thoroughly. Using matching cotton thread, begin at one end of the top row of the pattern. Bring the needle up through the hole, thread a bead on to the needle, and make a diagonal stitch across the block – making a half cross stitch. Repeat the stitch through the bead so that it is securely held in place and lies

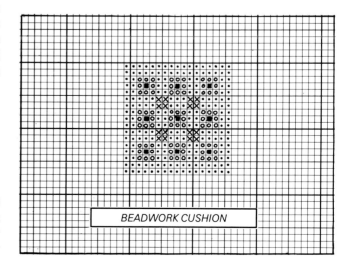

BEADWORK CUSHION

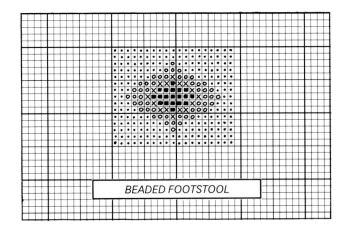

flat on the fabric. Work the pattern in rows, picking up the appropriate coloured bead as you go and stitching through each bead twice. When the pattern is complete, trim the fabric leaving an allowance of four holes outside the edge of beads. Fold in the fabric, in line with the outside row of beads, with mitred corners, and press. Cut a silk backing for the cushion with ¼ inch seam allowance all round, on the straight grain of the fabric. Turn in the seam allowance with mitred corners, and press. With wrong sides facing, place the beaded fabric and the backing together and slip stitch around three of the sides. Stuff the cushion lightly and slip stitch the fourth side closed.

BEADED FOOTSTOOL

(Shown on page 59)

This splendid beadwork footstool would grace any Victorian house. Dora has made our stool in pinks, gold, and green to match the cushion above, but you may prefer other colours. You will need a piece of ¼ inch thick wood, 1¼ x 1 inch for the stool seat, Aida with 14 holes to the inch for the cover, and ⅜ inch wide satin ribbon and picot braid to match the background colour for trimming. The stool might have bun feet made from brown or black round wooden beads, or you could use a set of commercial turned legs as Dora has done. For the best results, dye the Aida with drawing ink to match the colour of the background beads.

Paint a 4 inch square of Aida with drawing ink and allow to dry thoroughly. Using matching cotton thread, begin at one end of the top row of the pattern. Bring the needle up through the hole, pick up the bead, and make a diagonal stitch across the block – a half cross stitch. Repeat this stitch through

the bead to secure it firmly in place so that it lies flat on the fabric. Work the pattern in rows from the top downward, picking up the appropriate coloured beads as you go and working each stitch twice. When the pattern is complete, trim the fabric all round to four holes outside the outer row of beads. Cut a piece of Bondaweb (or similar) to fit, and iron it on to the back of the work. Cut a square notch, four holes deep, in each corner of the work so that the cover will fit over the stool seat.

Cut a piece of wadding (batting) or ¼ inch foam to pad the top of the seat and glue the padding on to the wood. Trim the top edges of the padding to make a rounded edge. Apply fabric glue to the outside edges of the underside of the seat cover and place the cover over the padding. Smooth the cover over the padding and press the glued edges firmly on to the sides of the wooden seat so that the notched corners of fabric meet neatly at each corner. Allow to dry, then trim the lower edge of fabric flush with the lower edge of the wooden sides. Glue satin ribbon around the sides of the stool seat to cover the fabric. Glue picot braid around the top edge of the ribbon to meet the beadwork – and around the lower edge as required. Glue the beads or turned legs to the underside of the stool seat.

RIBBONCRAFT

BELL PULL

(Shown on page 102)

This simple bell pull, used to summon the Victorian maid from the kitchen, is made from embroidered ribbon ¼ or ½ inch wide. You will also need a little stranded embroidery thread (floss) in a matching or toning colour and a small metal ring such as a jewellery jump ring. The method can also be used with strips of fabric (see Isobel's tapestry bell pull on page 154, which was made from a piece of fabric cut from an old handbag).

Cut a piece of ribbon approximately 6 inches

long. Stitch or glue a ½ inch hem at the top and fold and press the bottom end to make a point. Stitch or glue the point to secure. Make a small tassel in embroidery thread and stitch it to the point. Stitch the jump ring to the top of the bell pull.

Or cut a strip of fabric approximately 6 inches long and wide enough to turn in ¼ inch down both sides. Turn in and press the side edges, turn a ½ inch hem at the top and make a point at the bottom end, trimming as necessary and mitring the corners. Press, glue or tack (baste) to secure the folded edges and cut a backing in iron-on interfacing to fit. Iron the backing on to the bell pull. Make a tassel and stitch it and the jump ring as above.

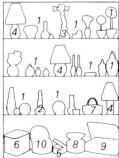

THE BEAD AND BASKET COLLECTION

1 Ornaments and accessories, 2 hookah pipe, 3 art-nouveau lamp, 4 bead-base lamp with lampshade, 5 raffia basket, 6 log basket, 7 baby basket, 8 lined sewing basket, 9 picnic hamper, 10 fishing creel (Chapter 8)

CUSHIONS AND ANTIMACASSARS

(Shown on page 59)

These simple cushions are made from scraps of ribbon 1–1½ inches wide. Almost any type of ribbon can be used including nylon, cotton, silk, satin, and velvet in plain colours or with woven or printed patterns. Plain cushions can be overlaid with lace or trimmed with embroidered motifs, and any cushion might have a fine cord edging or tassels made from embroidery thread (floss). Matching antimacassars, are trimmed with narrow lace.

Cut a piece of ribbon exactly twice as long as the width of the ribbon plus a small seam allowance, squarely on the grain of the fabric. Seal the cut edges with Fraycheck (or similar) and allow to dry. Seam the short ends of ribbon together, clip the ends, turn through, and press the seam open. Fold the ribbon so that any pattern is well centred on the front of the cushion, or the seam is at the centre of the back of the cushion, and press. Using matching thread and tiny stitches, oversew the edges together down one side, picking up only the outside woven edge of the ribbon. (To make a virtually invisible seam, use thread pulled from scrap ribbon.) Stuff the cushion lightly with kapok or polyester and oversew the second edge.

To make an antimacassar, mark a piece of ribbon approximately 2½ inches long, squarely on the grain of the fabric. Seal the cutting lines with Fraycheck (or similar), allow to dry, and cut. Stitch or glue narrow lace to one edge, centred carefully. Seal the lace ends and trim.

WORKBOX AND GLOVE BOX

(Shown on page 59)

These little boxes are made from thin stiff cardboard covered with embroidered ribbon. The patterns are designed for a workbox in ¾ inch wide ribbon and a glove box in ⅜ inch wide ribbon, but they can easily be adapted for other widths. The boxes are lined with plain ribbon in a matching or toning colour in the same width as the cover. To make needlework accessories to fill the workbox, see page 180, and for gloves see page 130.

Cut the patterns for box and lid in thin card, score the folding lines with a pointed tool, and fold the box to shape. Secure the corners with tape.

To make the workbox, cut two pieces of ¾ inch wide ribbon, 2½ inches long, matching the pattern on both pieces. Cover one side of the card lid with fabric glue and allow the glue to dry a little and become tacky. Place the ribbon strips on the lid so that they meet at the centre, with a ¼ inch overhang

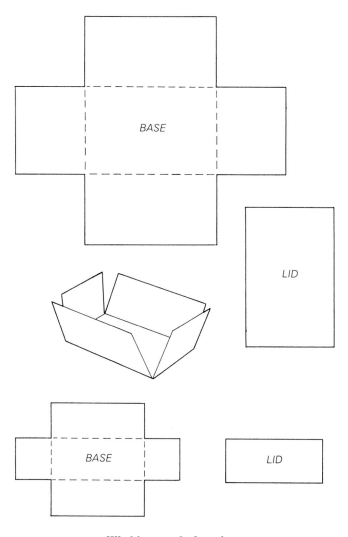

Workbox and glove box

on the back edge. Coat the other side of the card with glue, fold the ribbon over the front edge and smooth it on to the card so that the ends overhang the back edge. Glue the overhanging ends of ribbon wrong sides together, allow to dry and trim the overhang to ¼ inch – this will be the 'hinge' of the lid. Press the edges of ribbon together at the sides of the lid so that no card shows, and fold and press the hinge to the underside of the lid. Define the back edge of the card sharply through the ribbon by running your thumbnail or a pointed tool along the edge to score the fold.

To cover the box, cut a piece of ribbon 5 inches long with sealed ends. Apply glue to the sides and front of the box (not to the back), allow to become tacky, then wrap the ribbon around the sides and front, centring carefully so that the cut ends of ribbon will meet at the centre back of the box. Press the ribbon in place, leaving both ends free, and allow to dry. Fit the lid on the box and hold in place with a small elastic band. Glue the hinge to the back of the box, and allow to dry. Glue the free ends of ribbon to the back of the box, over the hinge, so that the ends meet at the centre back, and allow to dry thoroughly.

Cut a plain ribbon lining with sealed ends, and glue it around the inside sides of the box, with the cut ends meeting at one front corner. Cut a piece of ribbon to fit with sealed ends and glue it to the inside base of the box. Press the edges of the cover and lining together so that no card shows around the top of the box. Cut a piece of ribbon with sealed ends to line the lid and glue it in place, so that it does not cover the hinge. Add a small bead, stitched to the front of the box with a worked loop on the front edge of the lid, if required.

To make the glove box, cut three pieces of $\frac{3}{8}$ inch wide ribbon $1\frac{1}{2}$ inches long, and cover the lid and make the hinge as above. Cut a piece of ribbon $3\frac{1}{4}$ inches long and cover the sides and front of the box. Glue the hinge in place and cover the back of the box as above. Line the box and add bead and loop fastening as required.

 NIGHTDRESS CASE *(Shown on page 59)*

The nightdress case is made in $1\frac{1}{2}$ inch wide satin or silk ribbon, trimmed with narrow lace and a silk ribbon bow.

Trace the pattern on to the ribbon, squarely on the grain. Seal the cutting lines, allow to dry, and cut out. Glue narrow lace trimming on to the wrong side of the ribbon as shown, mitring or easing around the corners, and seal the cut ends of lace. Fold the untrimmed part of the ribbon, with wrong

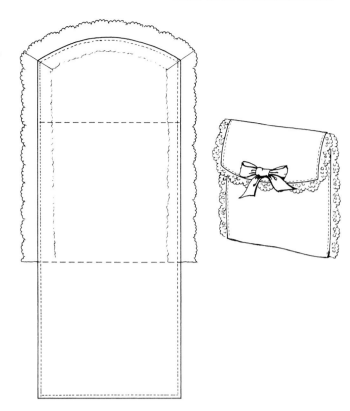

Nightdress case

sides facing, on to the trimmed ribbon and press. With thread to match the lace, and tiny stitches, oversew the side edges together, picking up just the outside woven edges of the ribbon through the lace. Fold the flap and press. Make a tiny ribbon bow and stitch or glue it to the centre of the flap.

MACRAMÉ

Our three macramé projects were designed and made by Heather Stringer who makes very skilful miniature macramé and teaches the craft. Heather recommends working the projects on a 2 inch thick block of polystyrene approximately 6 x 8 inches. You will also need glass-headed pins, a needle threader, and a darning needle. Given a basic knowledge of the craft, you should have no difficulty with these patterns as the technique in miniature is virtually the same as in lifesize.

 CURTAIN TIE-BACKS

(Shown on page 59)

These simple curtain ties will add a touch of elegance to window curtains or bed hangings in any house from the eighteenth century to the present day. Our curtain ties are made in Anchor (or similar) stranded cotton (floss) in two toning shades of crimson, but you could use any toning or contrasting colours you prefer.

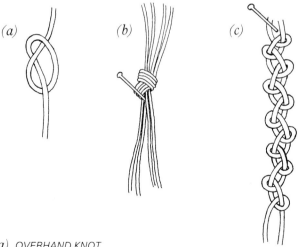

a) OVERHAND KNOT

b) TYING ON

c) ALTERNATING HALF-HITCH KNOT CHAIN

Curtain tie-backs

Cut two 12 inch lengths of each colour (four lengths) – these are referred to as 'cords'. Do not separate the strands in each cord. Knot the four cords together, approximately 4 inches from one end, with a loose overhand knot – do not tighten the knot (A). Push a pin into the polystyrene work-block and place the knotted cords over the pin, with one cord in each colour at either side of the pin.

Working both cords on each side as one, hold the right-hand cord straight downward and work the left-hand cord over it, then hold the left-hand cord straight downward and work the right-hand cord over it – to make an alternating chain of half-hitch knots (B). Note that for clarity, the knots shown are not fully tightened. Work 2½ inches of half-hitch chain, then remove the pin and untie the overhand knot at the beginning of the work. Fold the tie-back in half, ensuring that the ends are even, and tie all cords together with an overhand knot. Trim the ends and tease out the strands with a darning needle to make 'tassels'. Trim the tassels to length as required.

PLANT-POT HANGER *(Shown on page 59)*

Our pot hanger is designed to fit a commercial plant-pot approximately 1 inch in diameter which can be hung from a hook or bracket in the dolls-house kitchen, bathroom or conservatory. Our plant is made from a commercial kit and glued into oasis, or similar plant-arranging material, in the pot. You will need cotton crochet thread (Coats No 20 or similar), in the colour of your choice, six small glass or wooden beads, and a ¼ inch diameter metal ring – such as a jewellery jump ring.

Cut 24 inches of thread, and, using a darning needle, work blanket stitch around the metal ring,

Plant-pot hanger

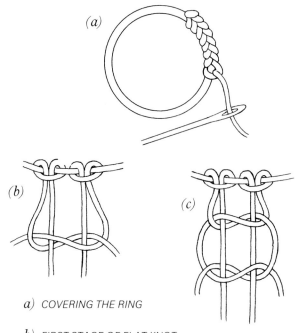

a) *COVERING THE RING*

b) *FIRST STAGE OF FLAT KNOT*

c) *SECOND STAGE OF FLAT KNOT*

Plant-pot hanger – method

working in the loose end of thread as you go (a). Fasten off by running the end of thread in and out of the outer edge, using the needle threader. Pin the covered ring on to the polystyrene work-block.

Cut six cords 48 inches long. Pass two cords together through the ring, ensuring that the four ends are equal, knot the cords together with an overhand knot, and tighten the knot close to the ring. Repeat with the other two pairs of cords so that you have three sets of four cords spaced evenly around the ring.

Working with each set of cords in turn, make ten flat knots as shown in (b) then thread a bead on to the two middle cords using the needle threader. Make a flat knot with the two outer cords under the bead. Make a twist by working only the first stage of the flat knot twenty times, then work one flat knot. Thread the next bead as before, then work ten more flat knots to complete the support. (Work all three sets of cords as above.)

Take the outside cords from the first and second sets and knot them together ½ inch down with an overhand knot (c), but do not over-tighten the knot. Repeat for each set of cords. Unpin the work at this stage and check that the pot fits into the holder with the knots just under the rim as shown, and adjust as necessary. Tighten the knots, with the pot in the holder, and work the remainder of the holder around the pot. Take the outside cords from each set and make another overhand knot ½ inch from, and between, the first round. Finish by bringing all the cords under the pot and knotting them together with an overhand knot. Trim the ends to the required length to make a tassel.

HAMMOCK

(Shown on page 15)

This splendid hammock is perfect for lazy summer afternoons in the garden, and during the winter it could be stored in the attic or the cupboard under the stairs. Our hammock is made in soft gimp thread (Strutts or similar), with stretchers of wooden toothpick or fine dowelling. You will also need two ¼ inch metal rings, four small wooden or plastic beads, and squared paper (graph paper or hand-drawn ½ inch squares).

Cut two pieces of toothpick or dowelling 2¼ inches long and glue a small wooden bead on to each end of each piece. Allow to dry, then sand the stretchers lightly to smooth off any roughness.

Cut a piece of squared paper approximately 8 x 4 inches and pin it on to the work-block as a guide for squaring up the work. Mark out the hammock as shown in (a) on the squared paper. Cover the metal rings with blanket stitch as described for the pot holder and pin one ring on to the work-block at top and bottom, as shown. Cut a cord 48 inches long, fold in half, pass the looped end through the top ring from front to back, pass the ends through the loop, and tighten in place.

Make an overhand knot above and below the top stretcher, at the left side, trapping the stretcher between the knots. Bring the cords down, and make overhand knots above and below the bottom stretcher in the same way. Pass the cords through the bottom ring from front to back and secure with a half-hitch knot. Make overhand knots above and

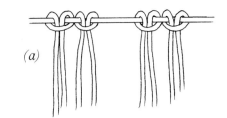

(a)

(b)

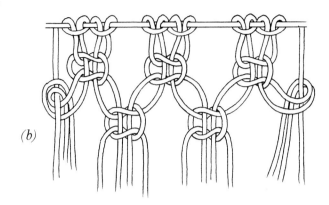

a) TYING ON

b) ALTERNATE FLAT KNOTS

Hammock – method

below the bottom stretcher at the right side, bring the cords up and make overhand knots above and below the top stretcher – as on the left side. Pass the cords through the top ring from front to back, secure with a half-hitch knot, trim the ends, and glue them securely behind the ring. This completes the support frame of the hammock.

Cut sixteen cords 48 inches long. Fold each in half and set on to the top stretcher as shown in (b). Take the first four cords and work a flat knot, then repeat across the row making a total of eight knots. Push a pin below each knot to hold it in place. To work the next row, take the first two cords, wind them around the support frame cords on the left side and pin in place. Take the last two cords of the first knot, and the first two cords of the second knot and make a flat knot. Repeat this across the row (c). Wind the last two cords around the side support frame cords on the right side. Push a pin above each knot as you are working so that you have something to tighten the knot against, and to keep the work even. Repeat these two rows, working down to the bottom of the hammock, then finish by repeating the first row, taking the first and second pairs of cords alternately over and under the bottom stretcher.

Unpin the work and turn to the wrong side. Working with four cords together, make an overhand knot tight against the stretcher, and repeat,

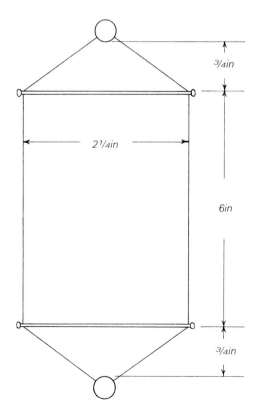

Hammock – working guide

2¼in

6in

¾in

¾in

working across the bottom stretcher. Trim the cords to 1½ inches to make a fringe at the bottom end of the hammock. To fringe the top end of the hammock, cut sixteen cords 6 inches long. Working on the wrong side, insert the needle threader through the first flat knot of the first row and pull two cords through the knot. With the four ends level, knot the cords together with an overhand knot. Thread and knot two cords through each of the remaining seven knots in the same way. Trim the fringe to 1½ inches. With a darning needle, tease out the fringes at both ends of the hammock and trim to length as required. Apply a small amount of craft glue to the side support cords at each end of the hammock in order to prevent them sliding along the wooden stretchers.

BASKETWORK

 ## LAUNDRY BIN

(Shown on page 39)

This simple laundry bin is made from a lidded plastic container approximately 2 inches tall and 1¼ inches in diameter. I used a container which is supplied with a spool of film for a camera. The laundry bin is covered with ³⁄₁₆ inch (4mm) hat straw which is available in a range of colours. You will also need double-sided tape or craft glue, and a small knob for the lid – I used a commercial wooden drawer knob.

Cover the side of the container with rounds of double-sided tape and press the straw on to the tape; or glue the back of the straw as you work and press the straw on to the container. Begin at the top leaving a small rim to accommodate the lid. Cut a tapered end on the straw and stick it evenly around the container. When you meet the end, lap the straw to cover the cut end and drop so that the top edge of the second round butts tightly against the lower edge of the first round. Continue working round and round the container, butting the edges tightly together and dropping to the next round in the same place all the way down. When you reach the bottom of the side, seal the end of the straw with Fraycheck (or similar) and cut the end at an angle to taper into the last round, in line with the drops on each round. This side of the container, where each round of straw drops at an angle, is the back of the laundry bin.

Cover the lid with double-sided tape, or glue the

straw as you work. Begin at the centre of the lid, pulling the thread woven into the edge of the straw to coil it tightly. Work outward from the centre, butting the edge of each round tightly against the previous round. Finish with a round on the side of the lid, sealing and cutting a tapered end on the straw. Glue the knob to the centre of the lid. Fit the lid on to the laundry bin so that the tapered end is at the back.

WASTE-PAPER BASKET

The waste-paper basket shown on page 99 is made in the same way, using the plastic cap from a furniture polish spray (or similar) as a base.

 ## STRAW MAT

(Shown on page 99)

The straw mat shown in our modern bathroom is made from ³⁄₁₆ inch (4mm) wide hat straw which is available from dolls-house and dollmaking suppliers. If you prefer, the method can be used with natural raffia, plaited (braided) into the longest lengths possible – but the plaited raffia should be ironed with a steam iron to flatten it.

Dampen the hat straw or raffia slightly to make it more pliable. Hat straw has a thread woven into the edge which is pulled to make the straw curve – the amount of tension on the thread controls the amount of curve. The mat is formed by coiling the straw or raffia outward from the centre and, traditionally, each round is secured by oversewing the edge to the previous round with small stitches in matching thread. The tension at the centre should be tight, gradually easing with each round as you work outward so that the mat remains as flat as possible. When the work is complete, gradually taper the last round of straw into the edge, secure firmly and cut the end at an angle. Seal the cut end with Fraycheck (or similar) as necessary. Press the mat on the wrong side with a steam iron to flatten it and iron a backing of heavyweight interfacing on to the wrong side if required.

The following method is quicker, and does not

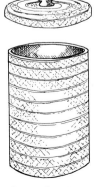

Laundry bin

require sewing:- Spray a piece of stiff paper or thin card with mounting spray (available from photographic suppliers and art shops), to make a tacky surface. Beginning at the centre and working outward, press the straw on to the tacky paper. Note that the upper surface of straw will be the finished underside of the mat. Butt the edge of each round to the previous round as tightly as possible and taper the end into the last round. Seal the end with Fraycheck and secure with a little glue. When the work is complete, iron heavyweight interfacing on to the upper surface and allow to cool. Peel the mat off the paper and press on the top side under a damp cloth. Allow to cool, then trim the backing flush with the outer edge of the straw.

RAFFIA BASKET

(Shown on page 171)

This little work basket is made from natural raffia (available from craft shops and garden centres). The method can be used to make almost any kind of basket as an alternative to the canvas baskets described below. The smaller the basket, the finer and tighter the raffia should be plaited (braided) but the method is the same whether you are making a shopping basket, laundry or log basket, Moses basket or picnic hamper.

Cut three strands of raffia as long as you can work with and knot them together at one end. Pin the knotted end to something stable (eg the arm of an armchair) and plait (braid) the strands together as tightly as possible. Knot the strands together at the end of the plait. Beginning at the centre of the base of the basket, coil the plaited raffia tightly and stitch with matching thread and small oversewing stitches. Work outward, stitching the edge of each round to the edge of the previous round and reducing the tension with each round to keep the work flat. When the base is the required size (our work basket is 1 inch in diameter), begin to work upward for the side. Work each round of the side with the same tension to keep the side straight. When the basket is the required depth, tuck the raffia end to the inside and secure firmly with small stitches before trimming. Make the lid in the same way as the base, so that it is very slightly larger than the basket, and taper the end neatly to the underside of the lid. Make a knob with a tiny loop of plaited raffia stitched or glued into the centre of the lid. Hinge the lid on to the basket with a few oversewing stitches in raffia through the top edge of the basket and the outside edge of the lid.

CANVAS BASKETS

The following baskets are all made from tapestry canvas shaped over a mould. This canvas is stiffened with a glue size which softens when it is wet so the canvas will take the shape of the mould, and stiffens again as it dries so that the shape is retained. The canvas can be single or double thread as you prefer, and no specific hole to the inch – though coarser canvas is more suitable for large baskets, and finer canvas for small ones. The natural colour of tapestry canvas is appropriate for most baskets, but you might like to try white for a baby's basket.

The moulds used to shape the baskets can usually be found around the house – bottle caps and lids, pieces of dowelling, plastic containers, etc, depending on the basket you wish to make. The patterns show an outline size of the base, and mention what I used as a mould, but this is an area where you can very much 'do your own thing' – anything that is the right size and shape for the basket you want to make will do. Non-porous moulds such as plastic can be used just as they are, but anything porous should be covered with cling film or aluminium cooking-foil so that the canvas does not stick to it.

The basic method is the same for any basket. Cut a piece of canvas a little larger all round than the mould and soak it for a few moments in tepid water. Place the wet canvas over the mould and smooth out any wrinkles. Put a small elastic band over the canvas at the position where the top edge of the finished basket will be, ensuring that the elastic band is straight, and lies flat. Gently pull the corners and edges of the wet canvas under the elastic so that they are even, and the weave of canvas threads is nicely spaced around the basket. Make sure any wrinkles are eased out, and leave the canvas on the mould to dry thoroughly. Remove the elastic band and lift the basket off the mould. Trim neatly around the top edge with small sharp scissors on the line defined by the elastic band.

To make a firm decorative edging, plait (braid) threads pulled from canvas – using three, six or nine threads depending on the thickness of the canvas and the size of the basket. Knot the threads together at one end and plait them tightly and evenly, knotting the end of the plait. Put the basket back on the mould, apply fabric glue to the back of the plait and press it in place around the top edge of the basket to cover the cut edge of canvas. Snip off the knot and glue the ends in place. On a large basket, you may wish to glue a second plait to the inside top edge for extra strength or decoration. To make handles, use plaited strands, with the ends glued inside the basket, or twist dampened threads of canvas together, allow to dry, then glue the ends inside the basket. If you use a plaited edge inside and outside the basket, glue the ends of the handles between the plaits.

To colour your basket, acrylic paint or spirit-based woodstain in walnut, blue, green, etc, can be painted on to the basket, on the mould. Allow to dry thoroughly before removing from the mould.

SHOPPING BASKET AND LOG BASKET

(Shown on pages 18 and 171)

These are simple versions of the moulded canvas baskets described above. I used a piece of dowelling covered with cling film as a mould for the small round shopping basket, and the plastic lid from a bottle of shampoo to make the larger oval shopping basket. The log basket was moulded over a small square plastic container. The finished log basket was painted with walnut woodstain.

Cover the mould if necessary. Cut a piece of canvas, wet it, and shape it over the mould as described above and leave to dry. Place the elastic band so that the finished shopping basket will be about ½ inch deep and the log basket 1 inch deep. Remove the basket and trim the top edge. Make a three or six strand plait (braid) for the shopping basket or a six strand plait for the log basket and glue around the top edge. Make a three or six strand twist handle for the shopping basket or a six strand twist to make two small handles for the log basket, and glue the handles to the inside of the basket. Put the log basket on the mould and paint with woodstain if required. Saw twigs to 1 inch lengths to make logs to fill the basket.

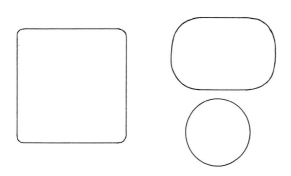

Shopping baskets and log baskets

PET BASKET

(Shown on page 127)

Our moulded canvas pet basket was shaped over a spray-can lid – but it can be any size you wish, suitable for a dog or cat, or any other pet who needs a cosy basket to sleep in.

Cut, wet and mould the canvas as described above. Place the elastic band so that the finished depth will be approximately ½ inch depending on the size of the basket. Remove the basket and trim the top edge straight round on the defined line, then trim the front to the shape shown. Make a six or nine strand plait (braid) as required and glue it around the outside (and inside) of the top edge.

Cut a square of woollen fabric for a blanket, or knit a blanket using the pattern in Chapter 1. Our dog lead (shown on page 138) is a length of jewellery chain with a tiny strip of leather glued into a loop through a jump ring at one end.

Pet basket

BABY BASKET AND NAPPIES

(Shown on page 171)

This useful little basket is made in white canvas shaped over a plastic cap from a roll-on deodorant, and will hold nappies (diapers) cut from single-sided towelling.

Cut, wet and mould the canvas as described above. Place the elastic band so that the finished basket will be about ½ inch deep. Make a six strand plait (braid) and twist handle and glue in place. Make tiny pink or blue silk ribbon bows around the handle as required. Trace three 1½ inch squares on to single-sided towelling and seal the cutting line

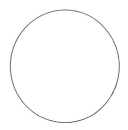

Baby basket

A DAY ON THE BEACH

Lady's swimsuit and jacket, children's swimsuits, cape, crocheted sun hats (Chapter 2), towels (Chapter 5), shopping bag (Chapter 6), picnic hamper and rug (Chapter 8)

with Fraycheck (or similar), and allow to dry. Cut the nappies and fold them one on top of the other. Tie narrow pink or blue silk ribbon around the pile of nappies and put them into the basket. Add talcum powder, baby lotion, safety pins, etc (available from dolls-house shops).

 ## MOSES BASKET

(Shown on page 15)

To make the Moses basket you will need a mould with an oval shape and a flat bottom – and if you are making the basket for a specific baby, check that the baby fits into the mould. I used the lower end of a Heinz squeezy bottle (salad cream or tomato ketchup) for our basket.

Cut, wet and mould the canvas as described above. Place the elastic band so that the finished basket will be about ¾ inch deep. Make a six or nine strand plait (braid) for the outside (and inside) top edge, and a pair of plaited handles.

Make a blanket for the basket from the pattern for the pet blanket in Chapter 1, or make a mattress, sheet, pillow, and quilt using the methods described for the draped-cradle bedding on page 145.

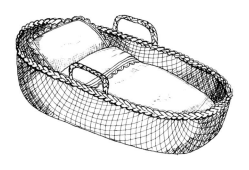

Moses basket

179

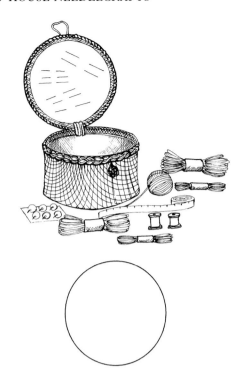

Lined sewing basket

LINED SEWING BASKET *(Shown on page 150)*

Our sewing basket was moulded over a plastic cap (from a bottle of after-shave lotion) which tapers slightly downward from the top – so that the top edge of the finished basket is slightly narrower than the base and the lid. Our basket is just over 1 inch in diameter, but you can make it larger or smaller if you wish, and I have lined the basket and lid with yellow silk.

To make the basket, cut, wet and mould the canvas over the inverted bottle cap (so that the widest part of the basket will be the base). Place the elastic band to make a finished depth of $\frac{1}{2}$ inch. When dry, ease the basket off the mould. Make a three or six strand plait (braid) and glue it to the top edge – with the basket OFF the mould. To make the lid, cut, wet, and mould the canvas over the inverted bottle cap. Place the elastic band as close to the top as possible. Make a three or six strand plait and glue it around the edge of the lid so that the top edge of the plait is level with the top of the lid. Trim away any excess canvas under the plait.

Make three knots, one tight on top of the other, in the centre of a thread of canvas to make a toggle. Thread the loose ends of the toggle through the side of the basket at the front and knot them together on the inside to secure the toggle. Iron medium-weight interfacing on to a piece of silk, and, using the mould as a pattern, cut a disc in backed fabric to fit into the base of the basket. Glue the disc, silk side up, lightly into the basket. Cut a strip of backed silk to fit, and glue it around the inside of the basket to cover the knotted inside ends of the toggle. Cut a disc of thin card (postcard) to fit into the lid. Glue the thinnest possible disc of wadding (batting) on to the card. Cut a circle of silk slightly larger than the card, make a row of gathering around the edge, pull up the gathering over the padded card and fasten off. Cut a disc of brown paper (from a thin manilla envelope or similar) and glue it on to the back of the card to cover the gathered fabric. Glue the paper side of the covered card into the lid. Fit the lid on to the basket, and make a hinge with four oversewing stitches in canvas thread through the plaited edges at the back of the basket and the lid. Make a canvas-thread loop at the front of the lid to fit over the toggle.

The contents of our work basket include 'needles' in the padded lining of the lid, made by threading fine fuse wire in a fine needle and stitching the wire through the fabric, snipping the needles to assorted lengths. Tiny skeins of embroidery silk are made by winding one strand of thread around card and securing with tiny paper bands. The skeins of knitting wool are made in the same way, and balls of yarn are wound and secured with a little glue. Knitting is worked on dressmakers' pins, patchwork in progress and small pieces of embroidery are all made in the materials and by the methods described in previous chapters. Stitch tiny beads or buttons, and wind darning thread on to little cards, and mark a strip of paper as a tape measure. Knitting patterns can be cut from magazine illustrations, but these and scissors, cotton reels (thread spools) and darning mushrooms are all available from dolls-house suppliers.

PICNIC HAMPER

(Shown on page 171)

The picnic hamper is shaped over a rectangular mould with slightly rounded corners. I used a plastic box, but a piece of balsawood cut to size and covered with cling film would work equally well. The hamper is lined with printed cotton or gingham and can be fastened with small toggles cut from a toothpick, or leather straps with tiny buckles.

Cut, wet and shape the canvas over the mould, placing the elastic band to make the hamper $\frac{1}{2}$ inch deep. Shape the lid on the same mould, making it $\frac{1}{4}$ inch deep. Make a six strand plait (braid) for both hamper and lid, and glue the plaits in place so that the ends meet at the centre back. Cut a short piece of plait for the handle, push the ends through holes in the canvas $\frac{1}{4}$ inch apart at the centre front of the hamper, and glue them flat to the inside. Tie and glue a strand of canvas around small pieces of toothpick to make toggles, and knot the toggles through the canvas at either side of the handle (or make leather straps and buckles later).

Using the mould as a pattern, cut thin card (postcard) to fit into the base of the hamper, and cover the card with fabric, wrapped and glued on to the back of the card. Cut a strip of card to fit around the inside sides of the basket and cover with fabric. Cut thin brown paper (manilla envelope or parcel wrapping paper), to fit the base and sides and glue on to the back of the covered cards to cover the raw edges of fabric. Glue the covered card (paper side down) lightly into the base of the hamper. Glue the covered strip (paper side out) into the sides of the hamper, so that the short ends meet with a butt join at centre back. Cut a card to fit into the lid and cover with fabric. Using doubled shirring elastic, stitch through the covered card, making a large cross stitch at each side, and small loops below (to hold plates and cutlery) as shown. Fasten off securely (or make leather straps later). Cut thin brown paper to fit, and glue on to the back of the covered card. Glue the covered card lightly into the lid.

Fit the lid on to the hamper and hold in place with an elastic band. Hinge the lid with oversewing stitches worked through the plaited edge of lid and hamper, 1 inch apart, at either side of centre back. Make three stitches for each hinge with a thread of canvas and fasten off securely. Make canvas-thread loops to fit toggles on the front edge of the lid.

If your hamper is to have leather straps, cut tiny strips of leather and glue the ends to the inside lid, crossed over the plates, and over the cutlery. Cut slightly larger strips of leather to fit the buckles. Glue straps to the lid, and buckles through straps to the hamper, at either side of the handle.

Our picnic basket contains crockery and cutlery, and a square sandwich tin from a dolls-house shop. The picnic cloth is a 3 inch square of the same fabric as the lining, with a fringed or sealed and stitched hem. The vacuum flask can be made by cutting a $\frac{7}{8}$ inch long piece from the bottom end of a fibre-tipped pen casing, with a $\frac{3}{8}$ inch long piece from the top of the pen cap for the lid. Glue the lid on to the flask with Superglue. Our tartan (plaid) picnic rug is made from fine wool or Viyella. Cut a piece 6 x 4 inches, squarely on the straight grain. Pull threads from both of the short ends in order to make a fringe and seal the long edges with Fraycheck (or similar).

FISHING CREEL AND EQUIPMENT
(Shown on page 183)

Our last basket is a leather-trimmed creel for the dolls-house fisherman, complete with a rod, nets, groundsheet, and a folding stool. The creel was shaped over a round mould with a flat back – I used a plastic container which held Sweetex sweetners, but if you cannot find anything suitable, trim a large cork (available from winemaking suppliers), with a craft knife and cover it with cling film. The rod and nets are made from stiff wire, such as the paper-covered wire sold by cake decoration shops. (Pass the wire through a match or candle flame to burn off the paper covering.) Handles are made from brown plastic-covered electric wire and the netting is ballet net or tulle coloured with greeny-brown poster paint. You will also need fine fuse wire, a few seed beads and tiny brass eyelets. The groundsheet is a small piece of waterproof fabric – my husband kindly donated one pocket from his jacket!

To make the creel, cut, wet, and shape the canvas over the mould, placing the elastic band to make a basket $\frac{3}{4}$ inch deep. Trim the top edge and bind it with a $\frac{1}{4}$ inch wide strip of fine brown leather, folded over the edge. Glue two or three strands of canvas around the outside of the base of the basket, and one strand around the lower edge of the leather binding. Tie and glue a canvas strand around a small piece of toothpick to make a toggle, and knot the toggle through the front of the basket. To make the lid, cut a piece of canvas approximately 2 x 3 inches, wet and fold the piece squarely so that the two layers bond together, and allow to dry flat. Using the mould as a pattern, cut a lid fractionally larger than the base of the creel with the folded edge of the canvas as the back (straight) edge of the lid. Make a six-strand plait (braid) and glue it around the inside edge of the lid. Make a three strand plait and glue it around the outside edge of the lid. Fit the lid on to the basket and hold with an elastic band. Hinge the lid with oversewing stitches in canvas thread, worked through the back of the basket and the back edge of the lid about $\frac{3}{4}$ inch

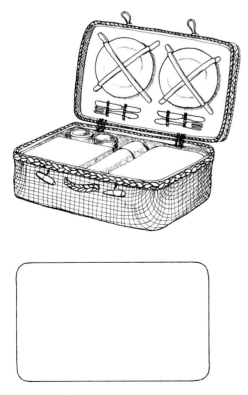

Picnic hamper

181

apart, and fasten off securely. Make a canvas-thread loop to fit the toggle at the front of the lid. Cut a 5 inch strip of leather for the strap, and thread it through holes in the canvas between the hinges. Glue on a tiny buckle and fasten the strap.

To make the flies, twist fine fuse wire into a tiny loop. Knot a piece of six strand embroidery thread (floss) through the loop, seal the knot with a drop of Superglue, then trim the thread to $\frac{1}{16}$ inch and fluff out the ends. Trim the fuse wire to length, glue on a seed-bead 'float' as required, and bend the wire end to a hook. Glue several fishing flies on to a strip of leather and glue the leather into the lid of the fishing creel.

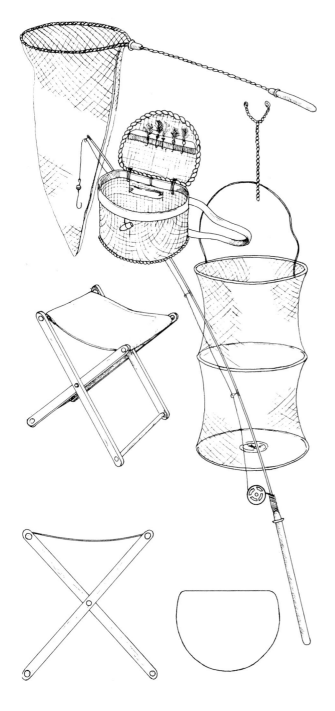

Fishing creel and equipment

FISHING ROD

Cut a piece of stiff wire 5 inches long. Cut a handle in plastic-covered wire 1½ inches long. Glue an eyelet on to one end of the handle with Superglue and glue and push the stiff wire through the eyelet into the handle. Pass the other end of the handle through a flame to soften the plastic, and roll the end between your fingers to mould the plastic over the cut end. Whip fine fuse wire around the wire of the rod and make tiny loops to carry the fishing line. Make one loop at the tip of the rod, another 1½ inches down, and another 1½ inches from the second. Secure these with a drop of Superglue. Glue the two halves of a press-stud together to make the reel. Wind doubled fine fuse wire around the reel and twist the fuse wire around the rod at the handle to fix the reel to the rod – secure with a drop of Superglue. Make a fuse wire and seed-bead hook as for the flies, thread a fine sewing thread line through the loop of the hook and knot the end. Pass the other end of the line through the loops on the rod and wind it around the reel several times, securing with Superglue.

FISHING NET

Bend a piece of stiff wire to form a loop approximately 1¼ inches in diameter and twist the ends together for approximately 2 inches. Thread the twisted wire through an eyelet and glue the eyelet to the base of the loop. Cut a ½ inch piece of plastic-covered wire and glue an eyelet to one end. Glue and push the twisted wire through the eyelet into the handle. Seal the cut end of the plastic handle as above. Paint the twisted wire and the eyelets dark brown. Cut a triangle of net or tulle approximately 3½ inches long and 4 inches wide. Seam the edges to form a cone, trim the seam, and turn through. Fold the top edge of the net over the wire loop and whipstitch (overcast) the net on to the wire. Mix a watery solution of sludgy brown-green poster paint in a saucer and, holding the handle, dunk the net in the paint and leave to dry.

KEEPING NET

Make three wire hoops, approximately 1½ inches in diameter. Cut a piece of net or tulle about 4¾ inches wide and 3½ inches long. Seam the shorter edges together to make a tube, trim the seam and turn through. Fit one hoop inside the net tube, about ¾ inch from the end, and oversew the net on to the wire around the hoop. Put the second hoop inside the net about 1½ inches from the first, and oversew the net on to the wire. Put the third hoop in the top end of the net, fold the net over the wire about ¼ inch and oversew the net on to the wire. Make a row of gathering stitches around the free edge of the net, beneath the first hoop, and pull up the gathering to leave a small hole in the centre.

TALES OF THE RIVERBANK
*Large umbrella (Chapter 6), fishing creel, fishing net,
keeping net, fishing rod, groundsheet, folding stool,
rug (Chapter 8)*

Buttonhole stitch around this hole working over the gathering thread. Make a thread loop handle from side to side of the top hoop, and buttonhole stitch along the length of the thread loop. Mix a watery solution of greeny-brown poster paint, dunk the whole net in the paint, and leave to dry suspended by the loop handle.

FOLDING STOOL

The stool is made from $\frac{1}{8}$ x $\frac{3}{16}$ inch woodstrip with wooden toothpick stretchers and a seat of beige cotton fabric. The stool is hinged with tiny brass pins. Cut four legs and four stretchers as shown. Drill holes in the legs to receive the stretchers and glue the stretchers in place. Drill holes through the legs to receive the pins as shown, and push the pins into the holes – securing the head only of each pin with a spot of Superglue – and trim the ends. Cut the seat 1¾ x 1⅛ inches in fabric with sealed edges, and fold and glue the seat around the seat stretchers.

GROUNDSHEET

Cut a 6 inch square in waterproof fabric. Fold and sew a small hem on each edge with the smallest machine stitch. Punch a tiny brass eyelet into each corner, just inside the stitching. Cut pegs from the ends of toothpicks if required. Our rod rest is simply twisted fuse wire, and the 'maggots' are grains of coarse-ground black pepper in a small glass jar with a button lid.

ACCESSORIES

BATHROOM AND KITCHEN ACCESSORIES

(Shown on page 131 and 186)

This collection of small accessories for the bathroom and kitchen are simply made from toothpicks or fine dowelling and oddments.

Our coathangers are made from coloured paper clips bent to the shape shown with a small pair of pliers. The loo brush is the end of a mascara brush, cut with wire snips, bent with pliers to form a loop, and glued into a handle of fine brass or aluminium tubing or plastic-covered electric wire. The loofah is the small sponge-pad from an eye makeup applicator glued on to a toothpick handle. The cork bath mat is sticky-backed cork drawer lining which is sold by the yard in craft and hardware (houseware) stores. Cut two pieces and put them together, sticky

Bathroom accessories

Kitchen accessories

side to sticky side, then cut the pattern with small sharp scissors or a craft knife.

To make the feather duster, bunch small feathers tightly together and push the glued end of a toothpick into the centre of the bunch. Bind the feathers tightly to the handle with cotton thread or fine fuse wire, secure with a drop of Superglue, and trim the ends of the feathers with a craft knife. Sand the toothpick sufficiently to push and glue a small eyelet up the handle to butt against the trimmed ends of the feathers.

To make the mop, cut strands of cotton thread approximately 3 inches long and bunch them together. Push a fine dowelling handle into the centre of the bunch and bind the middle of the threads tightly around the handle. Pull all the threads downward and trim to length. The dish mop is a tiny version with a twisted wire handle.

To make the carpet beater, use one strand of the finest cane, soaked to make it pliable, and follow the pattern to weave the cane as shown. Trim the end, bind tightly with thread or fuse wire and secure with a drop of Superglue.

To make the broom, cut a bunch of bristles from a lifesize brush and push a glued fine dowelling handle into the centre of the bunch. Bind the bristles tightly to the handle with thread or fuse wire and trim to the required length.

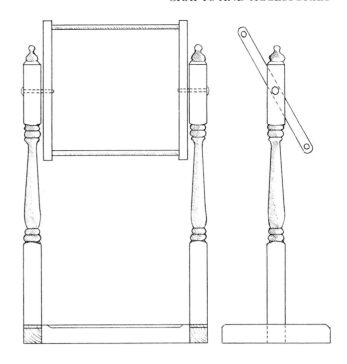

Tapestry frame – pattern

TAPESTRY FRAME
(Shown on page 102)

This simple tapestry frame is the perfect place to display the finished or unfinished work of the needlewoman in your dolls' house. Most of the small projects in the book, including cushion-fronts and samplers, will fit on to the frame, but it can easily be made larger if you wish. The frame is made from $\frac{1}{8}$ x $\frac{1}{12}$ inch wood and toothpicks, and supported on a pair of commercial turned baluster spindles with a base of $\frac{3}{16}$ inch square wood – available from dolls-house shops. The frame pivots on small brass pins.

Trim the spindles to length as shown on the pattern and sand gently but thoroughly. Drill a hole through each spindle to accept the pins. Cut two feet in $\frac{3}{16}$ inch square wood and chamfer the edges as shown. Glue the spindles on to the feet. Cut a stretcher in $\frac{3}{16}$ inch square wood, chamfer the top edges and glue it between the feet – ensuring that the spindles stand perfectly upright.

Cut two frame sides in $\frac{1}{8}$ x $\frac{1}{12}$ inch wood, round off both ends and drill $\frac{1}{16}$ inch diameter holes through each end to accommodate the frame stretchers. Sand two toothpicks to a diameter of $\frac{1}{16}$ inch, and trim them to fit into the frame sides, so that the frame will fit tightly between the upright spindles. Glue the frame stretchers into the frame sides, ensuring that the frame lies perfectly flat, and

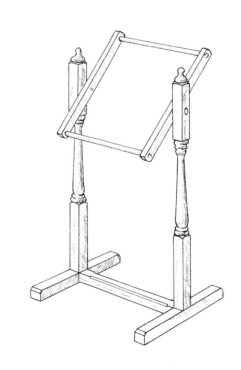

Tapestry frame – assembly

allow to dry. Drill holes into each side of the frame to accommodate the pins. Stain and polish the stand and frame as required. Push brass pins through the upright spindles and into the frame sides, and trim the ends of the pins to fit.

Apply a little fabric glue to the top and bottom edges of your needlework project, seal the sides with Fraycheck (or similar), and roll the needlework around the stretchers.

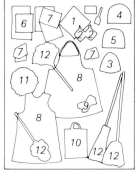

THE KITCHEN COLLECTION
*1 Dishcloth, 2 pot holder, 3 knitted tea-cosy
(Chapter 1), 4 ribbon-patch tea-cosy, 5 shell-pattern
tea-cosy (Chapter 4), 6 towels, 7 tea towels and
cleaning cloths (Chapter 5), 8 apron and pinafore,
9 rubber gloves, 10 shopping bag (Chapter 6),
11 beaded jug cover, 12 mop, broom, feather duster
and carpet beater (Chapter 8)*

DUMMY BOARD AND FIRE SCREEN

(Shown on page 62)

'Dummy board' or 'silent companion' are modern names for the lifesize cut-out figures which were popular in the seventeenth and eighteenth centuries. These figures often represented servants and seem to have had no practical purpose but were a fashionable decorative whimsey. You will need a suitable picture which might be a human figure or an animal, but should be more-or-less lifesize in $\frac{1}{12}$ scale, and it is most effective if it is of the period. I have used a picture of a real dummy board in the Victoria and Albert museum which was cut from the cover of a Shire booklet. Glue the picture on to a piece of $\frac{1}{8}$ inch thick wood and cut out the figure with a fret saw. Colour the cut edge with black or brown fibre-tipped pen. Cut a triangular support and glue it to the back of the dummy board, with the additional support of a piece of fine woodstrip if necessary.

Rectangular chimney boards, to screen the fireplace opening in summer are made in the same way. The pictures used usually show vases of flowers on a dark background – the chimney board in our Victorian drawing room is typical.

Dummy board

ACKNOWLEDGEMENTS

I would like to thank the following people whose help made *Dolls' House Needlecrafts* possible. Catalogues or price lists are available from these suppliers – contact them by phone for the current charge, or write to the addresses given, but *please enclose a stamped addressed envelope.*

**Isobel Hockey, 34 Cranmere Road, Higher Compton, Plymouth PL3 5JY
Tel: (01752) 708546**
Accepts commissions for miniature knitted garments and accessories in wool, cotton or silk.

Dora Lockyer, Willow Coign, Morebath, Tiverton, Devon EX16 9AR
Accepts commissions for miniature embroideries and supplies packs of materials to make her projects shown in the book. Please write for details.

Sue Bakker, 7 Craighall Gardens, Edinburgh 6   Tel: (0131 552) 1953
Accepts commissions for miniature needlepoint rugs and carpets.

Joan Ince, 13 Fowlers Close, Little Common, Bexhill-on-Sea, Sussex TN39 4JU
Accepts commissions for miniature upholstered furniture. Please write for details.

Most of the wallpaper, carpets, lighting and furniture shown in our rooms was chosen from the enormous range of inexpensive imported furniture and accessories supplied by Dijon Ltd. Almost every dolls-house shop in Britain stocks miniatures from Dijon or can order any item for you. A colour catalogue and a directory of stockists are available direct from:
**Dijon Ltd, The Old Print Works, Streatfield Road, Heathfield, Sussex TN21 8HX
Tel: (01435) 864155**

The 'oak panelling' in the Tudor bedchamber is from a range of interior and exterior moulded claddings available from most dolls-house shops or direct from:
**Reuben Barrows, 30 Wolsey Gardens, Hainault, Ilford, Essex IG6 2SN
Tel: (01992) 719593**

The packages and small accessories shown in our rooms are supplied by Thames Valley Crafts and are also available from most dolls-house shops. In case of difficulty contact:
Thames Valley Crafts, Mere House, Dedmere Road, Marlow on Thames, Bucks SL7 1PD   Tel: (01628) 890988

The costumed 'people' in our rooms are from a very wide range of exquisite dressed dolls made to commission by Sunday Dolls. For a catalogue showing the full range contact:
Sunday Dolls, 7 Park Drive, London SW14 8RB   Tel: (0181) 876 5634

The dolls' modelling clothes made from patterns in the book include:

The black couple on page 111 by
Ellen Beddington, 4 Dunbar Avenue, Beckenham, Kent BR3 3RQ

The granny having breakfast in bed on page 83 by
Whitehead Miniatures, 61 Castle View Road, Chiseldon, Swindon, Wiltshire SN4 0NS   Tel: (01793) 740709

The baby in the Moses basket on page 15 by
Theresa Macarty, 57A Pembroke Road, Erith, Kent DA8 1BY

The little boy on the beach on page 179 by
Nostalgia, 147a Nottingham Road, Eastwood, Notts NG16 3GK

The couple wearing Victorian bathing costumes on page 34 by **World of My Own, 18 London Road, Farningham, Dartford, Kent DA4 0JP
Tel: (01322) 862680**

The lady in the hammock on page 15 and the little boy opening presents on page 90 are by Christina Rhodes who is unable to accept commissions.

Thanks also to Heather Stringer for the macramé projects.

STOCKISTS

The following stockists supply the items used in the book. Most of them have a mail order service and/or a catalogue – but *please enclose a stamped addressed envelope with any enquiry* or you cannot reasonably expect a reply.

Knitting yarns, size 19 knitting needles and buttons are available by post from:
Golden Key Miniatures, PO Box 128, Lightcliffe, Halifax, W. YORKS HX3 8RN Tel: (01422) 201275

Fil à Dentelle yarn, size 16 and 18 knitting needles and 0.60 and 0.75 crochet hooks are available by post from:
Joan Nerini, 20 Court Close, Patcham, Brighton, Sussex BN1 8YG

Fil à Dentelle cotton yarn, DMC Medici embroidery wool and Gutermann silk thread are available from the shop and by post from:
Shades at Mace and Nairn, 89 Crane Street, Salisbury, Wilts SP1 2PY   Tel: (01722) 336903

Bleached white 1-ply 'cobweb' wool yarn is available by post from:
Jamieson and Smith, 90 North Road, Lerwick, Shetland Isles, Scotland ZE1 0PQ

Silk gauze for embroidery is available by post from:
Elizabeth Anderson Miniature Embroideries Rosedale, Tall Elms Close, Bromley, Kent BR2 0TT

Silk wadding for quilting is available by post from:
Dora Lockyer, Willow Coign, Morebath, Tiverton, Devon EX16 9AR

Fabrics, ribbons, lace and trimmings, buttons, beads, eyelets and buckles, also rose and bow-making tools and pleaters are all available by post from:
The Dollshouse Draper, PO Box 128, Lightcliffe, Halifax, W. Yorks HX3 8RN Tel: (01422) 201275

Tiny brass pins, basswood and balsa are available from the shop and by post from:
The Model Shop, 44-46 Hounslow Road, Whitton, Middlesex TW2 7EX

Wood, woodstrip and mouldings, turned legs and spindles are available by post from:
Borcraft Miniatures, 8 Fairfax View, Scotland Lane, Horsforth, Leeds LS18 5SZ Tel: (01532) 585739

An enormous range of beads in wood, metal, glass and ceramic is supplied through a catalogue available from W.H. Smith and direct by post from:
Janet Cole, Perdiswell Cottage, Bilford Road, Worcs WR3 8QA   Tel: (01905) 755888

BIBLIOGRAPHY

If you are building, decorating and furnishing a dolls' house, you may find the following books useful:

Atkinson, Sue, *Making and Dressing Dolls' House Dolls* (David & Charles, 1992)
Calloway, Stephen, *The Elements of Style* (Mitchell Beazley, 1991)
Dodge, Venus and Martin, *The New Dolls' House DIY Book* (David & Charles, 1993)
Dodge, Venus and Martin, *Making Miniatures* (David & Charles, 1989)
Hardyment, Christina, *Home Comfort* (Viking/National Trust, 1992)
Lodder, Carol and Nigel, *Making Dolls' House Interiors* (David & Charles, 1994)
Nickolls, Brian, *Making Dolls' Houses* (David & Charles, 1991)
Yarwood, Doreen, *The English Home* (Batsford, 1979)

DIRECTORIES AND MAGAZINES

The dolls-house hobby has grown so popular in the UK and US, and more recently in Australia, that there are now stockists everywhere and it would be impossible to list them all. If you are new to the hobby, we advise that you subscribe to one of the dolls-house magazines or directories listed here, where you will find information about dolls-house stockists in your area. Please include a SAE or IRC with all enquiries.

UK SUPPLIERS AND MAGAZINES

For a comprehensive list of UK craftspeople and suppliers, we recommend that you contact:

The Dolls' House Information Service, Avalon Court, Star Road, Partridge Green, West Sussex RH13 8RY   Tel: (01403) 711511
or
The Dollshouse Hobby Directory, 25 Priory Road, Kew Green, Richmond, Surrey TW9 3DW

The following magazines are specialist dolls-house publications which contain a wealth of information including articles, how-to projects, advertising and listings of dolls-house fairs around the country. They are available on subscription from the following addresses:

***Dolls' House World*, Avalon Court, Star Road, Partridge Green, West Sussex RH13 8RY   Tel: (01403) 711511**

***The International Dolls House News*, PO Box 154, Cobham, Surrey KT11 2YE Tel: (01932) 867938**

***The Home Miniaturist*, Avalon Court, Star Road, Partridge Green, West Sussex RH13 8RY   Tel: (01403) 711511**

***Dolls' House and Miniature Scene*, 5 Cissbury Road, Ferring, West Sussex BN12 6QJ   Tel: (01903) 506626**
(also available from W.H. Smith)

For a wide-ranging catalogue of books on dolls' houses, miniatures, architecture, crafts and furnishings, contact:
The Mulberry Bush, 9 George Street, Brighton, Sussex BN2 1RH Tel: (01273) 493781/600471

US SUPPLIERS AND MAGAZINES

In the US, the dolls-house hobby is so widespread that there are literally thousands of suppliers. The beginner is advised to look for a local miniatures shop which will probably stock most things needed for the projects in this book. For more information, there is an annual mail order suppliers directory called *The Miniatures Catalogue* which can be ordered from: **Hobby Book Distributors, 3150 State Line Road, North Bend, Ohio 45052.** This address is also the US Office of *Dolls' House World* magazine.

Small advertisements can be found in all the miniatures publications for suppliers of the tools and materials required for the projects in this book, but in case of difficulty, the following are recommended:

Wool, cotton and silk yarns, and needles, etc required for miniature knitting and crochet, by mail order from:
Jeanne Bell, 53 Millar Road, Bethany, CT 06525

Lace, ribbons, braids, tools and trimmings, etc for miniature sewing, by mail order from:
Sandy Staker, 2001 Highwood, Pekin, IL 61554

Ribbons, beads, buttons, laces and trimmings, etc by mail order from:
Viv's Ribbons and Laces, 2395 Pleasant Hill Road, Pleasant Hill, California 94523

There are several American magazines, but the best known is: *The Nutshell News*, available from: **Kalmbach Miniatures Inc, 21027 Crossroads Circle, PO Box 1612, Waukesha, WI 53187.**
UK magazines (see above) can also be sent to subscribers in the US, and contain much information which is relevant to them. Most UK suppliers will send catalogues and goods to the US, but please enclose an IRC with all enquiries.

AUSTRALIAN SUPPLIERS AND MAGAZINES

In Australia, the dolls-house hobby is fairly new but growing rapidly, and there are many specialist shops, mail-order suppliers and craftspeople. As the country is so large, we suggest that you contact *The Australian Miniaturist Magazine* as a starting point. The address is: **PO Box 467, Carlingford, New South Wales 2118, Australia.**

UK magazines (see above) can also be sent to subscribers in Australia, and contain much information which is relevant to them. Most UK suppliers will send catalogues and goods to Australia, but please enclose an IRC with all enquiries.

INDEX